Text.1

pp. 130 ff

//
Eco-efficiency and Beyond
Towards the Sustainable Enterprise

Edited by Jan-Dirk Seiler-Hausmann, Christa Liedtke
and Ernst Ulrich von Weizsäcker

Eco-efficiency and Beyond

TOWARDS THE SUSTAINABLE ENTERPRISE

EDITED BY JAN-DIRK SEILER-HAUSMANN, CHRISTA LIEDTKE
AND ERNST ULRICH von WEIZSÄCKER

Greenleaf
PUBLISHING
2004

© 2004 Greenleaf Publishing Limited
except Chapters 2 and 5, copyright of which is retained by the respective authors

Published by Greenleaf Publishing Limited
Aizlewood's Mill
Nursery Street
Sheffield S3 8GG
UK

Printed on paper made from at least 75% post-consumer waste using TCF and ECF bleaching.
Printed and bound by William Clowes, UK.
Cover by LaliAbril.com.

All rights reserved. No part of this publication may be reproduced, stored in a retrieval system, or transmitted, in any form or by any means, electronic, mechanical, photocopying, recording or otherwise, without the prior permission in writing of the publishers.

British Library Cataloguing in Publication Data:
  Eco-efficiency and beyond : towards the sustainable enterprise
    1. Sustainable development
    I. Seiler, Hausmann, Jan-Dirk   II. Liedtke, Christa
    III. Weizsäcker, Ernst U. von
    338.9

  ISBN 1874719608

Contents

Acknowledgements 8

Introduction 9
      Jan-Dirk Seiler-Hausmann, Christa Liedtke and
      Ernst Ulrich von Weizsäcker

  **1. Thinking about sustainable production and services
     in a globalised world** 13
      Ernst Ulrich von Weizsäcker, Member of the German Parliament,
      former Chair of the Bundestag Select Committee on Globalisation

  2. Promoting the life-cycle economy—time to act! 18
      Jacqueline Aloisi de Larderel, United Nations Environment Programme,
      Division of Technology, Industry and Economics, France

  3. The next sources of innovation 21
      Claude Fussler, World Business Council for Sustainable Development,
      Switzerland

  4. Sustainable politics 28
      Jan-Dirk Seiler-Hausmann, Wuppertal Institute, Germany

  5. Germany's Sustainable Development Strategy 34
      Hans Martin Bury, Member of German Parliament;
      German Minister of State for Europe

  6. The German Council for Sustainable Development 38
      Volker Hauff, Chair of the German Council for Sustainable Development

7. **Think—communicate—act. *Econsense* Forum for Sustainable Development: a German business initiative** 48
   Jürgen Zech, former member of the Board of Gerling and spokesperson for *econsense*, Germany

8. **Launching the ISS Sustainable Development** 52
   Raymond van Ermen, European Partners for the Environment, Belgium

9. **Sustainable business development** 64
   Michael Kuhndt, Wuppertal Institute, Germany

10. **Deloitte Sustainability Reporting Scorecard** 73
    Markus Lehni, Deloitte & Touche, Global Environment and Sustainability Services, Switzerland

11. **Sustainability management? Don't bother! Practical steps for bringing sustainability into core management practice** 93
    Peter Zollinger, SustainAbility, UK

12. **Sustainable accounting initiatives in Japan: pilot projects of material flow cost accounting** 100
    Katsuhiko Kokubu, Kobe University, Japan;
    Michiyasu Nakajima, Kansai University, Japan

13. **The BASF eco-efficiency method as a sustainable decision-making tool** 113
    Andreas Kicherer, BASF AG, Germany

14. **Toward sustainable products and services** 123
    Christa Liedtke, Wuppertal Institute, Germany

15. **Climatex® LifeguardFR™ upholstery fabrics: chronicle of a sustainable product redesign** 130
    Albin Kälin, Rohner Textil AG, Switzerland;
    Alain Rivière and Ralf Ketelhut, EPEA Internationale Umweltforschung GmbH, Germany;
    Michael Braungart, EPEA Internationale Umweltforschung GmbH, Germany, and McDonough Braungart Design Chemistry, LLC, USA

16. **Eco-effective design of products and production systems: eight theses on methodological and institutional prerequisites** .. 146
    Michael Braungart, EPEA Internationale Umweltforschung GmbH, Germany and McDonough Braungart Design Chemistry, LLC, USA;
    Alain Rivière and Ralf Ketelhut, EPEA Internationale Umweltforschung GmbH, Germany

17. Efforts in the electronics industry toward creating a
recycling-based society.. 152
  Nobuhisa Itoh, Matsushita Electric Industrial Co. Ltd, Japan

18. Ten years of sustainability at Henkel: innovative products
as a basis for long-term business success 163
  Rainer Rauberger and Michaela Raupach, Henkel, Corporate Sustainability
  Management/Reporting and Stakeholder Dialogue, Germany

19. Toward sustainable banks and insurance companies........... 177
  Thomas Orbach and Timo Busch, Wuppertal Institute, Germany

20. The challenge of sustainability for financial institutions 182
  Paul Clements-Hunt, Head of Unit, UNEP Finance Initiatives, Switzerland

21. Sustainability: the new paradigm in value-based corporate
management 196
  Hanns Michael Hoelz, Global Head of Sustainable Development,
  Deutsche Bank

22. Can pension funds drive sustainable development?........... 205
  Inge Schumacher, UBS Global Asset Management, Socially
  Responsible Investments, Switzerland

Bibliography 221
Author biographies 229
List of abbreviations 235
Useful websites 239
Index 241

Acknowledgements

This book would not have been possible without our families. The editors would like to thank all the authors for their contribution and the Wuppertal Institute for Climate, Environment and Energy, Germany, as well as the Institute for Global Environmental Strategies, Japan, for their support. Professor Peter Hennicke and Morishima-sensei made my research stay in Japan possible, and I am equally indebted to my colleagues at home and abroad for their transcontinental collaboration. Monika Kieslich gave invaluable assistance and helped co-ordinate the project. Nina Hausmann helped devise the book's structure, read its entire text and made valuable suggestions for the introduction. Last, but certainly not least, our thanks go to John Stuart of Greenleaf Publishing for his unflagging patience and confidence.

Jan-Dirk Seiler-Hausmann
January 2003

Introduction

*Jan-Dirk Seiler-Hausmann, Christa Liedtke
and Ernst Ulrich von Weizsäcker*

Sustainable enterprises are companies that manufacture products and provide services according to certain economic, environmental and social standards. So far, no definition has been set up to measure sustainable performance in companies, and in fact sustainable companies are constantly seeking to improve their performance. This book aims to clarify what sustainable companies are. Our choice of title, *Eco-efficiency and Beyond*, shows that, while the concept of eco-efficiency is a starting point that some companies may not yet have reached, others are already taking their initiatives much further.

As early as 1997, the Düsseldorf Trade Fair decided to incorporate eco-efficiency into the programme of the trade fair, making a term not often heard at that time in Germany the topic of in-depth debate at one of the biggest environmental technology fairs. Reading the signs of the time, the Düsseldorf Fair asked the Wuppertal Institute to organise the First International Eco-Efficiency Conference in 1998, and again in 1999, when the Wuppertal Institute joined forces with the World Business Council for Sustainable Development (WBCSD) to organise a second eco-efficiency conference held in 2001 and called 'From Eco-Efficiency to Overall Sustainability in Enterprises'. Only three years after the first conference, the idea of eco-efficiency was established well enough to be considered a starting point for further progress, toward that new, much-touted and often only vaguely defined goal of sustainability. This is where Greenleaf Publishing stepped in and asked the Wuppertal Institute to document developments in the book you are now holding in your hands.

Eco-efficiency as a way to reach sustainable development was brought forward no less than ten years ago by the Business Council for Sustainable Development (BCSD)—now WBCSD. During preparations for the Second United Nations Conference on Environment and Development in 1992 and the book *Changing Course* (Schmidheiny 1992), the WBCSD helped to focus attention on the concept of eco-efficiency. However, despite these positive beginnings, there has been little significant growth in public or political awareness of the concept outside interested groups of environmentalists, economists and business people. More than 150 leading multinational enterprises have joined the WBCSD in order to implement sustainable development by means of the eco-efficiency approach. But for the vast majority the concept is unknown.

So, what is eco-efficiency? Eco-efficiency is achieved when goods and services satisfy human needs, increase the quality of life at competitive prices and when environmental impacts and resource intensity are decreased to a degree that keeps them within the limits of Earth's expected carrying capacity.

Eco-efficiency is a management approach that allows enterprises to carry out environmental protection measures from a market-oriented point of view. Eco-efficiency shows that ecology and economy do not need to be a contradiction. On the contrary, when they are working together they present a gain for enterprises. The motto is to produce more with less. This is not sustainable development *in toto*, which goes further in that it also includes social considerations. The concept of 'corporate social responsibility' (CSR) integrates this aspect.

Eco-efficiency is being applied as a yardstick by financial institutions on the stock market. The Dow Jones Sustainability Index, which aims to list the most sustainable enterprises for stakeholders, includes companies, such as Badische Anilin- & Soda-Fabrik AG (BASF), Climatex, Henkel and Matsushita/Panasonic, that are implementing eco-efficiency measures. A number of business and political initiatives have also been formed. In December 2001, the German government suggested a national sustainability strategy to measure Germany's sustainable development. While this is not yet an accepted political target or even law, it shows that politics is moving toward the kind of binding aim for increasing efficiency as proposed by von Weizsäcker *et al.* (1997). Indicators and well-defined goals help to explain what sustainable development means; the ideas floated in the political sphere are about to be carried into the field of business, where abstract goals turn into solid facts.

Eco-Efficiency and Beyond approaches its subject from five different directions. If only two of the five continents are represented, however, that is because the book took shape in the context of German–Japanese research co-operation. The insights gained from juxtaposing German and Japanese approaches in the light of the standpoints concentrated in international organisations make us hope that this book will be only one of many to bring widely different cultures together. For, notwithstanding all the clichés about the loss of cultural diversity, different people still do have very different backgrounds, and it often takes a change of scene or the presence of a stranger to make us aware of what we take for granted, and of the deeper structures underlying surface similarity. Communication is the answer, and we are deeply grateful to our research partners at home and abroad for putting and pondering hundreds of questions.

The first chapters of the present book examines the framework set by globalisation, underlining the emerging importance of civil-society initiatives to balance the power of state and economy identified by classical political science. Globalisation has increased not only global trade links but also the awareness of our globe as one single system where, in the words of Edward N. Lorenz, the flap of a butterfly's wings in Brazil may set off a tornado in Texas. Sustainable development requires an economy adjusted to Earth's carrying capacity, with benefits for both present and future generations. Only intense innovation in technology, consumer behaviour, social relations and policy frameworks can make this undertaking successful.

How do individual nations shape the framework for sustainability? If innovation is to be steered toward sustainable development, policy-makers need to offer companies stable and beneficial frameworks for their planning decisions. The book then moves on to explore the political conditions for sustainability in Germany. Law-makers involved in shaping German sustainable policy discuss its development, and two business non-governmental organisations (NGOs) shed a light on the practical implications.

We then take the question of workability even farther, in presenting management tools that actually enable managers to measure development toward sustainable and therefore profitable business practices. Organisations such as the United Nations (UN), the Organisation for Economic Co-operation and Development (OECD) and the European Commission have introduced sustainability targets and indicators at the macro, that is, economic, level but concepts for practical implementation such as cleaner production, Factor 4/10, eco-efficiency, environmental and social accounting, corporate citizenship and corporate social responsibility have also been proposed. Chemical giant BASF here presents its sustainable decision-making tool, while Katsuhiko Kokubu and Michiyasu Nakajima discuss the various sustainable accounting initiatives emerging in Japan. Two consulting agencies describe why and how they seek to push their clients toward sustainability.

Some companies have already made significant progress. This book also presents companies on their way to sustainability—in industries ranging from upholstery fabrics to electronic appliances, adhesives, surface technologies and washing powders. While current practice predominantly focuses on short-term product cycles and high sales margins, short product cycles have proved to overtax management and product development, with profit margins getting smaller and clients becoming more and more dissatisfied. An individualisation of products or services—made-to-measure rather than mass-production—is a possible model for a future that uses human and natural resources more efficiently and orients the creation of wealth on human needs. The enterprises making themselves heard here gain their profits from intelligent, innovative services, from the use phase and reintegration, re-use, recycling, treatment and further use of resources or product parts.

Whatever form economic development takes, the financial services sector will be closely involved in the allocation of capital on the macro and micro levels. Decisions made at financial institutions have an enormous influence on individual entrepreneurs and their attitude toward the idea of sustainable development, so they are crucial in determining whether an economy will succeed in following a sustainable path. The final four chapters of the book discuss developments in the area of banks and insurance companies.

Only a few weeks before Greenleaf suggested the title *Eco-Efficiency and Beyond*, one of my colleagues at the Institute for Global Environmental Strategies (IGES) had lent me his video of *Toy Story* as a first step towards an initiation in Japanese animated movies. Those of you who know the film will understand that my first association was the hero's battle cry, 'To infinity and beyond!' The toy spaceman finally comes to terms with the fact that he is a toy and cannot really fly, but he learns to use the resources he does have and to rely on his fellow creatures in saving their own little world. In a similar vein, just citing eco-efficiency and sustainability will not lend us wings. These concepts need to be filled with less abstract meaning before they can take off. We will have to examine what we have to work on, whom we need to convince and who is there to help us.

The aim of *Eco-Efficiency and Beyond* is to trace developments so far and outline the concept's potential for the future. The great challenge we face now is the step beyond the factory gates, from eco-efficient production to sustainable products and services. In the last century, companies made their production lines more and more efficient, so that, today, emissions are ceasing to be a problem linked exclusively to manufacturing locations. At the same time, the emissions produced during the lifetime of products and services are increasing rapidly in a negative 'rebound' effect that policies, companies and consumers will have to address.

1
Thinking about sustainable production and services in a globalised world

Ernst Ulrich von Weizsäcker
Member of the German Parliament,
former Chair of the Bundestag Select Committee on Globalisation

Over 200 years ago, when Adam Smith set about forming his moral ideas of the free market, he made it clear that the wealth of nations requires a strong state, not a weak one. The state needs to guarantee at least three conditions:

- External peace
- A reliable legal framework—let us call it good governance
- Healthy infrastructure that benefits all competitors but is not paid for by any individual player (Adam Smith gives lighthouses as an example)

Another grandfather of modern economists, David Ricardo, also presented assumptions for healthy trade and an international division of labour. One of his assumptions was that capital was not moving. Is it very far-fetched to suspect that David Ricardo, were he alive today, would be among the protesters in Seattle, Genoa or Barcelona? These protesters say nothing in principle against international trade but do not like the élite power structures of today's capital 'markets'.

The fall of the Iron Curtain produced the globalisation paradigm

For how long have we been speaking about globalisation? Some believe that globalisation started with the ancient Phoenicians or at least when Cook sailed around the world. This is untrue. Globalisation is a brand-new term. It emerged after 1990 and the collapse of the Iron Curtain, which we all applauded, and in the context of the Internet revolution (German Parliament 2002).

Until 1990 international capital had to seek consensus with national governments and parliaments in the North and South. In the South, governments used to play on East–West tensions to solicit official development assistance (ODA). In Europe, the spectre of 'Finlandisation' spelled the dangers of rapprochement with the Soviet Union. Clearly, the owners of capital considered a consensus society with some elements of a welfare state the more attractive option.

After 1990, despite a massive reduction of military budgets (by roughly USD300 billion annually), the amount of funds available for development aid and other public goods started to shrink. We have seen a steady reduction of capital taxation in all OECD states. The OECD talks about 'harmful tax competition'.

Global governance

The private sector benefited and boomed. It may be high time to re-establish a healthy balance between public and private goods. To be sure, private capital accumulation is a public good in itself. It is a major part of the wealth of a nation. Moreover, international trade helps preserve international peace better than the nation-states have been able to do.

Nevertheless, I see a need for the world to establish an equivalent to democratic state authorities, this time on a global scale. The idea is to have a power structure matching the powers of the private sector and committed to defending public goods—in line with Adam Smith's concepts. In effect, we are speaking about global governance (not global government!).

Three pillars

Let me outline three pillars to support global governance. Classical political science has identified the duality between the state and the private sector, constituting two of the three pillars.

- The state must seek to extend its reach to global affairs by, *inter alia*, strengthening the UN system, international treaties, regional authorities (notably the European Union [EU]). It must also secure a meaningful participation of parliaments. The International Parliamentary Union (IPU), though established as early as 1889, is far from being an adequate institution in this regard. One fascinating initiative is called e-Parliament and tries to link up parliamentarians via Internet to help them in their local and national needs to learn about parallel developments in other countries. The idea is to enhance the level of competence and, in the end, the clout of parliaments.

- The private sector has its black and white sheep. UN Secretary-General Kofi Annan has invited the 'white sheep' to help with the UN agenda. Many enterprises have joined his Global Compact (UNGC).[1] Another road is investment portfolios focusing on 'white sheep'. Both the British and German parliaments have adopted legislation obliging private pension schemes to declare whether they adhere to ethical or ecological criteria. It is a rather new and exciting market with growth rates approaching 10% per annum (see Schumacher in Chapter 22).

- The new pillar is civil society. International civil-society organisations are booming. Although incredibly diverse, they can be strong.

We have witnessed several struggles between private-sector corporations and civil society. Perhaps the most famous struggle in the United Kingdom pitted Shell against Greenpeace over a North Atlantic oil platform. Legally, Shell was in the right: the British authorities had agreed to the oil company's plan to dump the platform. However, for moral reasons, Greenpeace objected and forced Shell to bow to them instead of the British authorities. In a sense, this event encouraged both parliamentary and civil-society actors to join forces for the common good.

A public goods democracy

The democracies of this world need to redefine their field of legal action. While technological developments should not be stopped, the political dimension of globalisation must be shaped. We should try to establish incentive structures rewarding states and companies seeking to preserve public goods. Social fairness, environmental protection, constitutionality, long-term orientation (education and science), international fair competition regulations and international solidarity are keywords for public goods.

The protection and development of public goods must be the aim of an international regulation politics, global governance. Foreign policy must make global governance a central issue.

One way nations can develop global governance based on common goods is by setting up international agreements on these goods. Such agreements were the aim of conferences such as the one for the Framework Convention on Climate Change (FCCC), which defined the protection of our climate as a public good. If our international policy goals are based on global governance, what part do companies play?

---

1 UN Global Compact 2002, www.unglobalcompact.org.

Companies in a globalised world

The United Nations Conference on Environment and Development (UNCED) in Rio de Janeiro in 1992 opened up new possibilities in environmental politics in the 1990s as companies started to move from mere reaction to action, from end-of-pipe to front-of-pipe solutions. To document this shift, companies recorded their environmental activities in environmental reports, today called sustainability reports. As yet only a small flock of 'white sheep' report on their activities, though some even publish corporate social responsibility reports to take social activities into account.

The case of Greenpeace versus Shell pointed to the even wider responsibilities that companies have for the future—the protection of our common good. Companies such as Shell and BP have changed their corporate governance and instead of rejecting now accept their responsibility for protecting a public good such as the climate. BP, for example, in 1997 committed itself to reducing carbon dioxide (CO_2) emissions by 10% by 2010 compared to 1990. To achieve this, BP in 2000 voluntarily launched a group-wide emissions-trading system for its 150 companies across the world. Surprisingly, only two years later BP announced that it had already achieved its target and that it would now stabilise emissions up to 2012 (Browne 2002). BP actively furthered global governance by proving that the Kyoto Protocol aim could be achieved.

Politics, private companies and society need to achieve a new balance as globalisation limits the possibilities of national parliaments and opens new room for action by private actors (companies, NGOs) and international institutions (UN, UNFCCC, etc.). Companies use this phase to find competitive locations: that is, unregulated free markets. But markets need regulations if social and environmental impacts are to be avoided. National parliaments and private actors (companies, NGOs, citizens) need a new world regulation system to stay in working order. According to Messner (2000), all the questions raised about the market economy in the last 250 years will be raised again from the local to the global level:

- How much imbalance is socially acceptable?
- How can social balance be achieved?
- How much economic power can democracy take?

Companies should therefore start addressing not only their stakeholders but also broader social questions that will be central to legitimising the global economy.

Unless civil society can be persuaded that private-sector companies act morally on the global market, public suspicion will persist and anti-WTO protests such as in Seattle may reoccur in future. Parliaments will remain alert to global pacts or alliances between states or international organisations and the private sector, but we need active companies that commit to reducing their CO_2 emissions. In this new international regulation system, states, on the one hand, will have to give up power to intergovernmental structures, but also to companies and the international civil society, which, on the other hand, have to accept this international regulation system. Only an agreement between currently unequal actors can secure democratic processes in a global context much changed after the fall of the Berlin Wall and, more recently and tragically, September 11.

For companies this will mean that they have to produce more sustainably not only in the sense of resource efficiency but also in terms of social responsibility. Global players will have to ensure equal opportunities for all employees worldwide. Democratic processes for companies means endowing employees with the right of co-determination, just as shareholders have a right to information on companies' economic development. The International Corporate Governance Network is one example for international efforts toward corporate governance standards.[2] In Germany, a national corporate governance codex became law in 2002.[3] In view of the failure of US companies such as WorldCom and Enron, the need for a more transparent reporting system is more pressing than ever. A new regulation system will have binding regulations making the Global Reporting Initiative (GRI) or the UNGC law, rather than a best-practice initiative dependent on companies' goodwill. A first step in this direction is a French law on environmental and social reporting for companies listed on the stock market.

In future companies will, besides setting up sustainable production lines and services offers, have to accept more corporate responsibility in national and international processes. Governments will have to organise these processes and include an international civil society. This seems to be the only way to save our planet Earth.

2   International Corporate Governance Network at www.icgn.org
3   www.corporate-governance-code.de

2
Promoting the life-cycle economy—time to act!

Jacqueline Aloisi de Larderel
United Nations Environment Programme,
Division of Technology, Industry and Economics, France

The recent United Nations World Summit on Sustainable Development (UN WSSD) held in Johannesburg brought forward a plan of implementation intended to set the world's environmental agenda for the next ten years. It will generate many activities and partnerships on the global, regional and national level to implement the activities needed to promote sustainable consumption and production patterns. Decoupling environmental degradation and economic growth was among the key objectives discussed. Concepts such as cleaner production, eco-efficiency and functionality can contribute to that broad goal.

In its work programme on changing production and consumption patterns, the United Nations Environment Programme (UNEP) emphasises the importance of facilitating a shift from addressing supply- and demand-side tools as separate entities, to looking at the functionality of production processes, products and services. The new Global Network on Energy for Sustainable Development (GNESD), the UNEP (United Nations Environment Programme) Society of Environmental Toxicology and Chemistry (SETAC) Life-cycle Initiative and the Sustainable Alternatives Network (SANet) are instrumental in enhancing the use of life-cycle approaches to develop better materials for the advance and the implementation of sustainable technologies by and for business, government and civil society.

At UN WSSD the development of a ten-year framework with programmes in support of sustainable consumption and production patterns, based on science-based approaches and life-cycle analysis, has been agreed.

UNEP's work programme on promoting sustainable consumption and production patterns aims at achieving the Millennium Development Goals (by 2015) within the carrying capacity of the Earth. The five key areas that will be addressed are water and sanitation, energy, health, agriculture and biodiversity ('WEHAB'). Many activities have already been carried out by various stakeholders, but much remains to be done in mainstreaming sustainable production practices along the entire value chain. It has become increasingly clear that there is a need to look at the functionality of products or services as opposed to the product itself.

Sustainability implies major industrial and social transformation and the creation of new systems of production and consumption. Eco-efficiency—achieving more with less—has reached the level of being an endorsed goal for business organisations and international agencies concerned with industry, economics and the environment. There is now a need for a paradigm shift, a shift where functionality and systemic thinking are at the centre of progress.

As products are produced more efficiently with less material and energy input, it has become clear that this has been offset by increased consumption in a rebound effect. A more holistic and integrated approach is needed that applies life-cycle thinking. Industry needs encouragement to change its production methods and consumers need to be empowered to send the right signals to pull production in the right direction.

A life-cycle perspective on the environmental impacts of a product captures the whole production–consumption chain. A significant percentage of the (life-cycle) impacts from some products, counting both the production and the use phase, is determined at the design stage. When product-related impacts are made explicit in the design process there are well-tried design strategies for reducing them. A focus on products and services is a way to engage business interest and action because it focuses on the products' market susceptibility. For instance, UNEP will identify specific industry sectors in the functional areas to be involved and play a lead role. For many, serving the specific needs of consumers is their core business and thus provides a challenging new business opportunity, while at the same time responding to societal needs.

UNEP has taken the initiative to approach several partners for promoting sustainable technologies, eco-efficiency and functionality, including:

- Work programme on changing production and consumption patterns
- UNEP/SETAC Life-cycle Initiative
- GNESD
- SANet
- National Cleaner Production Centres (NCPCs)
- Various industry sector initiatives

These partnerships seek to contribute to the application of tools such as:

- Cycle assessment and life-cycle management
- Environmental technology assessment (EnTA)
- Environmental impact assessment (EIA)
- Product service systems (PSS)
- Eco-design

- Environmental management systems (EMS)
- Eco-labelling, environmental product declarations

The UNEP/SETAC Life-cycle Initiative was launched at UNEP's Seventh International High-Level Seminar on Cleaner Production (CP7), which was held in Prague in April 2002. The initiative promotes cleaner production and sustainable consumption by facilitating assessments over the whole life-cycle of a product or service, and by developing integrated tools and strategies, based on transparent and harmonised product criteria.

The Life-cycle Initiative will benefit all actors involved in the product chain: consumers, business and governments. Individual consumers and consumer organisations have demonstrated their interest in the 'world behind the product'. Consumers want to know more about the environmental burden of a product. They want to know how and where a product has been produced, for example. The average consumer is not interested in detailed findings but in information at a glance—through a label, for instance.

For business and industry, the challenge is to secure and increase market shares, to protect and expand business values, including shareholder value, and to achieve competitive advantages that go beyond legal compliance and short-term cost savings. Incorporating life-cycle and sustainability management will improve image and brand value for world-market players as well as for smaller suppliers and producers. By integrating the life-cycle perspective into overall management and moving product and process development in a more sustainable direction, business can harvest benefits to environmental and occupational health and safety, risk and quality management, as well as developing and applying cleaner process and product options. Clear harmonised product criteria, to be used for designing, labelling and reporting, help industry to achieve sustainability in a cost-efficient way while potentially benefiting from the business opportunities arising from the global increase in consumers' awareness of sustainability.

Governments set the framework and conditions for production and consumption patterns. Government initiatives to stimulate markets for greener products will not only secure and strengthen the position of the industrial and service sectors on regional and global markets but also assure overall environmental benefits to society—balanced with economic and social aspects. Transparent and reliable data, based on life-cycle analysis, help governments in establishing the right signals for legislation and pricing.

In short, a shift from looking at supply- and demand-side tools as separate entities, to looking at the functionality of production processes, products and services, is essential. UNEP promotes the need to assess—from a life-cycle perspective—the environmental, social and societal consequences of the current production processes, products and services and the associated material and energy flows. This is facilitated through the UNEP/SETAC Life-cycle Initiative. The First Materials Science Forum on Future Sustainable Technologies, which took place in September 2002, provided an important input to the ongoing work to identify and discussed state-of-the-art concepts of functionality and eco-efficiency by highlighting the role that systems approaches and technologies can play in achieving these goals.

3
The next sources of innovation

Claude Fussler
World Business Council for Sustainable Development, Switzerland

To make development sustainable we need to design an economy that works for all and forever within the limits of this planet. Only intense innovation in technology, consumer behaviour, social relations and policy framework can make this undertaking successful.

Hooked on growth

We have been hearing this message for 15 years now. Yet, on the whole, it seems that we have moved in the wrong direction. We still retain a pattern of development that uses more natural resources and creates more waste than it should, now and in the long run. In the most simplistic description our economy is a process that, on the supply side, uses natural resources to produce infrastructures, consumer goods and waste. On the demand side consumers use these goods, accumulate or dispose of them. They also need energy and water and natural space on that side of the process. This physical process is interlinked with a financial process worth about USD29 trillion in added value (1998 world gross national product [GNP]). Producers stretch the natural inputs to create value that is used for reinvestment in a more productive capacity, payment of the taxes levied by the state and for distribution to consumers, be they shareholders or employees.

This process is hooked on growth for three main reasons. The world population continues to increase. The need for financial security also increases as we continue to live longer with a larger proportion of our time spent in education or retirement relative to our time earning a living and saving. And our aspirations to a better quality of life and our dreams of who we would like to be are mainly expressed through the rituals of shopping for, giving and collecting material goods.

Tomorrow's markets

Some key statistics will help to assess the direction taken by this process. The WBCSD, the World Resources Institute (WRI) and the UNEP selected 19 key trends that will shape the global business environment (WRI *et al.* 2002). Here is a sample:

- In the last ten years the average annual population growth rate was 1.6%. Earth's population reached 6 billion in 2000 and is projected to reach 7.9 billion by 2025 and 9.3 billion by 2050, remaining nearly stable thanks to declining fertility rates; 98% of the projected growth will be in countries today defined as developing countries (WRI *et al.* 2002: 10).

- World average life expectancy rose from 47 years in 1950 to 66 years in 2000 and will approach 70 years in 2010 (WRI *et al.* 2002: 16).

- Rich countries with nearly stable populations will have a bulge of people aged 50–90 in 2020. The working-age population in developing countries will reach 5.2 billion in 2020 (WRI *et al.* 2002: 11).

- Seventy-eight per cent of the world population lives below the poverty threshold, and the wealthiest 1% receives as much income as the entire bottom 57% (WRI *et al.* 2002: 13).

- World economic output has averaged 2.9% per annum since 1975. At this rate it more than doubles every 25 years (WRI *et al.* 2002: 12).

- World energy production rose by 42% from 1980 to 2000, an average 2% per annum that demonstrates a small efficiency gain relative to economic output (WRI *et al.* 2002: 24). At this rate it would only double in 35 years.

- Water consumption is estimated to increase twice as fast as population growth and 2.3 billion people are exposed to water stress affecting sanitation, agriculture and freshwater fishing (WRI *et al.* 2002: 36).

- In the last decade the world lost 2% of its forested areas (WRI *et al.* 2002: 32).

- Estimates of the total material throughput of various economies indicate efficiency gains in North America and Europe while most other economies become more material-intense to satisfy the needs of a growing population.

What do these broad indicators tell us about the health and future of the system?

Getting better? Getting worse?

Many 'things are getting better', to paraphrase a chapter title in *The Sceptical Environmentalist* by Bjørn Lomborg (2001), a statistician who takes issue with doom-

and-gloom predictions of environmentalists and his particular *bête noire*, the Worldwatch Institute. We live more healthily and longer, wealth is up, energy and material efficiency are up, with an effect on air quality improvement and waste reduction.

But this is the world seen from the perspective of the richest OECD countries. If 'things are getting better' they are not even getting good enough by a long stretch. In absolute terms most environmental impacts continue to grow. In the rest of the world and for the large majority of its population, things are hardly getting better. Consumption and demographics increase the pressure on water and forestry resources and yet many are left below the poverty and hunger line.

While 'getting better' can be statistically verified, 'good' or 'not good enough' are harder to establish. With all the attention the planet gets, it is still difficult to agree on its real state and the risks of running our economy at the current material and energy intensity. According to WWF's *Living Planet Report 2000* (WWF 2000), we already outran available bio-capacity in the mid-1970s. Our economy's ecological footprint now exceeds the capacity of natural systems to regenerate resources at the rate we use them and absorb the wastes at the rate we generate them. A majority of environmental scientists agree that the scales are tilting dangerously.

A Factor 10 challenge

If things got somewhat better, it was because of the inexhaustible creativity of people with vision and foresight who learned from accidents and assimilated public pressure in a bid to improve the efficiency and safety of the production–consumption cycle. Even the most sceptical environmentalists would agree that we need more change to maintain what they see as improving conditions. Another doubling of economic output also needs a doubling of efficiency in resource use. But that would leave pollution levels where they are. We also need another efficiency gain of at least 30% to reduce what WWF estimates as the current overshoot of our bio-capacity. This would still leave about 80% of the population in poverty. Taking all the world's population into a similar, high quality of life range would require a significant boost to physical efficiency by a Factor 5. The most demanding perspective on a sustainable future therefore creates an efficiency challenge of a full order of magnitude.

Whether one is a proponent of Factor 10 or 2 will continue to be a matter of debate and how we look at the world we want to hand down to the next generation. But there is no denying that innovation will be at the core of all strategies that stand a chance of coping with the trends enumerated above. Incremental change alone will not get us where we should be in 2025.

Eco-efficiency triggers innovation

Innovation cuts through paradoxes. It is the creation of solutions to conflicting demands. Flying in a vacuum gave us rockets and satellites; switching electrons through insulators gave us Silicon Valley and the digital age. Sustainable development presents a similar field of paradoxical innovation forces—provide affordable products and services for the growing unmet needs of the world population while reducing environmental impacts. This is what eco-efficiency is about, an approach defined by the WBCSD in the early 1990s (WBCSD 2000a). The designer Craig Frazier once said: 'Discomfort is almost a prerequisite for a great idea' (Frazier 1998).

If Factor 10 is not an innovation challenge, nothing is. But how does one turn the challenge into a business opportunity? Successful business innovation depends on four critical elements:

- Creative people
- A stimulating work environment
- The competence to deliver cost-efficient solutions that exceed customers' expectations and competitors' solutions
- A compelling purpose or vision

When competent companies adopt the principle of eco-efficiency they turn out important innovations. Take the line of polymers from Cargill Dow that sets a new benchmark of cost performance for fibres and plastics from corn-derived natural sugars. Or Toyota's hybrid technology engines for the Prius, a car that doubled energy efficiency in no more than three years from concept to commercial launch. Or Aventis Pasteur's commitment to create affordable vaccines for immunisation in poor countries (Holliday *et al.* 2002).

Harvard Professor Michael Porter sums it up: 'Innovative corporate practices in the area of the environment, then, will often enhance international competitiveness. Products that address environmental scarcities will also have enormous market potential' (WRI *et al.* 2002: 4). Not all business people see this opportunity. The majority of managers aim for business objectives at the lowest cost. They are 'denominator managers': their pride is in achieving results at or below budget. They tend toward realistic objectives, proven approaches and incremental improvement. They are devoted to cost–benefit evaluation, they are trade-off believers and, yes, sceptical environmentalists. But the innovators drive for the highest business impact out of a given investment. They are 'numerator managers', a minority of leaders in their sectors. They often exceed their goals and sometimes budget. They are not afraid of extreme goals, 'going to zero' waste, accidents, defects or greenhouse gas emissions. They are masters of paradox who see a creative connection between conflicting demands. Both types of manager confront the same business situations with similar budgets. Yet their different world-views bring large differences in results and competitive strength. The challenge of sustainable development (a concept itself often labelled an oxymoron) needs the world-view of the innovators.

Case study

DuPont: 'zero' targets driving innovation

Founded in 1802, DuPont is a science company, delivering science-based solutions from operations in 70 countries with 83,000 employees. The DuPont mission is to achieve 'sustainable growth', which is defined as creating shareholder and societal value while reducing footprint throughout the value chain. Paul Tebo, vice president for safety, health and environment, has been a driving force behind implementing sustainable growth within DuPont. Tebo has been spreading the vision to DuPont businesses worldwide, setting challenging targets based on the elimination of all injuries, illnesses, incidents, wastes and emissions throughout the value chain. In short, the goal is zero. The critical aspect is that businesses must still grow while driving toward zero.

'The goal is zero' impacts on each of DuPont's core strategies from improving productivity to increasing knowledge intensity, and finally to delivering new products through integrated science. The mission of sustainable growth is creating alignment between business strategies and societal expectations and the 'goal is zero' is driving new innovations within the company.

Innovations include progress on reducing waste and emissions at DuPont sites. A global team developed a new technology for manufacturing Terathane® brand PTMEG, a key raw material for Lycra®. The innovation increased yields, resulting in additional revenues of USD4 million while eliminating 2 million kg of waste per year.

Another team developed and implemented methods to reduce approximately 3 million pounds of annual releases of hydrofluorocarbon-23 (HFC-23) through process optimisation. The innovation saved USD20 million in capital investment and reduced greenhouse gas emissions on a CO_2 equivalent basis by 18 million tonnes. In Asturias, Spain, the Sontora® business determined that second-quality material could be used productively rather than be disposed of as waste. With the assistance of DuPont and local organisations, a group of unemployed women formed Novatex SA to take the second-quality Sontora® and produce disposable products for medical and laboratory applications. Novatex is now a stable business with 13 direct and stable jobs for women who previously had difficulties being hired into the local economy, while material that was formerly waste is now a valuable product (Holliday *et al.* 2002).

Innovators move before they have to, guided by foresight or vision. They assume that events, customer preferences and public policy will erode their current product portfolio. Where then are the next sources of growth? Bet on dematerialisation, energy and freshwater conservation, safe and healthy food, all at no price premium. Bet on meeting the needs of the billion poorest for sanitation, health and housing. Bet on mobility with little or no carbon combustion, on agriculture without nitrate run-off. Bet on knowledge, design skills and new partnerships rather than mines, oil fields or smelters.

But before getting carried away, let us note that great market potential is not yet great market share. The 3 litre car (Volkswagen Polo) and the cleaner hybrid engine (Toyota Prius) do exist, as do mobility services that substitute car ownership with elegant rental solutions, and compact fluorescent light bulbs. Rapid innovation has brought those products and services to the market with energy efficiency gains ranging from Factor 2 to 5. Yet large market success is still wanting. Although many will claim that energy is expensive, its price is not sufficient to make consumers turn toward technologies that would save them costs and energy. Hybrid-powered cars or compact fluorescent light bulbs carry a price premium that is soon recovered after some months of use. Mobility services or 3 litre cars even present a cash flow advantage from day one, but require a significant adjustment in the driver's habits and self-image. At the current price level of energy or road and parking access (if any), the majority of consumers do not feel an incentive for change. In most cases eco-efficient products and services meet an early-adopters, fringe-market situation rather than storming the market to establish dominant eco-efficient patterns of consumption.

Beyond eco-efficiency

Eco-efficiency gains are critical to sustainable development, but not sufficient. Eco-efficient products and services must convince the majority of producers and consumers and out-compete less efficient solutions in the marketplace. But markets are human arrangements. They reflect human conventions and preferences. For ages, through war and peace times, our societies have ignored the value of water, space and clean air. They have channelled state subsidies toward fossil fuels, agriculture and transport intensity. In a study by the International Institute for Sustainable Development (IISD), Myers and Kent (1998) estimated the world's total subsidies toward unsustainable practices at up to USD1,895 million, with the lion's share to road transport. In this situation the market points us in the wrong direction; it is affordable to over-use water, energy or natural space. The economic consequences of waste and pollution are underestimated and rarely affect those who cause them. Likewise many common goods—clean air, stable climate, freshwater security, abundant fish stocks and marine life, pollinating insects or the stratospheric ozone shield—send no direct price signals. Their value remains unnoticed in monetary terms. They remain silent market externalities as long as there are no system breakdowns or not enough defenders of their integrity. Meanwhile consumers and suppliers will use and misuse common goods without an economic penalty. Science, breakdowns, regulations and the use of economic steering instruments may yet tip the balance. But we have become complacent with our current arrangements. In a 'free', albeit distorted, market attempts by governments to provide a competitive premium for eco-efficient solutions would necessarily shake the status quo. They are therefore slow and prudent in the face of resistance from consumers and business.

All-out innovation

Yet the challenge of sustainable development will not be solved in slow motion. While we need innovation in product and services design from the side of business, we also need innovation in policy-making to tackle the sticky challenge of getting the market to yield serious rewards for innovative behaviour. We need innovation in social and political debates to create transition scenarios where change does not create losers and social stress. On the contrary, these scenarios should act as incentives for companies, regions and states that invest in knowledge, skills and technologies to create eco-efficient products and services. In the poorest regions of the world the challenge of eco-efficiency is rendered even graver by the challenge to jump-start economic development and functioning governance. This requires significant breakthroughs in the affordability of eco-efficient solutions. Consumers with USD2 a day or on microcredit are an opportunity for innovators who can think about new pricing schemes and cost structures.

When business people and politicians embrace the goals of sustainable development to contribute to an economy that works for all within the limits of our ecological base, they embrace innovation as a way of life. It will not just be about technology and economics but also about framing the market and about creating new partnerships across the traditional boundaries of business and politics.

4
Sustainable politics

Jan-Dirk Seiler-Hausmann
Wuppertal Institute, Germany

What is sustainable politics and what does it mean for companies? How do they react to or pre-empt sustainable policy strategies? When the world's nations met in 1992 in Rio de Janeiro at the 2nd UNCED, nearly all participants agreed to promote sustainable development. Sustainable policies were thin on the ground back then, but nearly ten years later law-makers still have not found a way to ensure their nations' sustainability.

What does sustainable development mean? The Brundtland Commission defined it as 'development that meets the needs of the present without compromising the ability of future generations to meet their own needs' (WCED 1987). The United Nations Framework Convention on Climate Change (UNFCCC) was the first official document to lay down sustainable development as a principle. The UNFCCC stipulated that CO_2 emissions be stabilised at a level enabling future generations to live on this planet. Indirectly, the participants admitted that continuing present economic policies would burst the limits of sustainable resource use.

Since that time, policy-makers have faced the challenge of developing a sustainable policy strategy—not only to go along with the agreed CO_2 reduction, as later decided in the Kyoto Protocol in 1997, but also to achieve the aims set up in the Rio Declaration and Agenda 21. To phrase sustainable development in more concrete terms, different policy levels began discussing indicators to describe sustainable development (UNSD 2001; World Bank 2001; Eurostat 2001; CEC 2002; EEA 2002). Though national and international agreements on indicators are few and far between, Germany has taken the lead and passed a cabinet decision defining 21 indicators to gauge economic, environmental and social development.

When the Rio participants agreed to promote sustainable development, a small group of companies had already presented a concept. In the mid-1990s, Maurice Strong, then General Secretary of UNCED, asked Stephan Schmidheiny to develop a global company perspective to achieve sustainable development. The group, then called BCSD, included some leading companies that during UNCED declared sustainable development to be their goal. In the book *Changing Course* (Schmidheiny 1992) the BCSD introduced the term 'eco-efficiency'. According to BCSD, 'corporations that achieve ever more efficiency while preventing pollution through good housekeeping, materials substitution, cleaner technologies, and cleaner products and that strive for more efficient use and recovery of resources can be called "eco-efficient" ' (Schmidheiny 1992: xii). Since the Rio conference, more than 150 companies joined the group now called WBCSD and worked on implementing sustainable management strategies (see also Chapters 3 and 8). The WBCSD uses seven elements to describe the eco-efficiency concept. Sustainable companies should:

- Reduce material intensity
- Reduce energy intensity
- Reduce dispersion of toxic substances
- Enhance recyclability
- Maximise use of renewables
- Extend product life
- Increase service intensity

The WBCSD, however, never defined to what extent companies should reduce their environmental impact. While one should assume that the details could safely be left to the member companies, so far few environmental and sustainability reports even mention workable targets. The WBCSD, in turn, developed a method using indicators to measure and report eco-efficiency in companies (WBCSD 2000b).

In 1995 A.B. Lovins, L.H. Lovins and E.U. von Weizsäcker proposed quadrupling energy efficiency by 2045, based on 1995 figures (von Weizsäcker *et al.* 1997). Schmidt-Bleek (1993) had even called for increasing resource productivity by ten in the next 50 years to reduce our material input. They all aimed to clarify what sustainable development means by setting open policy targets. The message reached the right people: the 'Factor 10' concept was mentioned as a way to achieve sustainable development in the final declaration of the United Nations General Assembly Special Session (UNGASS) in 1997, a Rio follow-up conference.

In 2001, nearly ten years after Rio, the German government set up the National Council for Sustainable Development (RNE 2001) and in December published a national sustainable development strategy, which the cabinet approved on 14 April 2002 (Deutsche Bundesregierung 2002). By due procedure, it is now up to the government ministries to develop policies that implement the national strategy. Already in 2001, the Commission of the European Communities (CEC) suggested a sustainable development strategy for the European Union (EU) (CEC 2001a). The Austrian government early in 2002 published a national sustainable strategy similar to Germany's (Österreichische Bundesregierung 2002), all of which involve economic and social as well as environmental indicators.

Germany's national sustainable development strategy lists 21 indicators designed to measure sustainable development, giving companies a targeted guideline (Table 4.1).

The strategy follows the Factor 10 concept. The main economic and ecological indicators besides CO_2 emissions are energy and resource intensity, land use, innovation investment, transport intensity and air quality. Social indicators are health, education, employment, family support, equal pay and integration of immigrants. The government plans to publish a biannual report on the status of German sustainable development, measuring future policies on indicators and aims that also set the direction for companies. This will be the task of the statistical office. Companies are now expected to develop their own indicators and aims and adapt them to national sustainable policy. A binding standardised national reporting system based on the 21 indicators and aims could be a good instrument to monitor developments. At the moment, environmental and social reporting happens exclusively on a voluntary basis. Japan is already discussing national reporting guidelines (see also Chapter 12).

The future challenge for the German government and companies is to achieve these 21 goals. What are the options open to them? Kuhndt and Liedtke (1998) suggested one way of translating Factor 10 into workable tools: companies in the same industry sector agree realistic and concrete aims that they engage to reach within a certain time, but with the means and methods each company deems best. One example for such an agreement is the commitment of the European Automobile Manufacturers Association (ACEA), a grouping of 13 European car manufacturers, to reduce CO_2 emissions from passenger cars from 185 g/km to 140 g/km CO_2 emissions in 2008 (ACEA and Commission Services 2002). The first step is setting relatively abstract Factor 10 targets. Ministries, companies and sectors then analyse and measure the distance to the targets before defining them more closely. The next step happens at the company level. Here, management tools come in that use national, sector- and company-wide goals to steer innovation at research and development (R&D) departments toward sustainable products and services.

In *Sustainable Solutions* Charter and Tischner (2001) have shown possibilities for designing sustainable products and services. Their examples illustrate that some indicators are useful guides for new products and services. Such indicators include not only energy and resource intensity but also toxic intensity, an aspect not mentioned in the national strategy. Innovation investment may not be quite as important as the national strategy supposes, and is hard to control. The German government suggests increasing innovation investments by 0.5% of the gross domestic product (GDP), from around 2.5% to 3% of the GDP. But how can the government ensure that further investment goes into sustainable R&D research projects and is targeted toward achieving the main indicators? In 2000 German companies invested two-thirds of R&D expenditure in innovation, around EUR32.7 billion. That makes up 65.5% of German investment in innovation. In the same year, the government supported research institutions with a total of EUR15.9 billions, 34.5% of total innovation investment, of which a mere EUR2.6 billion went into company research projects. That means German companies mostly fall back on their own finances to fund R&D. Every EUR3.5 of R&D investment in German companies goes to third-party commission, and every EUR5 of company

4. Sustainable politics Seiler-Hausmann

	Indicators	Aims
	Fairness for future generations	
1	Resource conservation (energy/material)	Increase by Factor 2 until 2020 baseline 1990–94; the eventual goal is Factor 4
2	Climate protection (CO_2 emission)	Reduction by 21% by 2010 baseline 1990
3	Renewable energy (primary energy/electricity)	Increase by 4.2%/12.5% by 2010
4	Land use	Reduction from 130 hectares to 30 hectares a day by 2020
5	Biodiversity	Increase of species to the 1995 baseline
6	National debt	Balanced state budget by 2006; decreasing national debt from 2007 on
7	Sustainable economy (state/companies)	Investment around 23% compared to the GDP
8	Innovation (state/companies)	Increasing of investment to 3% of the GDP
9	Education	Reduction of high-school dropout rate from 12% to 4%; increase of student beginners to 40% in 2010 compared to 30% in 2000
	Quality of life	
10	Economic prosperity	Sustainable increase of the GDP
11	Mobility (cargo and passenger traffic)	Reduction of transport intensity by 5%/20% by 2020 baseline 1999
12	Food	Increase of organic food production to 20% by 2010 compared to 3.2% in 2000
13	Air quality (SO_2, NO_x, VOC, NH_3)	Reduction by 70% by 2010 compared to 1990
14	Health	Increase of average age reached to 65 years
15	Crime prevention	Continuous decrease of crime

Table 4.1 **21 indicators for the 21st century** (continued over)
Source: Deutsche Bundesregierung 2002; author's compilation

	Indicators	Aims
	Social context	
16	Employment	Increase of the labour force participation rate to 70% by 2010 compared to 65% in 2000
17	Family support	Increase of daytime nursery schools and primary schools
18	Equal opportunities	Adjustment of payment rates for male and female working population
19	Integration of immigrants	Reduction of school dropout rate of immigrants from 16% in 1999 to 8% in 2020
	International responsibility	
20	Development aid	Increase of development aid to 0.33% by 2006, later to 7% of the GDP
21	Free trade	Increase of imports from developing countries

Table 4.1 (continued)

investment in R&D goes to German universities (BMBF 2002: 206). That gives companies considerable clout in determining what research is pursued at German universities, while the influence of the German government in the same area is decreasing. The same ratio can be observed in Japan and the United States (CEC 2001b: 26).

We have now seen how innovation policy works in Germany. What are the conclusions? Would a rise in government innovation investment really benefit sustainable development in Germany? One could argue that it would be better to orient spending on the national indicators, encouraging future research projects to find solutions that, for example, increase resource productivity. Since government influence on company R&D is low, policy-makers now need a management tool to influence innovation processes and outcomes, accelerating the development of technologies and maximising the contribution technology can make toward sustainable development. The fact that it takes decades to turn a sustainable idea into a viable product in the market is an essential consideration for such a tool. Experience with The Netherlands' 'sustainable technology development' (STD) tool could prove useful. STD focuses on planning and achieving objectives through multi-actor interactive processes. Co-operation between public policy-makers, business and knowledge institutions closes the gap between the businesses' need for short-term profit and the societal need for R&D on sustainable ideas in the long run. STD applies a set of tools, including backcasting, Factor 10, life-cycle assessment, constructive technology assessment and social niche management. STD enables companies to pursue sustainable development, and policy-makers to design sustainable policies and link up policy-oriented R&D with business and knowledge institutions (see Weaver *et al.* 2000).

In Germany, for example, BASF is developing a management tool to measure the eco-efficiency of processes and products or services (see Chapter 13). Research toward connecting the political and company-level decision-making processes is gaining impetus.

However, besides long-term strategic innovation management tools, policy-makers have to consider short- to mid-term policies that address the present market failure, which stems from subsidies, non-internalised costs and ineffective taxes. Subsidies, a complicated network of indirect funding, must be restructured along the lines of the national sustainable policy and generally thinned out in the long term. Wuppertal Institute (WI) researchers have suggested shifting taxation from labour to resources (WI 2002). According to Kemp, a wide range of instruments is available to promote sustainable innovations in companies, but each instrument requires specific framework conditions. Sometimes the threat of regulations can be the simplest and best way of stimulating technological innovation (Kemp 2000: 36, 52).

So what is sustainable politics and what does it mean for companies? While policy-makers often focus on short periods, sustainable politics is based on mid- to long-term goals. Sustainable politics would therefore mean combining short-term measures with a wider perspective, translating the familiar 'Act locally, think globally' slogan into a temporal dimension: 'Act now, think of the future'. This gives companies a long-term investment security under which they can operate. To measure sustainable development, governments have to enhance national indicators with long-term aims. These developments have to be reported to the public to indicate the stage of development. To steer innovation toward sustainable development, policy-makers should develop multi-actor processes to offer companies strategic options and promote them with policy instruments.

The following chapters show that Factor 10 policy is still in its early stages, but also reflect attempts to give the abstract concept of sustainable development a more concrete shape in measurable indicators.

5
Germany's Sustainable Development Strategy

Hans Martin Bury
Member of German Parliament; German Minister of State for Europe

In spring 2002 the German government adopted the National Strategy for Sustainable Development. The strategy goes back to a mandate from the 1992 Rio conference and is Germany's contribution to the World Summit on Sustainable Development in Johannesburg in August/September 2002.

However, this is about more than honouring our international obligations. Our current mode of producing and consuming can neither be carried on indefinitely nor can it be copied on a global scale. We must therefore further develop our model for fostering prosperity in such a way that enables both future generations and people in other parts of the world to take advantage of their opportunities for growth and prosperity. This is not about relaunching the old debates about possible growth limits. We need continued growth, particularly in order to enhance the development opportunities of countries in the South. This is about how we can maintain and/or create the prerequisites for sustainable growth and lasting prosperity under the conditions prevailing in the 21st century.

The strategy 'Prospects for Germany' is the German government's response to this challenge. At the centre of the strategy stands the model for sustainable development, with which we have intentionally moved away from the usual well-worn topics of the sustainability debate. To date the discussion has been oriented toward the three pillars of ecology, economy and social issues. Although this approach underlines the equal importance of the key challenges in these three spheres, it cements structures of thought that the sustainability debate is actually intended to overcome. Depending on the focus of interest, the political debate all too often considers the ecological, social or economic dimension in isolation.

A sustainability strategy requires an integrated approach. We have therefore introduced four parameters, each of which covers cross-sectoral issues, to describe the guiding principles for a good future: intergenerational fairness, quality of life, social cohesion and international responsibility.

This attractive model deliberately takes the issue out of the ecological corner and transforms it into a comprehensive reform and modernisation approach. Sustainability has become the common thread running through all our policies from budget consolidation to tax reform, legislation on old-age assets, education and research, better energy management and a reorientation of agriculture.

The National Strategy for Sustainable Development is not confined to describing nice goals but, rather, outlines the way forward and names concrete pointers. Indicators make clear where we stand and what action must be taken in future.

For example, we want to double our energy and resource productivity by 2020 and the share of renewable sources of energy by 2010. By mid-century we aim to meet half of our energy requirements with renewable sources of energy, both worldwide and here in Germany. By 2020, we intend to reduce land use from the current level of 130 ha per day to a maximum of 30 ha per day, and by 2010 our objective is to bring about a decrease in the excess nitrogen in agriculture to 80 kg per ha. We want to see a steady rise in public and private expenditure on research and development to 3% of GDP by 2010. And, during the same period, full-time childcare facilities for children in the western German states should be increased to cover 30%. At present, it is just under 3% for some age groups.

As yet, there is no sustainability indicator comparable to the Deutsche Aktienindex (DAX) for the stock market or the inflation rate for the value of money. However, the 21 objectives for the 21st century reflect more than a mere trend. In contrast to the sustainability debate in the past, they deal openly with conflicting objectives and suggest how to balance them out in keeping with the idea of sustainability.

The strategy's core idea is increasing energy and resource efficiency. Our planet's reserves of raw materials are limited. The raw materials that we consume today will no longer be available to future generations. The economical and efficient use of scarce resources is therefore a fundamental prerequisite for sustainable development, not only on ecological but also on economic grounds. In view of the world's growing population and the strong increase in demand from emerging market economies such as China and India, we can expect prices for raw materials and energy to rise in future. Those who use increasingly scarce resources more efficiently will have a better chance of holding their own in global competition. In future, energy and resource efficiency will be the hallmark of successful economies worldwide.

For many decades companies have largely focused their rationalisation efforts on labour. For example, labour productivity grew by a factor of 4.2 in the western German states between 1950 and 1991. In the same period, however, energy productivity only increased by a factor of 2.1. Future rises in productivity must therefore primarily be in energy and resource consumption. We need a revolution in efficiency here similar to the one we have already achieved in labour productivity.

During the last few years, we have achieved a very welcome development in this field and decoupled economic growth and energy consumption. While energy productivity in the EU only rose by 1.1% annually between 1991 and 2000, we in Germany have achieved annual increases of 1.9%. We want to continue this trend. By 2020 energy productivity is to be doubled compared to 1990 levels. That means that roughly twice as much will be produced with any given amount of energy in 2020 as was produced in 1990. In the long term, the Factor 4 vision shows the way ahead, toward creating twice as much prosperity using half the amount of natural resources.

The less energy and fewer raw materials we have to use in production or services, the higher the 'profit margin' will be for the environment and industry. The efficient use of resources will thus result in sustainable growth and jobs with secure future prospects.

Demand for such resource-saving products and processes is growing steadily. Germany has a good chance of capturing this market of the future. As we endeavoured to advance our national climate policy very early on, many German companies now have an advantage over their competitors. In energy technology, for example, the Renewable Energy Act, the '100,000 roofs' programme and other measures have created the framework for a massive expansion in environmentally sound renewable sources of energy.

The upswing in this field has been of particular benefit to small and medium-sized enterprises, among them engineering and planning offices, manufacturers of components for wind wheels or photovoltaic units, and companies that install and service such units. The renewable energy sector currently employs approximately 120,000 people in jobs that, by and large, cannot be exported. The products, in contrast, can be exported worldwide. However, we are not focusing exclusively on the renewable energy sector. With the promotion of modern combined heat and power stations and fuel cells, we are creating incentives for much greater energy efficiency.

Potential for increasing efficiency is not restricted to the energy sector. Increases in water consumption efficiency demonstrate the possibilities of 'dematerialised' production. Around 1900 a tonne of water was required to produce one kilogram of paper. In 1990, it was only 64 kg of water. Today the most modern paper factories are working with almost closed circuits that need no more than 1.5 kg of fresh water.

The more resolute we are in pursuing this course, the greater the chance that we can maintain and increase our lead when it comes to know-how on energy and resource efficiency.

Government programmes and agreements on targets create the framework and provide the necessary impetus for sustainable development. The task of players in industry and society is to flesh out this framework for sustainability in their own area of responsibility. The belief that sustainability is mainly achieved through state action merely reveals an unrealistic reliance on the state. For the way in which consumers and entrepreneurs consume and invest has just as much of an impact as laws, ordinances, promotion programmes and agreements on targets.

To gain widespread approval for the strategy and benefit from the experiences of different players, we deliberately opted for a participatory approach in drawing up the National Strategy for Sustainable Development. It therefore also symbolises a new political style. For the first time, citizens had the opportunity to play an active role in drawing up a government strategy paper. The main points, as well as a first draft of the strategy, were posted for discussion on the Internet forum 'Dialogue on Sustainable Development'. Proposals and ideas suggested here were taken into account in the strategy just as much as the reports of numerous social groups. The Council for Sustainable Development, established by Chancellor Schröder in April 2001 under the chairmanship of Volker Hauff, made particularly important contributions.

Volker Hauff proposed that a world commission on sustainable development and globalisation should be set up, pointing out that the idea of sustainable development supplies answers to critical questions on the social and ecological consequences of globalisation. The National Strategy for Sustainable Development provides Germany with guidance on what action to take and contributes toward international understanding. We are deliberately focusing on increasing efficiency and not primarily on sufficiency. For who wants to deny other countries the chance to participate in growth and prosperity? As the economic practices and way of life of industrialised states cannot be adopted globally without destroying our planet's sources of life for everybody, we are responsible for developing a model for fostering prosperity (and welfare) that is attractive here and elsewhere and thus helps to avoid a development where the countries of the South merely strive to catch up. With this strategy, we are moving the chances for sustainable development to the fore: jobs with secure future prospects, economic growth that is lasting because it does not burden the environment, the preservation of an intact natural environment for our children and grandchildren. For only if we succeed in convincing people that more sustainability also means more quality of life for them personally, will we gain the necessary acceptance, both nationally and internationally.[1]

---

1 The German government provides English-language information at http://eng.bundesregierung.de. Choose 'Sustainable Development' in the pop-up menu for 'Background Information'.

6
The German Council for Sustainable Development

Volker Hauff
Chair of the German Council for Sustainable Development

The work of the German Council for Sustainable Development[1] shows ways of pursuing what may be called sustainable politics. This chapter addresses the following questions: What is the mandate of the Council and who are the members? Why establish a Council for Sustainable Development? What have we achieved so far? What are the next steps in the Council's work?

The Council's mandate and members

On 26 July 2000 the German Federal Government agreed to formulate a National Strategy for Sustainable Development to be presented at the UN WSSD in Johannesburg in 2002, as required by the UN General Assembly in 1997. As a working body the German government established a 'green cabinet' on the level of state secretaries of ministries involved in sustainability politics. At the same time the government established the German Council for Sustainable Development to provide proposals for the National Sustainable Development Strategy, particularly objectives, timetables and indicators, to suggest projects designed to demonstrate some of the major elements of sustainable development in Germany, and to set the agenda for a broader understanding of 'sustainability' in society. Both bodies, the green cabinet and the Council, focused on priority issues such as energy and climate change, mobility and transport, and agriculture, food, health and environment. The third task of the German Council for Sustainable Development is to

---

1 German Council for Sustainable Development at www.nachhaltigkeitsrat.de.

foster social dialogue and achieve consensus between different social pressure groups, and to raise public awareness of sustainability as a political issue and concept.

The 17 members appointed by the German government are: Philip Freiherr von dem Bussche (President of the German Agricultural Society [DLG eV]), Jochen Flasbarth (President of the Association for the Protection of Nature of Germany [NABU eV]), Wolfgang Franz (President of the Centre for European Economic Research [ZEW], Mannheim), Rainer Grohe (Managing director of VIAG invent!), Volker Hauff (Member of the Board of KPMG Consulting AG), Roland Heinisch (Chief Executive Officer [CEO] of Deutsche Bahn Netz AG [DB Netz AG]), Claus Hipp (Hipp GmbH & Co. Vertrieb KG, Vice President of the Association of German Chambers of Industry and Commerce), Eberhard Jochem (Fraunhofer Institute for Systems Technology and Innovation Research [ISI], Karlsruhe, Centre for Energy Policy and Economics [CEPE], Swiss Federal Institute of Technology [ETH], Zürich), Margot Käßmann (Regional Bishop of the Protestant–Lutheran Regional Church Hanover), Edda Müller (Chair of the Federal Association of Consumer Associations [vzbv]), Matthias Platzeck (Mayor of Potsdam, capital of Brandenburg), Heinz Putzhammer (Member of the Federal Executive Committee of the German Federation of Trade Unions [DGB]), Josef Sayer (General Manager of the Bishop's Relief Organisation [MISEREOR]), Klaus Töpfer (Executive Director of UNEP), Fritz Vahrenholt (CEO of REpower Systems AG), Hubert Weinzierl (President of the German League for Nature Conservation and Environmental Protection [DNR]), Angelika Zahrnt (Chair of the Association for Environmental and Nature Conservation in Germany [BUND/Friends of the Earth]). Replacing von dem Bussche, Flasbarth, Hipp and Platzeck, in 2003 a further five members were appointed: Horst Frank (Lord Mayor of the City of Konstanz), Hermann Graf Hatzfeldt (Chairman of the Forest Stewardship Council Germany), Jürgen Rimpau (Member of the Board of Deutsche Landwirtschaftsgesellschaft eV Hannover), Holger Tschense (Mayor and Councillor of the City of Leipzig) and Eggert Voscherau, Vice Chairman of the Board of Executive Directors of BASF AG.

Why a Council for Sustainable Development?

A German Council for Sustainable Development—a consensical-nonsensical talking shop or an instrument for rational conflict solution and promoter of sustainable development? Secret doubts assailed many involved in the process of establishing the German Council and, in the time before April 2001, even the designated members of the Council shared this critical view.

These reservations had their roots neither in the Council's task, nor in the issue of sustainable development (which is quite close to my heart, having been a member of the United Nations World Commission on Environment and Development [WCED] headed by Gro Harlem Brundtland in 1987). No, the problem was the Council's composition. Its members represent very different public spheres. They are engaged in sustainable development policies either in enterprises, environmental and consumer organisations, the churches, sciences, local authorities or the unions. Would a certain corporate manner result in the kind of trench warfare that often blocks political progress?

On the other hand, Council members are appointed *ad personam*. This seemed to open a window of opportunity. They were explicitly appointed *not* as representatives of their respective organisations, but as individuals with knowledge in certain fields, with perspectives and backgrounds of which our work soon proved able to make good use. The Council's sessions proceed in an atmosphere of openness and willingness to find shared positions that reach far enough to promote sustainable development, and take economic, social and political constraints as well as environmental basics into account.

Outputs and impacts

How does the Council work in the context of eco-efficiency and sustainable development? Let us take a look at the substantial outputs and impacts of the Council's work: that is, policy recommendations for the German government, efforts to promote public debate about sustainable development, but also discussions in the Council on what sustainable development is all about.

The German government tasked the Council with developing proposals for indicators, targets and objectives to be integrated into a National Sustainable Development Strategy (or rather, initially, the government draft for this paper), and designing some basic projects implementing the sustainable development strategy. A dialogue paper duly introduced proposals for indicators, targets and objectives as a basis for further debate. In 2002, the Council issued some in-depth recommendations focusing on key issues of sustainability, such as energy, consumer policies and international trade.

The Council also proposed projects to implement sustainability strategies, commented on the government's draft for the National Sustainable Development Strategy and recommended some amendments to crucial points of the strategy paper. One important goal is to raise public awareness of sustainable development.

Sustainable development: targets and objectives

What is the Council's definition of sustainable development?

Social dialogue on a large scale is crucial for sustainable development. When we describe overall concepts and goals, we communicate what it is that we wish to achieve. Sustainable development is a concept that reaches far beyond the borders of Germany, and far beyond the life-span of a government. Economic development in an intact environment, quality of life and social cohesion as matters of global responsibility—these objectives are rooted in all aspects of social activity, and they demand new approaches to the integration and co-ordination of political initiatives. They also contribute to peace in the world.

Sustainable development looks forward to a future in a bigger and more colourful world, a world with a healthy and clean environment that has kept its natural diversity, with more democracy and greater well-being, and with a common cultural heritage cared for by all. It is an important principle of sustainable development not to live at the expense of future generations or of people in other parts of the world. In order to ensure a good quality of life, an intact natural environment, social and cultural cohesion, and international responsibility in a globalised world, it is essential to find a proper balance between the needs of the present generation and the prospects for those born after us.

Agreement on objectives, mostly quantified objectives, is in the Council's view the most important feature of sustainable development. This is the core element of a policy of sustainable development. Apart from the state with its regulatory and finance policies, the Council also intends to involve other players.

Quantifying objectives serves a valuable purpose, for quantified objectives can be monitored and accounted for. They are politically enforceable. Commitment to objectives entails a special responsibility, and the extent and social commitment with which objectives are determined also tells how serious a project is. In the Council's view a sustainability strategy for Germany must rely on quantified objectives. The Council accordingly recommended that the German government

- Make quantified objectives the cornerstones of a strategy for sustainability
- Apply these objectives to the main issues: that is, energy, mobility and agriculture, food, environment and health and, in addition, to the issues of land use and building and the German contribution to international development aid

The national climate objective shows how important objectives are politically. Political commitment here has resulted in the creation of jobs, new economic and political initiatives, and has promoted research and citizen activities. The Council therefore proposes a more ambitious climate objective designed for a longer time-frame.

Another example is land use for settlement and transport purposes. There is a necessity to reduce land use from today's 130 hectares per day to 30 by 2020, an objective that, it must be admitted, has not so far been very successful. The Council is addressing this issue because it demonstrates more than any other that previous environmental thinking has been too narrow-minded. It is in a way characteristic that environmental experts propose a wonderful objective without discussing it with other players who are literally on the spot. 'Do not obstruct future possibilities' is a slogan that could be adopted as a sensible guiding principle to avoid using for settlements and transport land and agricultural areas that will be needed for a new, future agricultural system.

The dialogue paper

The Council began its work by establishing three working groups to concentrate on the three priority areas defined by the German government: that is, energy and climate change, mobility and transport, and agriculture, food, health and environment, plus the issue of land use. The working groups agreed on goals, objectives and indicators summarised in a dialogue paper.

Proposed goals for energy policies are the reduction of CO_2 emissions by 40% from 1990 to 2020, renewed efficiency efforts to achieve an annual efficiency rate of 3%, phasing out mineral coal subsidies by 2010, and further developing renewable energy sources.

Agricultural goals proposed by the Council highlight the importance of farming families in Germany's tradition of entrepreneurial and sustainable farming. Apart from the production of healthy foods in an intact environment, other forward-looking business activities and sources of income should help sustain and develop rural areas. Conflicts of interest with the EU and the World Trade Organisation (WTO) should be solved with a view to global justice, in a way that also gives developing countries a fair chance.

The Council has also pointed out that the transport sector must contribute toward CO_2 reduction objectives. Trading in CO_2 certificates opens up new perspectives for sustainable mobility. Technical innovations such as the zero-emissions car should be linked to social and entrepreneurial innovations. Supplementary legal guidelines will make concrete goals clearer. To give impetus to sustainable development in rail transport, the volume of goods transported by rail should be doubled. For the proportion of motorised individuals, the Council suggests an interim target of a reduction to 70% by the year 2015.

As an overarching aspect of settlement policy, the Council calls for reducing the amount of land used for roads and settlements to less than 30 hectares per day by 2020 and to zero by 2050; at the same time, an active development of spatial structures is needed to reduce transport demand.

The Council attaches great importance to linking up local and global activities. Concrete action in Germany goes hand in hand with a global view. As a first global measure, the Council in its dialogue paper recommended German government initiatives at the highest political level to set up a World Commission on Sustainability and Globalisation at the World Summit on Sustainable Development in September 2002 (see the final section of this chapter).

At the end of 2001, the Council ran a two-month dialogue forum inviting the public to comment on the Council's dialogue paper.

The Council's project proposals

The State Secretaries' Committee (green cabinet) outlined several pilot projects. In addition, the Council in November 2001 proposed five projects to implement sustainable development in the three priority areas defined by the German government.

Energy and climate change

The Council has proposed a project for modernising old buildings, which hold an enormous potential in economic and energy terms as nearly 95% of total heat energy is used in flats in old buildings. In addition, renovating old buildings helps revitalise cities. Approximately 24 million of the 34 million dwellings in Germany are in need of renovation. Currently, only about 1% of this potential is realised each year. Despite the efforts of the German government to provide encouragement by allocating grants for renovation, progress in this area is still lagging behind what is both feasible and necessary if climate protection objectives are to be attained.

The project has two parts, one of which is concerned with government-owned buildings, the other with projects to be conducted in co-operation with private housing associations and homeowners or tenants.

- Energy contracts for all government property are to be put out to tender. The aim is to equip existing government properties with better plant technology and insulation so that, on average, heating will consume no more than an average of 4 litres of heating oil per square metre of floor area per year ('4 litre building'). More-efficient energy services help conserve resources and in the end save money in spite of higher upfront costs.

- A project group for housing, energy and climate protection will carry out model projects in all German states to bring existing residential buildings up to the 4 litre standard with the most economical means possible. These examples are to demonstrate that energy modernisation is not a luxury but advantageous to all involved. This second part of the project will be integrative in nature, bringing together the responsible state authorities and players in the construction and housing industries so that an intelligent combination of measures may ensure efficient realisation of goals.

Mobility

'Intelligent transport services make mobility fit for the future' is the motto of the project, which aims to create and increase demand for an environmentally friendly combination of transport providers that are socially innovative in their organisation. A pilot project is to show that providing specific personal advice on the one hand, and establishing new mobility services on the other, significantly changes the choice of transport means and improves both quality of life in the cities and mobility. Travelling with public transport, by bike, on foot and by car— that is the image of modern transport in an intermodal city. Simple appeals and warnings of congestion do little to change behaviour patterns, and the project therefore concentrates on services and demand. On the one hand, the services offered should be tailored to the needs of the population; on the other hand, individual information and personal advice breaks down prejudices against alternative transport options. The project proposal includes new transport services and service packages as well as active mobility advice. The first step requires finding a suitable model city.

In a beacon effect the project reaches various levels: individual advice for road users can easily be realised at the regional level and then transferred to other regions. At the same time, the project adopts approaches that, by optimising the interface between transport providers, show how access to all means of transport can be improved. In providing a mix of transport means, pedestrian and cycle traffic will be given special consideration. In this context, measures can be implemented directly as first components of an overall concept. The result is a learning process for politicians and citizens that effectively alters behaviour. The project combines technical and social innovations in a model for sustainable transport policy.

Agriculture and food

The Council made two proposals in this field: one focusing on consumer behaviour, the other aimed to combat world hunger by promoting sustainable, locally adapted land use.

The aim of the first project is to encourage consumer demand for food produced in sustainable agriculture, by conceiving and implementing a long-term awareness and information campaign. The long-term information campaign is aimed at increasing the demand for products produced and marketed with sustainable methods, and at reducing deficits revealed by consumer research. Sustainable development is rarely taken into consideration in price-oriented competition, consumer choices are seldom made on an altruistic basis or with long-term aims in mind, and produce does not come with information on manufacturing conditions. The content of the campaign is conceived to address different consumer classes. Ultimately, the campaign is aimed to become a cult in itself—regardless of the contents conveyed—and this with as many social groups as possible. Within Europe, television would seem to be the most appropriate medium, with advertising broadcast in optimum slots for the various target groups. Poster and cinema advertising and other media should also be considered.

The aim of the second project is to disseminate and exchange know-how on sustainable, locally adapted land-use systems that have proved successful in practice, in order to provide food security in developing countries. The idea is to avoid a one-sided transfer of knowledge from the North to the South, or vice versa, and instead increase South–South exchanges. Locally adapted land-use systems can be described as sustainable when they maintain the income of the rural population and the productiveness of the country in the long term, without having a detrimental impact on the environment (erosion, reduction in soil fertility, etc.) or on the population (e.g. loss of a sufficient basis for living). The land-use system must be adapted to the respective cultures to make it economically, ecologically and socially sustainable. Priority is given to the application of adapted local knowledge. Sustainable land-use systems rely on the local population, taking into account disadvantaged groups. In this context, women play a particularly important role.

The government's strategy

The government's National Sustainable Development Strategy, presented in 2002, introduces indicators and objectives for sustainable development. The Council praised the integrated viewpoint and emphasised that the 21 indicators, which allow the measurement of development, make it a milestone in the German sustainability discourse. However, the Council also voiced critical remarks. In its comment, the Council recommends reframing the concept of sustainability in the strategy draft in three respects. First, the perspective should shift from a national to a more global one. The Council asked the government to put more emphasis on international responsibility and define concrete objectives such as earmarking 0.7% of the GDP for ODA. Second, the Council called for more ambitious objectives and indicators: for example, a long term-objective to reduce CO_2 emissions until 2020 and 2050, phase out mineral coal subsidies, and fix concrete targets rather than phrasing goals in terms of reduction of energy and resource intensity. Third, account should be taken of technology as well as social components and changes in behaviour patterns.

Raising awareness

One of the Council's core tasks is to disseminate the idea of sustainable development as widely as possible. In Germany, only 28% of the population know what sustainable development is. To combat this downward drift, the Council produced a booklet that explains what sustainable development means, what and who the Council is and what it does.

An Internet-based project forum was set up at the Council's website, which also features a search engine to give quick and easy access to databases of sustainability projects, and a youth project for young people to express their wishes, ideas, thoughts and fears concerning the future. These texts were included in the portfolio that the German delegation for the UN WSSD took to Johannesburg.

At its first conference in September 2001, the Council's members talked to more than 300 people about sustainable ways of living. The Council broke new ground in presenting a topical issue in an appealing, emotive way, with a live band that garnered enthusiastic audience response for its sustainability song. The song was released on a give-away recording included in information packages on the Council's work.

More than 600 people attended a conference in May 2002, where participants discussed sustainability policy ten years after the Rio summit and 100 days before the Johannesburg summit. And, perhaps even more importantly, the conference addressed the next steps *after* the summit. The conference also set the scene for a broader media campaign. In 2003, there was also an open annual conference with a similar attendance.

Where do we go from here?

The Council outlined the core fields of its work in 2002 to include an initiative for a World Commission on Sustainability and Globalisation, an ecological tax reform, the cultural aspects of globalisation, world trade relations in agriculture, a basket of sustainable goods (in contrast to the statistical basket of goods for calculating the consumer price index), and questions relating to the transfer of technological and consumption patterns.

World Commissions such as Willy Brandt's North–South Commission and the Brundtland Commission have played a major role in developing the political agenda. The globalised deregulation of financial markets during the 1990s was rash and wrong. Sustainability and globalisation must be seen in context: it is important to find the right regulatory framework. We must, therefore, talk about new governance and corporate governance, and that is why the Council asked the German government to raise a proposal along those lines at the World Summit in Johannesburg.

Globalisation and sustainability are linked more closely than many assume. Globalised flows of capital and information raise new expectations. Furthermore, globalisation leads to a convergence of lifestyles with Western, industrialised patterns of consumption, which is often linked with environmental problems. On the other hand, globalisation offers enormous opportunities and holds the promise of prosperity and stability, universal human rights and an increasingly global sense of responsibility.

The World Commission on Sustainability and Globalisation would continue the successful work of the Brundtland Commission. The concept of sustainable development dates back to the report issued by Gro Harlem Brundtland's World Commission on Environment and Development (WCED 1987), which was the first to point to the connection between global environmental problems and the North–South conflict.

The Commission's basic aim according to the Council's proposal is to promote sustainable development in a globalised world. It will analyse the main forces of social and environmental change in relation to a globalised economy, assess policies put forward by global players in business and industry, and suggest ways of facing the challenge of sustaining the global development process. The Commission will look into the social and environmental responsibility of globally operating business corporations, the policies of nations and the global civil society on the one hand, and the understanding of global environmental, economic, social and cultural development on the other. The importance of sustainable development and globalisation is still growing. The Commission is to explore how both processes interrelate.

By no means the first to take up work, the proposed new World Commission will also examine why its predecessors made so little progress in reducing poverty and upholding human rights, arresting or reversing environmental degradation and socioeconomic exclusion, in fighting corruption and establishing good governance. The Commission is to articulate a vision of sustainable global development that will inspire business corporations, nations and NGOs—leaders and people—to intensify their collective endeavours. Another concern of the Commission is global collective social security, including the financing system and global food and environmental security.

While sovereign states remain the primary units of the international system, the nature of state sovereignty and the relationship between national autonomy and international responsibility is changing. The Commission will need to evaluate how the existing regulatory frameworks of the global rule of law can be improved, and examine the role of contradictory policy issues.

As an issue of governance, sustainable development requires the regulatory framework underlying participatory democracy to be improved and greater attention to be paid to the role of civil society in different sociocultural settings. The Commission will be concerned with the globalisation of participatory rights and explore how democratic accountability—and credibility and legitimate decision-making institutions—can be fostered in all cultural settings without destroying cultural, intellectual and spiritual diversity.

7
Think—communicate—act
Econsense Forum for Sustainable Development: a German business initiative

Jürgen Zech
Former member of the Board of Gerling and spokesperson for *econsense*, Germany

Since UNCED in 1992, internationally linked scientific institutions, companies, environmental organisations and other NGOs have been working intensively to promote the concerns of sustainable development. Political framework guidelines based on this model are increasingly being set at national and particularly European and international levels. Ten years after Rio, sustainable development was again on the international agenda at the World Summit in Johannesburg.

Taking responsibility

Industry recognised its responsibility in this process at an early stage. Its representatives regard sustainable development as a challenge to their technological competence and management ability and therefore consider it an opportunity. In recent years numerous initiatives have been launched that work toward realising the sustainability idea. Sustainable development is now a frequent item in corporate objectives, and the problem-solving competence of companies for implementing sustainable development has increased and reached a high level. Sustainability-oriented company initiatives (e.g. the Responsible Care programme of the chemical industry, the UNEP insurance initiative, the initiative for employment) and industry bodies have formed at national and international levels (e.g. WBCSD, Entreprises pour l'Environnement, Austrian Business Council for Sustainable Development).

In 2000, 19 leading German companies and organisations that have integrated the model for sustainable development into their strategy founded *econsense* as a forum for sustainable development in Germany. Currently, 24 companies are represented in *econsense*.[1] The project was initiated by the Federation of German Industries (Bundesverband der Deutschen Industrie eV [BDI]).

The initiative wants to make an active and constructive contribution to creating a sustainable future in which life is worth living. The primary objective is to influence political framework conditions to enable and promote innovation, but the member companies also form a network for exchanging knowledge and know-how.

Econsense is

- A platform for open dialogue between industry, politics and stakeholders—in national as well as international contexts
- A think-tank that produces workable concepts for sustainable management and policies and focuses industry's problem-solving skills
- A workshop set up to develop and test scenarios
- A competence centre that supplies knowledge and experience at national and international levels
- An active and distinct voice in the political debate, which puts issues on the political agenda and suggests new solutions

Focus on dialogue

We regard open dialogue with political decision-makers and stakeholders from NGOs, science and society as essential for successfully framing and implementing the sustainability concept. The key issue for us is to develop scenarios for our future society, and this requires intensive exchange with representatives of social groups. We need to get to know their way of thinking, their motivations and aims as well as their needs. Our aim is to join forces and find sustainable solutions that make the most of the capacities of industry, politics, science and non-governmental organisations, and link them in a dense network. We want transparency with regard to conflicts, goals and topics, instruments and achievements.

The Forum for Sustainable Development has firmly set its sights on this aim. Throughout the past year *econsense* has provided opportunities for intensive discussions with representatives from industry at meetings and international conferences, within the framework of workshops on selected issues, in small groups at round-tables and in talks with political representatives.

1 The member companies of *econsense* are: Allianz, BASF, Bayer, BMW, Bosch, Daimler-Chrysler, Deutsche Bahn, Deutsche Bank, Deutsche Telekom, E.ON, Gerling, Heidelberg-Cement, Henkel, Lufthansa, Munich Re, RAG, Ruhrgas, RWE, Siemens, Tetra Pak, ThyssenKrupp, TUI, VCI (Association of the Germany Chemical Industry), Volkswagen.

During the first project phase, project groups have worked on various focal topics such as climate protection and sustainability, sustainable energy and sustainable products (sustainable consumption). We will now move on from topics with a primarily environmental focus to other issues that are important aspects of sustainable development. The present sustainability discussion does not yet go far enough, particularly where the social dimensions of sustainability, flexible work systems, social backup systems or even education are concerned. *Econsense* will therefore shift its focus toward topics such as sustainable mobility, the social dimension of sustainability, financial services, sustainability management and sustainability indicators, education and qualifications, globalisation and corporate governance.

Sustainability

'Sustainability' is a term that is on everybody's lips at the moment. Correctly so, for this important concept is in fact a big opportunity for our society and may help to overcome the reform build-up. Unfortunately, 'sustainability' is frequently used without a clear definition, and there is a risk of the term becoming a meaningless catchword.

Econsense has explained in detail how the member organisations understand sustainability. Their view of the sustainability concept is summarised in the following four core ideas.

Sustainable development strives for a balance between economic, social and ecological goals

One of the fundamental beliefs of *econsense* is that sustainable development requires a balanced consideration of economic, social and ecological aspects. So far the discussion has clearly focused on ecological problems. However, such a one-sided view is inadequate and does not do justice to the idea of sustainability. Economic growth and appropriate social framework conditions are prerequisites for developing a society fit for the future.

Sustainability is an essential, strategic competitive factor for industry

Sustainable development is recognised by the *econsense* member companies as a competitive advantage. The challenge is to secure economic growth in the long term, to recognise the important role cultural and social corporate involvement plays and to guarantee long-term availability of resources.

Sustainable development is a continual searching and learning process

We must constantly review our decisions and problem-solving concepts and correct them if necessary. We need the courage and readiness to take risks for individual solutions and time and time again must think over ideas and concepts relating to sustainable economy and politics. For what seems sustainable may change with time. Solutions are not universally applicable and by no means ultimate; they must be specifically defined for each individual case and have to be updated in line with societal awareness.

Shaping a sustainable future requires new political approaches

Management action is not oriented on political cycles. Innovations essential for sustainable development belong in a long-term perspective, so innovative entrepreneurship and sound investment strategies need the planning security provided by reliable political framework conditions.

The members of *econsense* wish to help ensure that future as well as present generations have the freedom to realise their right to shape their lives in a secure future.[2]

---

2 *Econsense* provides English-language information at www.econsense.de.

8
Launching the ISS Sustainable Development

Raymond van Ermen
European Partners for the Environment, Belgium

Let us take the International Space Station (ISS) as a model. The designers and engineers who created it hail from all corners of the globe. The time has come for all parties concerned with a more equitable globalisation to form a team of social engineers for a new endeavour—to create a working model of sustainable living and business styles. Lester Brown, founder of the Earth Policy Institute, has pointed to the need to accelerate the transition to sustainable development (Brown 2001). A 'network of excellence' should take the lead in a project following a systemic and holistic approach. Europeans have an essential contribution to make.

The challenge of moving toward sustainable development is of the same order of magnitude as the conquest of outer space, and the ISS makes a compelling metaphor. Both endeavours require a systemic approach and the development of synergies. The difference is that—intense competition in space and continuing battles on Earth notwithstanding—Russians, Americans (USA, Canada and Brazil), Japanese and Europeans have learned to share knowledge and to trust each other enough to collaborate aboard the same vessel. We seem to be unable to do so when it comes to addressing the complexity of moving Earth toward the new paradigm that is sustainable development.

What is needed is a partnership between science, industry, technology and trade on the one hand and human rights, solidarity, equity, protection of the global commons and the rights of future generations on the other. Such a partnership will have to address first and foremost the agenda of the poor.

Hawken *et al.* (1999) explore the lucrative opportunities for businesses in an era of approaching environmental limits and explain how the world is on the verge of a new industrial revolution—one that promises to transform our fundamental notions about commerce, in which business and environmental interests increas-

8. Launching the ISS Sustainable Development *van Ermen* 53

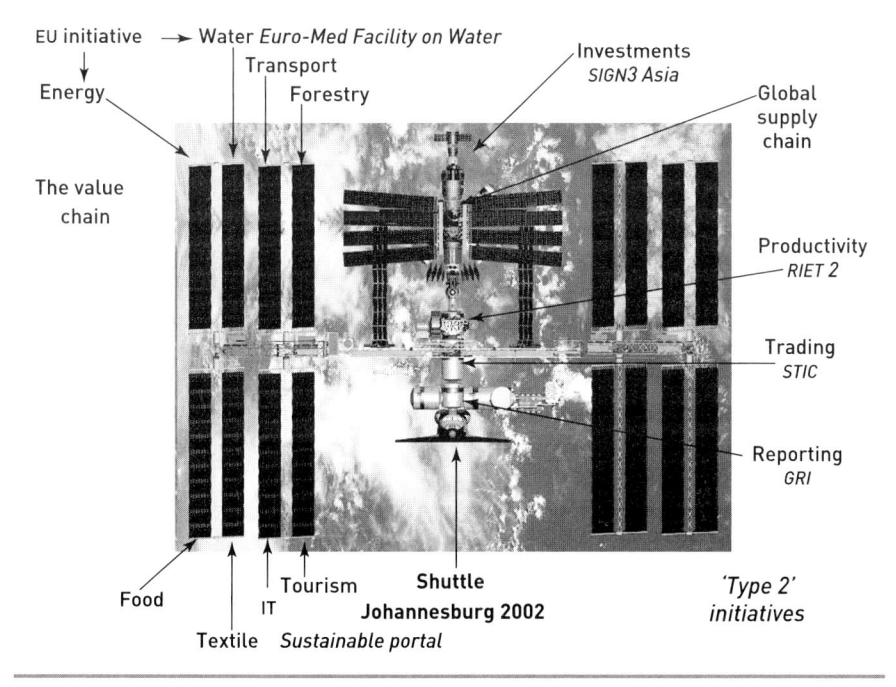

Figure 8.1 ISS sustainable development

ingly overlap, and in which businesses can better satisfy their customers' needs, increase profits and help solve environmental problems all at the same time.

The lessons learned from the European Eco-Efficiency Initiative (EEEI) process confirm that a network of excellence would have to address several critical issues and bring together European and non-European research networks dealing with:

- A co-development model
- A new entrepreneurial model
- A new governance scheme (how to improve synergies between institutions and networks)
- A dematerialised, service-oriented, knowledge-based economy (how to reach total resource productivity/eco-efficiency)
- A European industrial policy in support of sustainable development
- A new investments policy
- An ecological and fair purchasing and trade strategy
- A fully integrated, ecologically based land and water use policy

Globalisation should be fully inclusive and equitable. This is not the case at present. The world today is neither equitable nor sustainable. The continued existence of absolute poverty in many parts of the world undermines the advancement of basic human rights. Cultural and natural diversity are key issues. The challenge has moral, ethical and spiritual dimensions.

Time is running out. The central question facing our generation is whether it is possible to meet the needs of the poor and reverse environmental deterioration before it spirals out of control. The answer is yes! As Lester Brown (2001) indicated, 'almost all the component goals of a sustainable economy have been achieved by at least one country'.

We need to shape new synergies between stakeholders to foster the necessary shift toward an inclusive globalisation through partnerships. A coalition 'pro-poor, pro-peace and pro-planet' should take the lead, and Europeans have a specific contribution to make here. Such a coalition should

1. Ensure that developing-country stakeholders play a leading role in the development of WSSD partnerships from the beginning of the process
2. Involve intergovernmental organisations and support them in co-ordinating their activities at an informal level
3. Engage high-level stakeholders, such as heads of government, CEOs and leaders of civil-society organisations, to ensure the full commitment of governments and other organisations to the implementation strategies developed in the new partnerships

Elements of ISS design

Of course, engineering an 'International Sustainability Synergy' requires the best experts! In the framework of the Sixth Framework Programme for Research and Development of the EU, it would be useful to launch a network of excellence addressing the basic components of the ISS we are concerned with, the international sustainable society.

Such a network of excellence should play a key role in helping to shape a strategy of synergies, building bridges between current initiatives and players in order to assemble contributions to the design of such an endeavour. Another issue is how to 'engineer' the first ISS nucleus that the elements of the value chain will lock onto in a way that orients investments, productivity (eco-efficiency), purchasing, trading and reporting toward sustainable development.

A co-development

Let me present two of the many Type 2 initiatives that might offer a vehicle for partnership toward co-development, and in which European Partners for the Environment (EPE) is involved.

Sustainable Trade and Innovation Centre

The integration of developing countries into the global economy and addressing development needs were central objectives of the new round of multilateral trade negotiations in the WTO. Part of a potential package for technical assistance and capacity-building in the trade and environment area is the Sustainable Trade and Innovation Centre (STIC),[1] a market-driven initiative launched in Johannesburg. Promoted jointly by developing and developed countries, its main beneficiaries would be local sustainable enterprises. A feasibility study has been conducted under the guidance of an international advisory board headed by Minister Ngubane of South Africa and supported by the EU and the Commonwealth Science Council. The Centre's objective is to facilitate exports of sustainable goods and services from developing countries to OECD countries. Sectors of primary focus are textiles, agri-food and electronics.

Sustainable Investments–Global Network for Asia

Another initiative, called Sustainable Investments–Global Network for Asia (SIGN),[2] has been launched with EU financial support by a cross-sectoral consortium including the Asia–Pacific Development Centre and UNEP. Its core concern is to balance a rapidly diminishing level of ODA with the increasing amount of financial resource flows associated with foreign direct investment (FDI) and trade. Its broad aim is to assist in catalysing a paradigm shift in the way in which private capital, institutional investments and ODA flow into Asian developing economies, thus boosting sustainable investment. Convergence between international trade, FDI and development aid unlocks and redirects private capital to address concerns over escalating poverty and a deteriorating environment. Since the donor aid pathway appears to be eroding under the weight of global circumstances, there is an urgent need to leverage sources of private capital, in particular foreign direct investment and trade. Bringing FDI to bear on donor aid projects has served as a mechanism to achieve convergence and in the process has harmonised activities around a trade–poverty–environment nexus.

SIGN Asia is designed to assist low- and middle-income countries in overcoming their deteriorating economic and environmental conditions through a more efficient allocation of an ODA–FDI–trade pathway. Its realisation helps to create a new order for economic co-operation between developed and developing countries of the world.

It seems to me that this project is perfectly in line with the conclusions of the round-table that Minister Moosa co-chaired in Monterrey on 'Financing Environment and Sustainable Development'. We expect that this initiative will be replicated in other regions of the world.

1 STIC at www.johannesburgsummit.org/html/sustainable_dev/p2_means_implement.html#transfer.
2 SIGN Asia at www.epe.be/sign3/summary/sign3summary.html.

A new entrepreneurial and business model

The sustainable development economy will become a successful new business paradigm. The time has come for enlightened players to cross the threshold and make the old model obsolete. Accelerating the transition is vital for achieving peace and prosperity for all. A new approach is required.

An increasing number of European companies are promoting their CSR strategies as a response to a variety of social, environmental and economic pressures. They aim to convey a message to the various stakeholders with whom they interact, to employees, shareholders, investors, consumers, public authorities and NGOs. In so doing, companies invest in their future, and they expect that their adoption of voluntary commitments to sustainable development will help to increase their profitability.

It requires new entrepreneurial and business models to bring essential products to markets in the developing world, to introduce new technologies, to implement new work and employment systems, for new commercial approaches, and for effective partnership structures to deliver sustainable development. The modelling exercise should address which developments are related to responsible enterprise (the way companies operate) and which developments are related to the business contribution to society (what they provide), as well as strategic managerial issues, such as relations with stakeholders/shareholders, branded products, mergers, franchising, eco-fair trade and the value chain.

A new governance scheme for a Europe of synergies

Success in a networked knowledge society is more likely to be secured if a public authority is designed into the coalition of institutions and networks. The UN is very advanced in developing this approach. Within a European context, EU institutions should be able to play a leading role and be one of the major partners of a Europe of synergies.

The EU could become, or could once more be, the community it was under the leadership of Jean Monet: 'the leading post-modern state, [leading on the basis of values that are] peace, not blood, co-development, not competition, synergy, not superpower or empire, social commitment with coherence within the society' (Luyckx 2001).

However, several experiences, including the EEEI, show us that the EU is not, today, aware of this potential or able to convert it. Symptoms include lack of leadership, lack of continuity, loss of institutional memory, disparate and lost databases, attempts to manipulate stakeholders and over-cumbersome procedures.

Here is a story to illustrate this point. Year: 2000. Place: Brussels, Office of the President of the European Commission. Sitting in front of the President were leaders of the business community (WBCSD President), trade unions (European Trade Union Confederation [ETUC]), environmental NGOs (European Environmental Bureau [EEB] President) and multi-stakeholder groups (EPE President). They were telling President Prodi about their joint proposal to launch a process involving companies and supporting the implementation of the European Union Sustainable Development Strategy, its macro-indicators and its targets. Building on the evidence of a recent Michael Porter report and the development of such initiatives as the Dow Jones Sustainability Index (DJSI) group, these businesses, trade unions and NGOs proposed to join efforts to follow up the first phase of the EEEI. There has been no response to this remarkable offer, neither during the meeting nor afterwards. How does one interpret this? Simply as a missed opportunity? No, as a strategic mistake by the Commission Services.

A dematerialised, service-oriented, knowledge-based economy

If a dematerialised, service-oriented and knowledge-based economy is our goal for Europe, what does that mean and how do we get there? As a minimum, it requires consensus on

- A 'target scenario' covering all dimensions of sustainable development (social, cultural, economic and ecological)
- New forms of governance, involving governments, business and civil society, integrated into this scenario
- The ways and means of meeting the target, time-lines and the role of the various partners in the process of developing
    - Systemic strategies for achieving sustainability
    - Massive technological innovation for new services, infrastructure and products
    - A mix of efficiency–sufficiency–compatibility strategies to avoid rebound effects
    - A better understanding of the systemic relationships between all aspects of sustainable development and of the dynamics of a service-oriented, networked-knowledge society

As Amory Lovins has noted (Hawken *et al.* 1999: 9):

> The first of natural capitalism's four interlinked principles . . . is radically increased resource productivity. Implementing just this first principle can significantly improve a firm's bottom line, and can also help finance the other three. They are: redesigning industry on biological models with closed loops and zero waste; shifting from the sale of goods (for example, light bulbs) to the provision of services (illumination); and reinvesting in the natural capital that is the basis of future prosperity.

The need for a visionary industrial policy

Europe has a huge potential but the institutional delivery of eco-efficiency does not meet the ambitious expectations some had of the EU. Why is this so? Undoubtedly because there is a lack of vision.

Within the DG Enterprise the mood is still that eco-efficiency is a burden, not an opportunity. European competitiveness is still addressed from a short-term perspective. The need to move toward new processes, products and services to meet the basic needs of the global population, especially the poor, and to foster innovation, new competitiveness and new markets, including in Central and Eastern Europe, are simply not on the agenda. It seems that sustainability for the Commission is not a successful business paradigm—as it is perceived by a growing number of companies—but a threat.

There is a technical explanation for this attitude, which is, however, no justification. It relates to the weight of old trading associations defending old-fashioned views and able to veto any project. In the EU we badly need a new approach toward an industrial policy, leveraging EU tools such as facilities development, subsidies, R&D and co-operation programmes with Asia and other regions of the world, to foster the implementation of the new business paradigm.

Various EU initiatives should be put in alignment with sustainable development objectives:

- The Commission should address responsible entrepreneurship as an overarching concept.

- The multi-annual Programme for Enterprise and Entrepreneurship should channel EU support into increasing the understanding of the competitive and environmental value of eco-efficiency and the convergence initiative.

- The European Charter for small and medium-sized enterprises (SMEs) should address the importance of (1) co-operation within the supply chain to maximise the competitive and environmental value of eco-efficiency, and (2) the importance of sustainable development indicators.

- An assessment of the contribution of public finances to growth and employment should address the context of sustainable development and explore how to support the convergence process.

- The updating of public procurement rules should encourage eco-fair and eco-effective procurement as a means of driving and rewarding responsible entrepreneurship. The tender procedure requirements should secure access to procurement markets only to those companies with performance records aligned with the rules and specific sustainable development targets.

- A review of the Regulatory and Financial Incentives Framework should encourage initiatives fostering responsible entrepreneurship, such as eco-efficiency, eco-effectiveness and ethical business practices.

- Trade provisions in the framework of WTO should be revised to ensure they are in line with existing international conventions on environmental protection, human rights and labour.
- Support of export credit agencies should be limited to projects in line with the convergence indicators.

A new investment policy

According to Nick Robins of Henderson Global Investors:

> There is now an increasingly widespread appreciation of the design flaws inherent in the 1990s model of corporate globalisation—even within the financial community. When the chief economist of Morgan Stanley [Roach 2001] points to the geopolitical tensions wrought by rising income inequality and highlights the tendency for globalisation to 'sow the seeds of its own demise' a significant watershed has been crossed. Yet, what is lacking is a coherent global framework that places investment in the over-arching context of sustainable development. As with so many areas where markets have overstepped the global governance, solutions are emerging from hybrid initiatives that bring together market innovation, social action and enabling regulation (Robins 2002).

New agenda issues

According to Nick Robins, further efforts should be explored (Robins 2002):

- **Mobilising new resources** to explore and recommend ways in which a portion of industrialised country pension fund assets would be 'channelled toward sustainable development funds in the South . . . These funds would have to meet the highest standards of financial probity and sustainability analysis, and could be particularly targeted towards the financial needs of small and medium sized enterprises, perhaps through partnerships with local banks.'
- **Extending stock market disclosure** 'to form a task force to agree core sustainable development disclosure requirements which could be adopted by all stock markets'.
- **New models of ownership**: launch a process to recommend new models of ownership for utility sectors where regulation alone can probably never wholly protect the public interest.
- **Building common standards** to support socially responsible investment (SRI) fund managers in North America and Europe in their dealings with the South, where they often operate 'with unclear legitimacy. Fund criteria are being introduced and implemented which could have pro-

found implications for developing countries—both positive and negative—with external input coming, if at all, from Northern environment and development NGOs. Just as with the tense and distrustful world of sustainable trade, so the SRI movement now needs to develop governance frameworks that allow for the co-evolution of standards in place of unilateral imposition . . . a first global SRI congress should be held (in 2004?) to agree governance principles for SRI against which different funds could be judged.'

An eco-fair purchasing and trade strategy: a fast track to new production and consumption patterns

EPE and WBCSD have welcomed the emergence of a framework and process within the EU that fosters efficiency by

- Adopting indicators (manage better what you measure)
- Developing benchmarking (respond and reward)
- Setting targets (achieve what has been agreed)

Claude Fussler of the WBCSD and EPE's past president proposed developing a 'convergence process for sustainable development' similar to the 'euro method' and comprising some indicators reflecting the triple bottom line, targets and timetable. 'The analogy of "sustainability convergence criteria" is the key as it aims to raise the profile of sustainability to that of the Euro, one of the key dimensions of European integration in recent years,' noted Nick Robins (Club of Rome 2001). A set of convergence criteria must be simple, compelling and accessible to every aware citizen. It must stimulate a desire to build a better society based on specific plans and strong co-operation among all actors.

Drawing some lessons from the successes and failures of the Fifth Environmental Programme, let me propose a 'fast track' to implementing the sustainable development strategy, with its indicators, targets and timetable, through a purchasing and supply chain management initiative. Indeed, today, a large part of trade is centrally managed, through intra-firm transfers and outsourcing. A multinational has easily more than 100,000 suppliers. The sustainable development convergence initiative, based on agreed indicators, targets and timetables, would innovate in two ways:

- Effective monitoring of follow-up action would be achieved by procurement guidelines, as well as records and assessments of procurement officers' purchasing decisions.
- Companies would join the process, adapt their purchasing procedures and report via their annual sustainability/environmental report.

The process would involve **two tracks**. The aim of the first is to set a framework involving the commission and member states in fixing the governmental agenda. The second track highlights companies as motors of development, harnessing market forces to support the convergence process of sustainable development (see Table 8.1).

	Policy	Instruments
Track 1	Setting the governmental framework	
EU	EU strategy for sustainable development	Indicators, thresholds, dates
Member states		
Track 2	Encouraging companies to act	
Value chain	Eco-fair purchasing in line with the six indicators	Negotiated agreement between vendors and institutional buyers
Companies	Commitments toward continuous improvement of environmental performance in line with the six indicators	WBCSD eco-efficiency indicators (reporting); GRI reporting; sustainable electronic platform reporting

Table 8.1 Fast-track sustainable development strategy

The sustainable development indicators should include criteria that address the following dimensions:

- Eco-efficiency: if the material efficiency of our economy increases at a higher rate than our economic growth, we produce more wealth with less environmental impact
- Energy and greenhouse gases: energy savings in line with our Kyoto targets
- Fresh water: more wealth and crops using the water resources we have

Eco-efficiency is a necessary but not sufficient condition for sustainable development. We recognise that responsible entrepreneurs want to contribute to the social success of the societies in which they operate. An encompassing sustainable development strategy must therefore also take into account:

- Poverty (the Portuguese presidency proposed poverty reduction from 18% to 10% by 2010)
- Public health

- Employee and other stakeholder involvement

The support policy should:

- Cover all industrial activities within the EU (no exclusion, no derogation)
- Provide accompanying measures for companies committed to sustainability
- Support partnerships in favour of sustainability
- Implement market-improving instruments such as
  - A subsidy reform to get rid of subsidies with negative environmental impacts
  - Environmental (and revenue-neutral, social) tax reforms.

A land-use management policy

Eco-efficiency requires a new approach to mobility and goods transport. Industrial estates should be designed to favour eco-efficiency, notably by incorporating the principles of industrial ecology, where the waste products of one enterprise are raw material for another. Eco-efficiency includes a more co-ordinated management of water and wastes at the level of industrial estates.

The possible environmental impacts of industrial estates are numerous: contaminated soil and lost future land use, disposal of solid waste, local irritants such as noise and transport, exposure to toxic chemicals, risks from hazardous waste, marine pollution, freshwater pollution, air pollution, habitat degradation, ozone-depleting and greenhouse gases, landscape disturbance, and spills.

Conclusions

The EU Sustainable Development Convergence Initiative as a follow-up of the EEEI is intended as a pilot initiative related to 'sustainability through the market', 'European and global governance' and 'sustainable supply chain and trade'.

For Europe, embracing sustainable development should become a turning point in economic competitiveness. 'Decoupling', 'eco-efficiency' and 'ecological footprint' are slowly entering EU policies, though of course not fast enough in the eyes of major European civil-society groups. The movement toward greening Europe, and in particular greening its purchasing policy, is becoming a major issue with an important evolution from a purely ecological to a sustainable-trade approach.

Key points are the pressure of emerging economies and the concerns of transnational corporations, now under heavy scrutiny by civil society and the financial community, in particular sustainable development rating agencies.

But perhaps the most promising sign in 2002 are the projects and joint ventures developed as part of 'cross-cultural innovation' initiatives. Indeed, to secure a 'better quality of life for everyone, now and for the future generations'—another definition of sustainable development—we need more than business as usual. Partnerships between local entrepreneurs (for example in India) and their counterparts in Europe are offering new opportunities in the textile sector as well as in information technologies and other sectors. A networked-knowledge society enables new synergies that lead toward a new economy. The new development model addresses ethics, spirituality, cultural diversity, dematerialisation, co-development, and allows room for exciting partnership opportunities, in particular between developing countries and Europe. A new civilisation project is emerging. From the roots of old civilisations the elements of a new paradigm are growing. Its fruit are peace and better quality of life for everyone.

9
Sustainable business development

Michael Kuhndt
Wuppertal Institute, Germany

Sustainable development remains a formidable challenge to the societies of the 21st century. A number of concepts have been put forward on how to reach sustainability at a macro-economic level. These concepts are based on different points of view of economic, social and environmental systems and their behaviour, and derive from economic and environmental theories. Different organisations (e.g. UN, OECD, European Commission) have already introduced sustainability targets and indicators on the macro level: that is, on the economic level. Furthermore, and this is the focus of this chapter, various concepts for implementation have been suggested, such as cleaner production, Factor 4, Factor 10, eco-efficiency, environmental and social accounting, corporate citizenship or corporate social responsibility. Sustainability agendas have been set up by different stakeholders such as political institutions, consumer associations, NGOs, the financial sector and the business sector. Some of the principal policy and business agendas now being pursued include: expanded application of economic instruments to environmental management; measures to encourage eco-efficient production patterns and corporate social responsibility; supply- and demand-side management strategies; increasing public participation in business and policy development; information and public awareness programmes; product performance targets; and policies and guidelines for reporting. The quest for sustainable consumption and production patterns requires a broadly accepted set of qualitative and quantitative targets, and indicators to measure and monitor progress. Table 9.1 provides an overview of some agendas (i.e. initiatives, tools or publications) relevant for sustainable business development.

To move toward sustainable development, businesses and in fact all actors in society will have to rethink their behaviour. Where environmental and social issues are concerned, companies start from various stages of development and corporate culture. The model in Figure 9.1, adopted from Klinkers *et al.* 1999, distinguishes five phases.

Leading organisation	Initiative/document	Core mission
United Nations (UN)	Agenda 21	• Provide a comprehensive plan of action to be taken globally, nationally and locally by organisations of the UN system, governments and major groups in every area in which there is human impact on the environment
United Nations Commission on Sustainable Development (UNCSD)	Indicators for Sustainable Development: Framework and Methodologies	• Provide a framework for the development and selection of sustainability indicators for monitoring progress toward sustainable development at the national level • Ensure a high level of practicality and acceptance through intensive pilot-testing
International Labour Organisation (ILO)	ILO standards	• Establish norms covering all aspects of working conditions and industrial relations • Ensure that member countries respect, promote and realise these norms, especially principles concerning fundamental rights at work
Organisation for Economic Co-operation and Development (OECD)	OECD Guidelines for Multinational Enterprises	• Encourage responsible business practices • Enhance multinational enterprises' contribution to sustainable development • Strengthen government–business relationships
Commission of the European Communities (CEC)	CEC Green Paper on Corporate Social Responsibility (CSR)	• Initiate a wide debate on CSR at all levels • Develop a CSR framework (in the long run)
UN Secretary-General	UN Global Compact	• Build the social and environmental pillars required to sustain the new global economy • Make globalisation work for all the world's people, based on commitment to universal principles

Table 9.1 Selected initiatives or documents for sustainable business development and their core mission (continued over)

Source: Kuhndt et al. 2002

Leading organisation	Initiative/document	Core mission
Global Reporting Initiative (GRI)	Sustainability Reporting Guidelines on economic, environmental and social performance	• Forge the link between environmental and economic performance • Elevate sustainability reporting to a level equivalent to financial reporting through a standardised reporting framework
International Organisation for Standardisation (ISO)	ISO 14031	• Offer an internal management tool designed to provide management with reliable and verifiable information on an ongoing basis to determine whether an organisation's environmental performance meets the criteria set by management
Social Accountability International (SAI)	SA 8000	• Improve labour conditions through a workplace standard, a verification system and public reporting
AccountAbility	AA 1000 series Consultation briefing 1	• Improve the accountability and overall performance of organisations by increasing the quality of social and ethical accounting, auditing and reporting
United Nations Environment Programme (UNEP)	UNEP's Financial Institutions Initiative	• Engage a broad range of financial institutions in constructive dialogue about sustainable development issues • Identify, promote and realise the adoption of best sustainability practice at all levels of financial institution operations
Dow Jones Sustainability Group Indices (partnership of Dow Jones & Company with Sustainable Asset Management [SAM])	SAM questionnaire	• Establish a ranking of sustainability leader companies for investment purposes according to their management of sustainability opportunities and risks

Table 9.1 (from previous page; continued opposite)

Leading organisation	Initiative/document	Core mission
International Chamber of Commerce (ICC)	ICC Business Charter for Sustainable Development	• Encourage continuous improvement in environmental management and practice • Commit the widest range of enterprises possible to the charter's principles • Assist enterprises in fulfilling their commitment
World Business Council for Sustainable Development (WBCSD)	Measuring Eco-efficiency	• Reduce business impact on the environment while continuing to grow and develop
	Corporate Social Responsibility: Making Good Business Sense	• Increase the understanding of CSR in the business community, including the following aspects: interdependent nature of the business–society relationship, contribution of CSR to long-term prosperity, the role of stakeholder dialogue • Offer a navigator to guide companies in the implementation of CSR in daily business practice
Corporate Social Responsibility Europe (CSR Europe)	Communicating Corporate Social Responsibility	• Encourage companies to commit to voluntary external reporting on social and environmental performance across all company operations • Encourage companies to use a variety of communication methods provide a CSR reporting approach
Amnesty International (AI) and Prince of Wales Business Leaders Forum	Human Rights: Is it Any of Your Business?	• Inform companies about business-relevant human rights aspects • Assist companies in developing adequate human rights policies

Table 9.1 (continued)

In the output-oriented phase 1, management emphasis is on outputs rather than processes. Errors here only become apparent after the event, so companies in this phase can be labelled reactive with respect to the environment. Process orientation is characteristic of phase 2, in which the focus has shifted to the production process and its management. Major errors here can be corrected on the basis of measurements and knowledge of the process. During phase 3, system orientation makes the entire organisation including support processes and their management the focus of performance improvement measures. In this phase, a system is set up

	Green entrepreneurship		Efficient entrepreneurship	Responsible entrepreneurship
Phase 1	Phase 2	Phase 3	Phase 4	Phase 5
Output-oriented	Process-oriented	System-oriented	Chain-oriented	Stakeholder-oriented

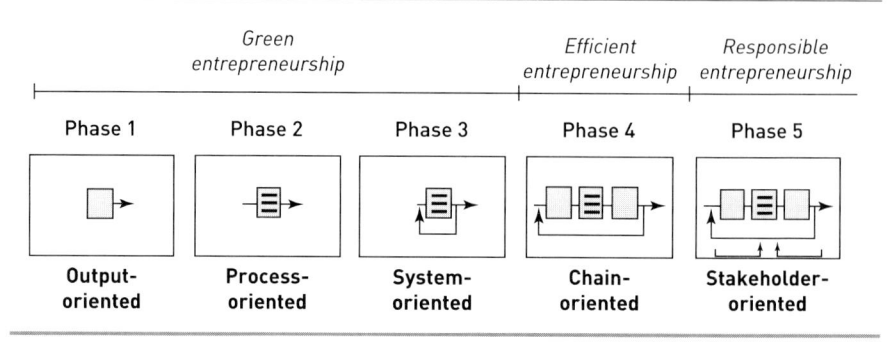

Figure 9.1 Different phases of sustainable business development

Source: Adapted from Klinkers *et al.* 1999

that controls production processes and aims at preventative measures including corrective action if mistakes occur. In contrast to the previous phases' internal focus, the chain-oriented phase 4 takes external effects within markets into account as companies relate the whole organisation to other actors. In a co-operative way, win–win situations are created for the entire chain. At the stakeholder-oriented stage (phase 5), companies base their vision and policy on stakeholder expectations, acting from a sense of responsibility toward society.

The order of the different phases (from green, to [eco]-efficient, and then responsible entrepreneurship) seems to be the path most companies follow on their way toward sustainable development. Companies often begin by addressing internal environmental issues (and realising cost-saving potentials by internal environmental management) before they go further and address environmental issues in the product chain and, finally, stakeholders such as the community, NGOs, etc. However, as Klinkers *et al.* (1999) point out, it is not necessary to focus on internal environmental management before taking the step into the chain. Companies can just as well bypass the first phases and start with phase 3 or 4.

A number of multinational companies and SMEs are as yet unfamiliar with the approaches taken in most phases. However, because of increased pressure from customers, authorities, mainly public procurement agencies, central wholesale organisations or industrial companies within the product chain, environmental and social concern is slowly increasing. In business-to-business customer relationships, matters that must be dealt with include the handling of environmental and social affairs and their management in general, the use of environmentally and socially sound solutions, as well as information on the product's environmental and social impacts during its life-cycle.

To promote sustainability at the enterprise and industry level, different stakeholders (e.g. governments, NGOs, companies) have started to translate broad sustainability concepts at the macro level into specific measures that are helpful in day-to-day business activities. Corporate policy, strategy and decision-making processes need to integrate economic (high profits, high competitiveness, low investment payback, etc.), ecological (high life-cycle-wide resource productivity, low toxicity, high biodiversity, low erosion, etc.) and social aspects (from employee satisfaction, a low unemployment rate to overall stability in society) (see Table 9.2).

9. Sustainable business development *Kuhndt*

Level	Business context	Examples of decisions where sustainability performance information is helpful
Strategic level	1. Strategic planning	• Corporate policy development • Long-term strategies for technological development • Strategies for research and development of a sustainable product portfolio
	2. Capital investment and acquisition	• Investment in new technologies or production lines improving sustainability performance
Tactical level	3. Design and development (products/services and processes)	• Product and service developments at different levels of improvement • Process development • Technological development
Operational level	4. Communication and marketing	• Marketing decisions: companies can use sustainability information to advertise their products as 'more sustainable' or to refute adverse claims about products by competitors, NGOs and consumers • Product labelling (ISO 14020, Type III) • Sustainability reporting for external communication, co-operation and networking
	5. Operational management (including operational purchasing and procurement)	• Internal monitoring • Identify and prioritise management opportunities • Compliance with existing or upcoming regulations or initiatives (e.g. EU Integrated Product Policy) • Sustainability management and auditing • Product stewardship and chain management • Supplier choice, especially relevant in view of issues such as chain liability • Benchmarking: companies can compare their own performance with their competitors', or may want to monitor their own sustainability performance over time

Table 9.2 Corporate decisions requiring sustainability information

Source: adapted from Wrisberg and Udo de Haes 2002

Several tools—for example, operational methods—have been developed for/at companies to support decisions oriented on sustainability (Elkington 1997; Kuhndt and Liedtke 1999; Kuhndt and van der Lugt 2000; Wrisberg and Udo de Haes 2002). These management tools provide essential support for green, (eco-)efficient and responsible entrepreneurship.

According to UNEP (1995), environmental management tools can be broken down into tools for analysis and evaluation, tools for action, and tools for communication and stakeholder relations. This typology is used to present tools relevant to the current discussion (Table 9.3).

Issues tackled	*Responsible entrepreneurship* — *Social, economic and environmental*		
	Efficient entrepreneurship — *Economic and environmental*		
	Green entrepreneurship — *Environmental*		
	Environmental	**Economic and environmental**	**Social, economic and environmental**
Analytical tools	• Ecological footprint • Environmental performance evaluation • Life-cycle assessment • Material flow analysis • Material input per service unit (MIPS) • Environmental auditing	• Full-cost accounting • Life-cycle costing • Resource efficiency accounting • Cost–benefit analysis • Eco-efficiency analysis	• Sustainability accounting (sustainable balanced scorecard) • Stakeholder value approach
Tools for action	• Environmental management systems • Eco-design tools	• Green procurement • Efficient entrepreneur calendar	• Companies' and sectors' pass to sustainability (COMPASS) • Sustainability assessment for enterprises (SAFE) • Suppliers' accreditation
Tools for communication and stakeholder relations	• Eco-labels • Environmental product declaration • Environmental reporting • Eco-benchmarking/rating	• Eco-marketing • Environmental aspects in financial reporting • Eco-efficiency–benchmarking/rating	• Sustainability reporting • Triple-bottom-line benchmarking/rating

Table 9.3 **Overview of corporate management tools**

Source: adapted from Henriques 2000; Kuhndt and von Geibler 2002

For green entrepreneurship there are a number of tools for each area of focus described above. These tools help to satisfy different informational needs. The nature and extent of the environmental information needed depends on the level of stakeholders' interest and the strategic level of the decision. A broad distinction can be made between the following levels of interest:

- Compliance with legislation and making agreements between parties (environmental legislation, covenants, international treaties)
- Market-oriented considerations (green consumerism, competitive advantage, pressure from customers)
- Proactive economic considerations (waste reduction, cost effectiveness, anticipation of future policy measures, environmental liability)
- Ecological/societal considerations (aiming at sustainable development)

The tools to provide such information have developed over time; some, such as environmental auditing, environmental management systems or environmental performance evaluation, have even achieved standardisation. The most important related standardisation processes within the European debate are the Eco-Management and Audit Scheme (EMAS) and the worldwide International Organisation for Standardisation (ISO) 14000 series. The elements within the 14000 series have different areas of focus (see Fig. 9.2). EMS, environmental auditing and environmental performance evaluation have a more organisational focus, whereas life-cycle assessment, the integration of environmental aspects in product development and environmental labelling are more related to products. All tools are conceived for the micro (companies and products) level.

Environmental management systems ISO 14001	Environmental auditing ISO 14010	Life-cycle assessment ISO 14040	Environmental labelling ISO 14020
	Environmental performance evaluation ISO 14030	Design for environment ISO 14062	

organisational focus → *Increasing level of* → *product focus*

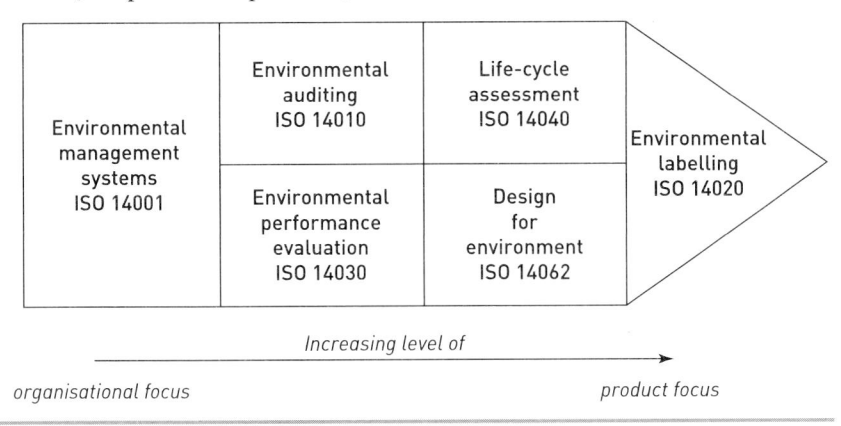

Figure 9.2 Elements of the ISO 14000 series: environmental management
Source: adapted from Lee 2000

Tools for efficient and responsible entrepreneurship have mainly been developed from the environmental toolbox including economic and social (and ethical) aspects. Several analytical tools for communication as well as action are now being developed. Their development reflects companies' and stakeholders' information demands of companies' triple-bottom-line (environmental, economic and social) performance.

Examples of tools incorporating environmental and economic aspects are full-cost accounting, life-cycle costing, cost–benefit analysis, resource efficiency accounting and green procurement. Other upcoming related tools are eco-efficiency rating and benchmarking. All these tools should be complemented and assisted by appropriate information systems (Orbach *et al.* 1998; Orbach and Liedtke 1998), incorporating the information linkages to 'higher' levels, that is, (inter)national sustainability goals and information requirements (Krcmar *et al.* 2000).

Corporate management tools with a social and ethical focus are, for example, social auditing, stakeholder analysis, shareholder value approach or social reporting. They have gained increasing importance in the European debate. Recent developments in corporate social reporting are presented in Figure 9.3.

- GRI (June 2000)
- OECD Guidelines for Multinational Enterprises (revised June 2000)
- EC Social Policy Agenda (adopted June 2000)
- AccountAbility 1000 (November 1999)
- European Business Network for Social Cohesion CSR Matrix (October 1999)
- Global Corporate Governance Forum (September 1999)
- Global Sullivan Principles (February 1999)
- UN Global Compact (January 1999)

Figure 9.3 Some recent developments in corporate social reporting
Source: McGregor and Peirce 2000

Different national and international governmental bodies, business and civil-society organisations play equally important roles here. Much effort has gone into agreeing standardised tools. However, so far only a few tools for responsible entrepreneurship have been standardised: for example, the Social Accountability (SA) 8000 or AccountAbility's AA 1000 for social auditing (see Table 9.1). Compared to tools for green entrepreneurship, the degree of standardisation for efficient and responsible management tools seems to be lower, perhaps because in the debate on sustainability there is most consensus on its environmental aspects (GRI 2002).

Parallel to the evolution of management tools toward sustainable industrial development, the actors engaged in the development of tools are changing. Actors developing tools for green entrepreneurship have mainly been academic institutions (natural science and engineering), business, environmental NGOs and governmental institutions. In the current debate on tools for efficient and responsible entrepreneurship, academic economics institutions and other NGOs (e.g. ethical, human rights groups), but also financial institutions and business consultancies are increasingly becoming involved.

10
Deloitte Sustainability Reporting Scorecard

Markus Lehni
Deloitte & Touche, Global Environment and
Sustainability Services, Switzerland

Corporate enterprises and other types of organisation are paying closer attention to their sustainability reports and for a good reason. More and more stakeholders—from regulators to suppliers and investors—use the reports in their decision-making. Businesses read them to decide on potential partners, consumers to choose whose products and services they want to buy, and students to evaluate prospective employers. Investors and financial analysts use sustainability reports as they are increasingly interested in non-financial information, such as social, economic and environmental impacts and related risks and opportunities, to support their investment decisions.

Companies are taking a more comprehensive approach to reporting than previously seen in traditional financial reporting to shareholders. There is also a move from isolated reporting on environment or health and safety toward sustainability, including environmental, social and economic aspects, and including direct and indirect influence on the economy and on society.

Stakeholders' demands for sustainability information have grown more exacting than ever before. Business enterprises are asked for information on their vision, values and principles, the management systems and actions they have in place to support these, their objectives and their past and current performance in comparison to their peers and their targets. They are asked to provide sufficient information on all the issues that stakeholders have identified as being important to them and which have an impact on society, the economy and on the environment.

The value of transparency and reporting

The world today is a place where transparency has become a prerequisite for acceptance in the marketplace and for the licence to operate. Indeed, reporting is a very effective approach toward making progress in sustainable development. External reporting to interested stakeholders enhances trust and acceptance. Internal reporting on progress against targets and on action plans to management supports companies' decision-making and helps to improve performance and business success overall.

Many business and non-business organisations make great efforts to achieve higher transparency and accountability and work together in initiatives such as the UNGC or the GRI to increase acceptance of reporting as an effective tool for making progress, to create a better understanding and enhance the use of commonly accepted reporting principles and formats.

The logic to the process of reporting

To make reporting and communication effective management instruments, it is important that reporting organisations, first and foremost, identify the target audiences of their communication and consult these audiences about their actual information needs and expectations, before they start writing or talking. It might also be important to know what the relevant problems and concerns of stakeholders are and how—as a business organisation—it could contribute useful products and services for solving these problems. Reporting organisations should also identify and characterise those issues of their activities and products that create an impact on any stakeholder group, either directly or indirectly.

Once relevant issues are identified and characterised, reporting organisations can describe to report users how they manage these issues by demonstrating their commitment and management methods, by addressing the sustainable development agenda in their relationship with the various stakeholder groups and by quantifying and progressing their performance. Organisations must demonstrate credibly in their reports that the key sustainability issues are core to their business strategies and objectives. Report users would be looking to see consistency in measures and actions, and to find a 'red thread' throughout their actions and throughout their report.

However, reporting makes sense only if reports reach their audience and are read, and if the information provided is understood. This information can then be the start of a dialogue that finally will lead to a change in behaviour or further improvement of the respective performance. Reports, therefore, must make good use of tools for communicating effectively and work toward creating credibility and trust from the viewpoint of the reader.

We believe that these are the essential steps in demonstrating the business case for sustainable development reporting: what will, finally, lead to a much more widespread acceptance and higher value of sustainability reporting.

A scorecard to assess the quality of reports

To date, environmental and sustainability reports have been largely experimental. Reporting awards have led to the development of scoring criteria that fit particular circumstances. GRI[1] is making great progress in developing a common framework for sustainability reporting and in formulating criteria that reflect current thinking or best practice of reporting. However, there is still a long way to go in making such reporting criteria widely accepted and broadly applied.

The Deloitte Sustainability Reporting Scorecard[2] is a step toward filling this gap.

Benefits from the Deloitte Sustainability Reporting Scorecard

The Deloitte Sustainability Reporting Scorecard concentrates on the quality of the report and the messages communicated, rather than on quantity of information or the completeness of the report in covering all areas and aspects. We intend to give guidance on the process of reporting, on the content of a report and on the format to make sure that the report is able to communicate effectively. We do not specify or require information on specific topics or impacts as these will always depend on the circumstances of the reporting organisation on the one hand and the needs of the report user on the other. This certainly makes assessment more challenging than just checking against a given list of impacts or indicators following a fixed format.

With this scorecard we can only assess how organisations report and what they state in their reports, and not how they perform on sustainable development. The scorecard is about the quality of reports, not the performance of the respective reporting organisation. However, it provides vast opportunities to learn about reporting practices and to improve effectiveness and quality. It also allows for benchmarking of reports over time, against each other, and against best practice.

An innovative tool based on international guidelines

The manual on which the scorecard is based builds on international guidelines established by leading international sustainability and reporting organisations. Many of the criteria evaluated refer to the sustainability reporting guidelines on economic, environmental and social performance of the GRI. Further input comes from the work being done by the WBCSD on sustainable development reporting

---

1 Global Reporting Guidelines (GRI) at www.globalreporting.org.
2 Deloitte Sustainability Reporting Scorecard at www.deloitte-sustainable.com.

and on measuring eco-efficiency (WBCSD 2000a) and on sustainability through the market (WBCSD 2001), as well as on work conducted by the International Auditing Practice Committee.

Deloitte Touche Tohmatsu is actively involved in these efforts in many different ways and through several of its most experienced experts. Some of them are also involved in the various national and international award schemes for environmental and sustainability reporting, which are also in many ways active forums for discussing and further developing reporting best practice.

Deloitte Touche Tohmatsu will continue to consult with these organisations and leading reporters, and to participate in reporting initiatives as part of the continual improvement process.

How we developed the scorecard

The Deloitte Sustainability Reporting Scorecard was created with input from many angles and with the active contribution of many experienced environmental and sustainability practitioners. It was developed in an interactive process, maintained by a robust and intensive methodology of sharing and consultation.

We built our development on a state-of-play analysis of report rating schemes and reporting guidelines. This study included not only the analysis of tools for report assessment and methodologies of report award schemes but also of governmental and institutional guidelines for reporting, performance assessment tools and process guidelines. It finally also built on manifold communication with corporate report writers and in-depth analysis of many corporate reports that were either winners of awards or were rated high in recent report rating studies.

Deloitte Touche Tohmatsu around the world is already successfully using a Corporate Environmental Report Scorecard that was originally developed in 1995 and revised in 1997. This is a scorecard particularly developed for environmental reports that is still valid and highly useful for this specific purpose. It is best used for and based on communication needs of corporations whose major impacts lie within the company's own operations.

The new Deloitte Sustainability Reporting Scorecard builds on the experience with this former tool intensively applied to environmental reports, as well as to additional formats that are used in various countries for environmental and social reports. The most valid input forms the vast experience that was developed throughout the Deloitte Touche Tohmatsu global practice in manifold client engagements on reporting.

The approach of evaluation and scoring

The scorecard's structure and rationale

The Deloitte Sustainability Reporting Scorecard follows the logic of the 'red thread' recommended for the process of reporting.

The scorecard first of all evaluates the effectiveness that report providers can expect to achieve with their communications to report users and the ability of the report to create credibility with report users. These criteria seldom refer to particular chapters in a report, but rather need overall evaluation.

Most importantly, the scorecard focuses on the relevant issues that a reporting organisation has to identify and build into its management and reporting. The scorecard then follows a logic of argumentation that starts with the identification of the relevant issues and respective stakeholders, covers commitment and management quality, addresses relationships to key stakeholders and concludes with quantifying performance. It is often the case that reporting organisations will assign particular sections of their report to these relevant issues; others will choose different structuring rules that they find more useful for effective communication and more suitable to their specific case.

The 30 criteria evaluated by the scorecard are grouped into six parts as visualised in Figure 10.1, illustrating the interrelationship between report provider and report user, the key elements of a report and the tool's six sections.

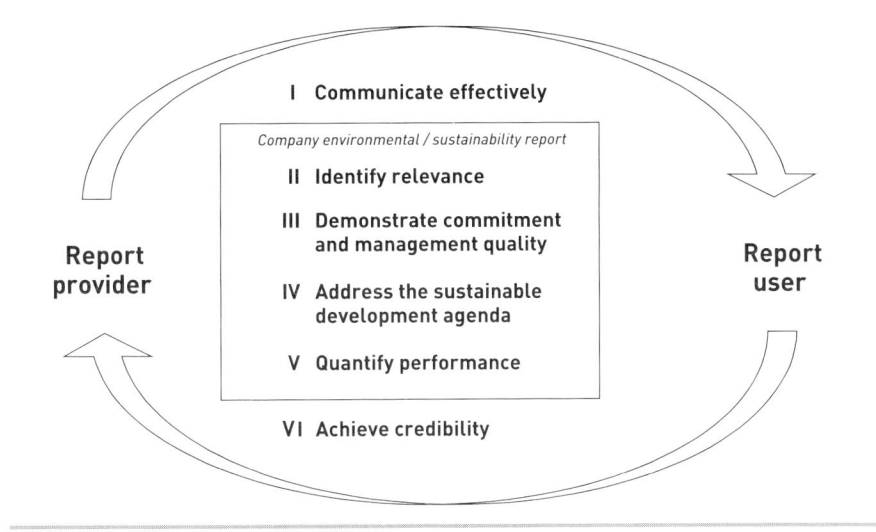

Figure 10.1 Deloitte Sustainability Reporting Scorecard

Source: Deloitte Touche Tohmatsu

We believe that a high-quality sustainability report—whatever it is called (for example, triple-bottom-line or corporate citizenship report)—should be designed to communicate a compact story on the reporting organisation's strategy and commitment, and its progress and contribution toward a more sustainable economy, environment and society. This should become visible as the 'red thread' tying together the organisation's aims throughout the report.

The scorecard tool provides detailed information and guidance for evaluating reports with respect to each of the 30 criteria. Such information—explanations, characteristics and examples—is most valuable in better understanding reporting practices and development trends.

In Box 10.1 these 30 criteria are listed and explained in brief to make their meaning understandable. The tool also asks for additional specifications to characterise the reporting organisation and the report assessed.

I   *Communicate effectively*
- Provide corporate context
- Follow basic principles of reporting (reporting period, scope and entity)
- Cover qualitative reporting characteristics
- Design an effective report structure (a 'red thread')
- Optimise readability (language, pictures, charts, explanations, navigation tools)
- Allow for quick reading (executive summary, key indicators)

II *Identify relevance*
- Identify and address key stakeholders and their concerns and challenges
- Identify and describe key relevant issues (significant aspects)

III *Demonstrate commitment and management quality*
- Include sustainable development vision and strategy
- Formulate top-management commitment (principles, values, policy)
- Characterise responsibilities and organisational structures (including corporate governance)
- Demonstrate action (objectives and programmes)
- Describe management system and integration into business processes
- Describe management of risks and opportunities (contingency planning, compliance management, etc.)

IV *Address the sustainable development agenda*
- Describe **innovation** for more sustainability (design, operations, markets)
- Demonstrate a sustainable **value/supply chain**
- Describe **financial implications** (costs, savings, investments, liabilities, winnings) and wider **economic impacts**
- Demonstrate **employee involvement/relationship** (including knowledge management)
- Include interaction and partnerships with **civil society** (communities, consumer groups, NGOs, authorities)
- Describe work on **framework conditions** and **public policies** for sustainability (local and global developments)

V   *Quantify performance*
- Use effective and meaningful metrics and indicators (absolute figures and ratios)
- Specify data quality and accuracy

Box 10.1 **The 30 criteria** (continued opposite)

V Quantify performance (continued)
- Show trends (performance over time)
- Provide targets (level of achievement and envisioned future performance)
- Include interpretation and benchmarks (context and comparability)

VI Achieve credibility
- Describe engagement with stakeholders (dialogues and outcomes thereof)
- Optimise balance of issues (relevant aspects, usefulness)
- Demonstrate connection to reality (stories, people)
- Enable accessibility and interactivity for contacts, feedback and for further information
- Use assurance services (verification)
- Additional specifications
- Reporting organisation
- Assessed report
- User of the scorecard

Box 10.1 (continued)

The meaning of the scores

Each of the 30 criteria of the scorecard is worth a score between 0 and 4 points corresponding to a level of fulfilment between 'no mention' or 'very insufficient' and 'pace-setting creative approach' or 'outstanding'.

Scoring should be conservative. We believe that conservative scoring encourages learning and improvement. The score of 4 points is reserved for truly extraordinary/innovative disclosure and explanation. The theoretical overall total of 120 scores or 100% would refer to a rather unrealistic maximum for ideal reporting of complete satisfaction.

In Table 10.1, the five scoring levels from 0 to 4 and respective percentages for the overall score are described with general qualification statements.

Scores	Generic qualification	Total
0	No mention or very insufficient/very little	0%
1	Some/little/partial mention or coverage	25%
2	Most important aspects covered, average	50%
3	Better than average, current state-of-the-art practice of several leading reporters	75%
4	Pace-setting creative new approach, outstanding, best practice	100%

Table 10.1 The meaning of scoring levels

The building blocks of the evaluation questionnaire

The scorecard gives detailed information and guidance for each of its 30 criteria on how to assess a report and how to do the scoring. This information (on all the 30 criteria) is constructed in a standardised way. In this section, the meaning and value of this structure and its elements are explained. The way to use it is demonstrated in Table 10.2.

Description of the criteria: A sentence to characterise and describe the item briefly.	
Scores: • Characterisation of the scores 0 to 4, based on generic scoring levels, additionally specified for the respective criteria.	*Explanations and characteristics:* • This section provides additional **explanations and definitions** of terms and key expressions used to describe this item. • It also includes **characteristics** that help understand the item and score the quality in which it is fulfilled by the report assessed. • Furthermore, there are some **qualifications** or **requirements** of current state-of-the-art practices of reporting. • Finally, the section gives important **references** to reporting standards/guidelines.
Examples: • Examples of practices applied in reporting • Examples from reporting standards/guidelines • Illustrative examples • Listing of options from the explanations and qualifications	

Table 10.2 Description of the criteria

The scorecard as a learning and improvement tool

The Deloitte Sustainability Reporting Scorecard is designed for the benefit of report providers in developing their reports, but it also benefits report users in evaluating the value and quality of published reports.

The application of the scorecard is not limited to any particular kind of report or reporting scope. However, the total score received may be reduced for a report of limited or incomplete sustainability scope.

In developing a report, report writers can use the scorecard either as a self-assessment tool or just as a source of learning and experience. Deloitte Touche Tohmatsu practitioners are using it to assist clients in report development. They assess—together with their clients—report drafts and identify gaps and options for further improvements.

In the detailed description of the 30 criteria, the scorecard includes a vast amount of know-how and explanations. Manifold examples illustrate the issue and provide possibilities others have used successfully.

Discussing the results of an assessment and comparing it, for example, to sector average or to best practice allows for a better understanding of the strengths and weaknesses of one's own report. Discussing it in comparison to reports of peers can offer options for improvement. Scorecard users will be able to learn a lot from such in-depth discussion and benchmarking.

Finally, the scorecard puts users in touch with Deloitte Touche Tohmatsu reporting experts to benefit from their experience and know-how.

The scorecard as an assessment tool

The Deloitte Sustainability Reporting Scorecard will also enable report users and analysts to assess and compare reports over time and with each other. Surveys and comparisons could be made within sectors, within regions and on other groups of reporting organisations or report types. Individual reports can be assessed against average or best-practice benchmarks.

The scorecard would also allow the establishment or strengthening of new national, regional or global benchmarks. It could serve to set up or further develop award schemes for sustainability reporting.

If users want to stress certain areas or set a particular focus, the tool is flexible enough for weighting the criteria or for parts of the scorecard to be adapted accordingly.

Use for different type of reports

The application of the scorecard is not limited to any particular kind of report. It can be used for printed reports and for Internet-based communication. Nor is there any limitation to the scope or purpose of a report. It can be applied to fully fledged sustainability reports, as well as for reports with a partial scope, such as environmental, environment health and safety (EH&S), social reports or reports limited to other aspects of sustainability. It may even be applied to an annual report if it includes information on sustainability, corporate governance, corporate citizenship or the like. Often, it is most helpful or expedient to apply the scorecard to a combination of reports that together compose a company's communication on sustainability. Finally, the scorecard could also be used on site reports or on reports of subsidiaries, regional organisations or brands, in the same way as it is applicable to corporate reports. Total scoring, however, will be influenced by a report's limited or incomplete scope.

Guidelines for using the scorecard

Users of the Deloitte Sustainability Reporting Scorecard are recommended to follow a sequence of steps when applying the tool to a report to assess its quality.

- It is recommended that assessors first read the entire report before starting the scoring. This reading should not cover all details but should allow a profound overview of what the report includes and what elements are covered (or not covered) in which parts and in what way.

- Making side notes in the report will help assessors track where they want to refer to which criteria of the scorecard and, on a scoring sheet with referenced page numbers, on which page of the report they found a particular criterion dealt with or specification fulfilled.

- Scores should be given conservatively. If only parts of the requirements of a scoring level (e.g. 3) are fulfilled, it is recommended scoring one level lower (i.e. 2 in the above example).

- It is further recommended to avoid half scores such as 1.5 or 2.5 wherever possible. A five-level scoring (here 0 to 4) is the most robust scoring from a statistical point of view. From half-level scoring it is only a very small step to even further differentiation of, for example, 2.25 or 2.75 or even finer.

- It might be advisable to go over the scores again, once the assessment is completed or later when other reports have been scored, as individually applied assessment criteria may change during the process because of experience gained over time.

We expect that approximately six to eight hours are necessary for careful reading and to provide a robust and sound assessment and scoring of a report.

We also recommend that a particular report be assessed by more than one person to balance out subjective views and create a sound basis for discussion of open points and differing views.

A tool such as this scorecard is never perfect, and there are plenty of arguments why it could be constructed in a different way and with a different way of grouping or describing the individual criteria and even scoring levels.

There are a number of dilemmas reflected in the structure and format of this tool as it is presented here. Deloitte Touche Tohmatsu has discussed these dilemmas to the extent possible in order to solve them or deal with them constructively. Difficulties in using the scorecard can be managed, we believe, by means of the rules provided in this section.

The process of evaluation

When evaluating a report with the scorecard, Deloitte Touche Tohmatsu specialists work together in a team. They carefully read the report and compare it with their experience and knowledge of sustainability reporting and with the detailed description provided in the tool for each of the 30 criteria.

A practical spreadsheet guides scorecard users—in conjunction with accumulating the scores—in compiling comments and elaborating recommendations for improvement on each of the 30 criteria.

Presentation of results

A summary of the individual scores for all 30 criteria is visualised in a scorecard chart. Figure 10.2 is an example to illustrate the results of an actual evaluation.

The criteria on which a report scores 3 and 4 referring to 'above average' and 'pace setting' respectively are easily identified in the chart. So are criteria scoring 1 and 0, referring to 'below average' and 'very little'. This chart, illustrating the relative strengths and weaknesses as described, forms an ideal basis for a discussion with the reporting organisation.

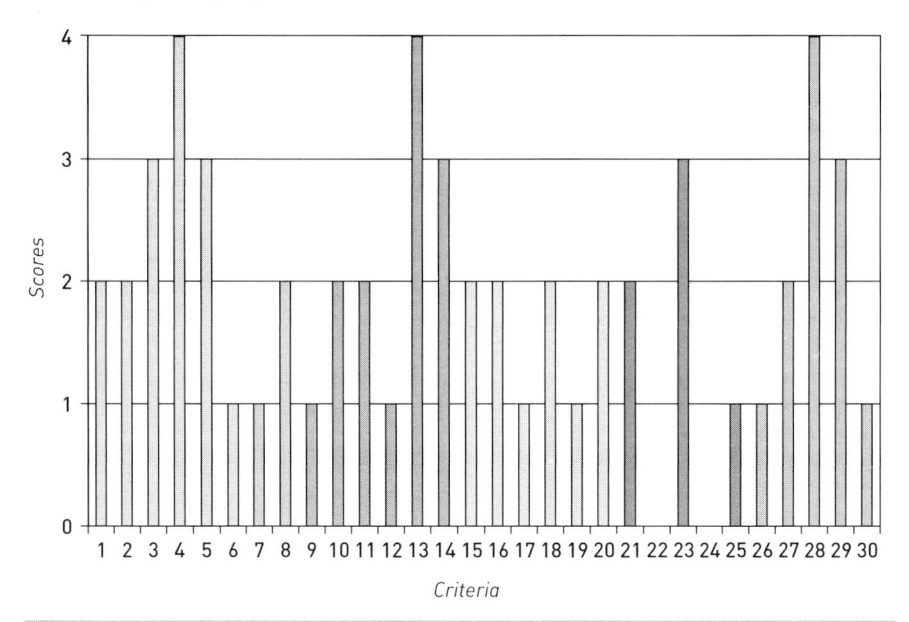

Figure 10.2 Scorecard chart: example of results

Source: Deloitte Touche Tohmatsu

84 Eco-efficiency and Beyond

In a summary chart, the results for the six parts of the scorecard are presented as percentages of the maximum possible in each of the six groups of criteria (see Fig. 10.3). The overall score is the arithmetic average (mean) across the six parts. Again, the reporting organisation can identify those areas that score the lowest and offer the greatest opportunities for improvement.

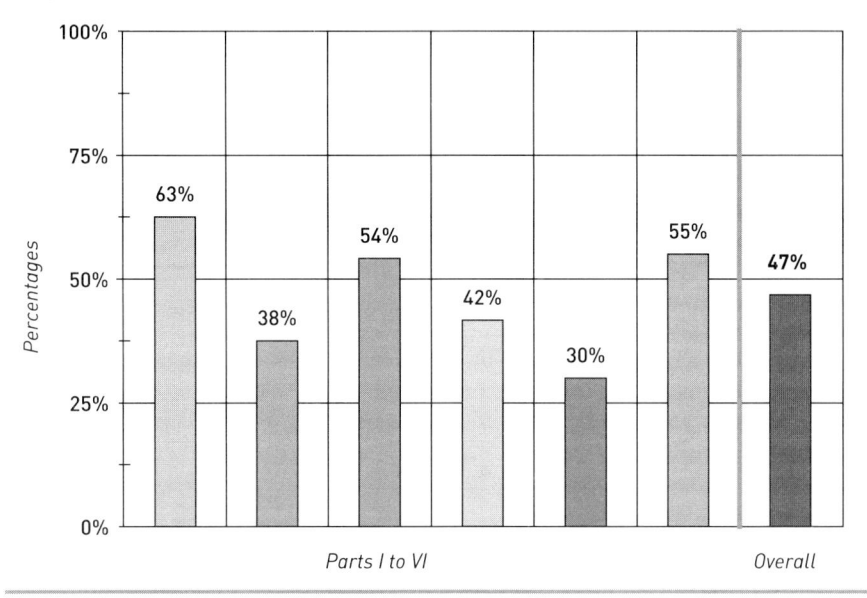

Figure 10.3 **Summary chart: example of results**

Source: Deloitte Touche Tohmatsu

It depends on individual results and circumstances, which of the two charts can serve the company better in the discussion to identify and define improvements.

Deloitte Touche Tohmatsu specialists can—in addition to the scoring and recommendations for improvement—also conduct a gap analysis that points out measures to be taken for a certain level of quality: for example, to achieve a scoring of a state-of-the-art report, referring to a scoring of 75% overall.

A description of the overall quality of the report and a benchmark comparison with, for example, a sector or another type of average complete the assessment package that Deloitte Touche Tohmatsu can deliver with the scorecard worldwide.

The Deloitte Sustainability Reporting Scorecard focuses on improvement potentials rather than on comparing reports and ranking them. Recommendations for improvement and measures to be taken for future reporting can be easily explored and specified by means of the tool.

Using the scorecard to survey reporting quality in various industry sectors

To develop a more comprehensive reflection of the quality of sustainability reporting, Deloitte Touche Tohmatsu occasionally conducts surveys based on the scorecard. These surveys may be intended for public use and may include most recent reports from major companies of a sector. The global database formed from the results of these surveys will provide Deloitte Touche Tohmatsu with a basis for evaluating current reporting practice and for characterising a best-in-class benchmark, as well as for collecting best-practice examples and learning.

Analysing the automotive sector's reporting quality

Deloitte Touche Tohmatsu evaluated the current status of environmental and sustainability reporting in the automotive industry during the year 2001. Analysing more than 20 reports from major automobile manufacturers, the survey provides a composite of the sector's reporting practice of today and progress made over time.

The study was based on the newly developed Deloitte Sustainability Reporting Scorecard. This tool measures sustainability reporting quality and effectiveness with respect to key success drivers. It focuses on relevance and on those principles and characteristics that make reporting effective and reported information credible. The study also covers aspects that are pre-eminent in today's debate on sustainability reporting, such as the development of social indicators and the integration of sustainability into business processes. In evaluating the results of the analysis of the automotive reports included in this study, we applied our sound experience in the international environmental and sustainability reporting field.

Benchmarking reports for improvement

With this study, Deloitte Touche Tohmatsu aimed to give automobile manufacturers an overview of reporting practice in their industry and to provide helpful guidance for further improvement. In addition to the overall results described in this brief, Deloitte Touche Tohmatsu is offering individual companies a detailed discussion of specific results for their report, benchmarked against sector average and best practice. The scorecard provides valuable information about 30 success drivers in reporting and enables discussion of suggested recommendations for report improvements based on individual scoring.

The scope of the survey

This reporting study includes the latest reports published in 2000 and 2001 from 15 automobile brands and three of their regional organisations. In five cases, the reports of two subsequent reporting periods were evaluated in order to trend information on improvements and developments over time.

Deloitte Touche Tohmatsu studied the following benchmarking reports for improvement:

- Audi, Environmental Report 1999
- BMW Group, Sustainable Value Report 2000–2001
- DaimlerChrysler, Environmental Report 2001
- Fiat Group, Environmental Report 2000
- Ford Motor Company, Corporate Citizenship Report 2000
- General Motors, Sustainability Reports 1999–2000 and 2000–2001
- Honda, Environmental Report 2000
- Nissan, Environmental Reports 1999 and 2000
- Opel, Environmental Report 2000–2001
- PSA Peugeot Citroën, Environmental Report 2001
- Renault Group, Environmental Report 2000
- Toyota Motor Corporation, Environmental Reports 2000 and 2001
- Toyota in North America, Environmental Report 2000
- Toyota in Europe, European Environmental Report 2001
- Toyota Australia, Environmental Report 2001
- Vauxhall Motors, Environmental Report 1999 and Sustainability Report 2000
- Volkswagen, Environmental Reports 1999–2000 and 2001–2002
- Volvo Car Corporation, Corporate Citizenship 2000

The value of sustainability reporting to the automotive industry

Mobility and the automobile are indeed of central importance to today's economic, societal and environmental developments around the globe. This places a primary responsibility on the automotive industry to develop a vision for sustainable mobility and to implement strategies and actions toward improved solutions for mobility needs.

Accepting this responsibility includes actively engaging with stakeholders, conducting open dialogue and exchanging information about commitments, objectives and performance. Such transparency and communication can help create the trust and credibility necessary in the industry for the companies' societal 'licence to operate, innovate and grow', and as a result will help address the evident sustainability challenges.

Sustainability reporting is an important instrument for the automotive industry: one that can add great value. Not reporting, on the other hand, may inhibit credibility and justify prejudice.

Observations on the evaluated reports

Do automotive companies make the best use of sustainability reporting? We think that the automotive industry delivers above-average-quality reports, compared to other industry sectors. The reports published demonstrate that sustainability reporting is beginning to command attention and resource allocation in the automotive industry.

Automotive companies already have significant reporting experience from publishing predominantly environmental reports on a regular basis for several years. However, improvements from year to year and adaptation to further needs and new trends appear rather modest.

- **Surely but slowly toward sustainability.** While five automotive companies intend to report fully on sustainability, nine others focus mainly on environmental issues, providing minimal information in social and economic areas. We believe that there are some gaps between reporting practice and users' expectations. Linkages between the three pillars of sustainability, particularly to economic implications and the multi-dimensional nature of sustainability, are not really addressed in automotive reports.

- **Low on the e-reporting learning curve.** The reports of all but two automotive companies are printed and distributed as hard copies. They are also available as PDF files from the corporate web pages. Two companies provide real web-based reports together with a printed executive summary, while two others offer additional content on their websites that is not included in the report. Flexibility of structure and sequence and options to obtain additional information through interaction are moderate and, where provided, they are not easy to navigate. Internet-based reporting remains a major challenge to both report providers and report users.

- **More like books than brochures.** Ten out of the 21 automotive reports analysed exceed 80 pages. The length results in difficulty of comprehension. Most reports provide a high level of technical detail. For those particularly interested, such detail may be a means to learn and better understand, while others may soon tire of the wealth of information and put the books down. Automobile companies generally provide attractive and visually appealing reports. Focused ideas assist the reader in navigating through the reports and understanding complicated language and technical charts.

- **Reporting is getting global, too.** Most automotive companies are operating globally. Some years ago, automotive reports were still focused on headquarters and provided information mainly on home-country operations, but environmental and sustainability reporting is gradually becoming global. Automotive companies implement global reporting strategies, including, for example, high-quality regional reports, or have subsidiary brands publish their own reports.

- **GRI adoption pays.** Several automotive companies are involved in some form or fashion in the GRI. Seven are aiming to adopt the GRI Sustainability Reporting Guidelines. There are indications that reports following the GRI Guidelines outperform the others. Their score outstripped other reports by an average 20%.

- **What's the matter with verification?** An unexpected result of the survey is the limited use of assurance-related services in the automotive industry. Few reports are verified with an independent statement from assurance professionals. Four out of 16 companies include a third-party verification statement in their reports and four more offer at least some commentary on the issue of assurance.

The strengths of the reports are:

- **Commitments and management quality are well described.** The automotive industry's top management seems to be honestly committed to the environment and to sustainability. The CEO statements illustrate this, and automotive companies are engaged in important global forums. They have developed corporate charters, policies and ambitious action plans and targets. They work to implement and maintain comprehensive management structures and procedures for their operations and business activities.

- **The entire life-cycle is covered.** The entire life-cycle of the automobile is covered in all reports analysed. Companies talk not only about production but also about product design and development, distribution, product use and vehicle end of life. Taking the relative importance of these phases into account, they might consider reducing the amount of detail in describing the manufacturing phase.

- **Innovation, technological options are very comprehensive.** All reports provide much detail about product design and development. Technical innovations for environmental improvements are explained in great detail. In the context of the search for the 'ultimate eco-car', reports describe various options for improvements on the most pressing environmental problems such as material use, recycling, noise, exhaust emissions and—probably most importantly—climate change.

- **Operational eco-efficiency improvements are demonstrated.** Automotive reports provide a good description of operational performance with manifold input and output indicators. Development over time of operational environmental data allows the reader to understand that the industry contributes its share to operational efficiency and environmental performance improvements. This is, however, less clearly demonstrated for supply chain and distribution channels.

Weaknesses are:

- **Some important issues are missing.** Only a few reports systematically attempt to identify and describe the relevant sustainability issues of the automotive sector. Pressing issues related to mobility, in particular to car-based private transportation and impacts in developing countries, are not well captured in the reports.

- **Stakeholders are partially addressed.** The stakeholders affected by the automotive industry are not always identified and target audiences for the reports are not clear. Reports do not demonstrate much engagement with external stakeholders. Most often, reports show interaction only with employees or with neighbouring communities. Reports give little evidence of external stakeholders' involvement in the process of report development.

- **Social aspects are still fragmented.** Social impacts are still rather fragmentally described in reports of the automotive industry. They are most often limited to philanthropic contributions, employee education and training and operational health and safety.

- **Financial implications are not demonstrated.** There is limited discussion of matters that have or could have a bearing—both risks and opportunities—on the organisation's short- or long-term financial performance, as well as an impact on the surrounding economy. More than half of the reports score low (0 or 1) on the description of financial implications of environmental or social issues.

- **Interpretation and benchmarking are limited.** Some 90% of reports received a low scoring on interpretation and benchmarking of quantified performance information. Providing context together with data, interpretation and rationale definitely assists report users in understanding the performance achieved. The ability to compare the indicators used and to benchmark results with peers are additional instruments that report users have for their decision-making.

Average scores as a sector benchmark

The summary and scorecard charts in Figures 10.4 and 10.5 show the average values of the 23 reports evaluated in the course of the study. The summary chart (Fig. 10.4) gives the average percentage of fulfilment for all six parts of the scorecard and the overall scoring. Even though this is slightly below the 50% level, we believe that the automotive sector's reporting practice is above average, as there are only a few companies who do not yet publish an environmental or sustainability report.

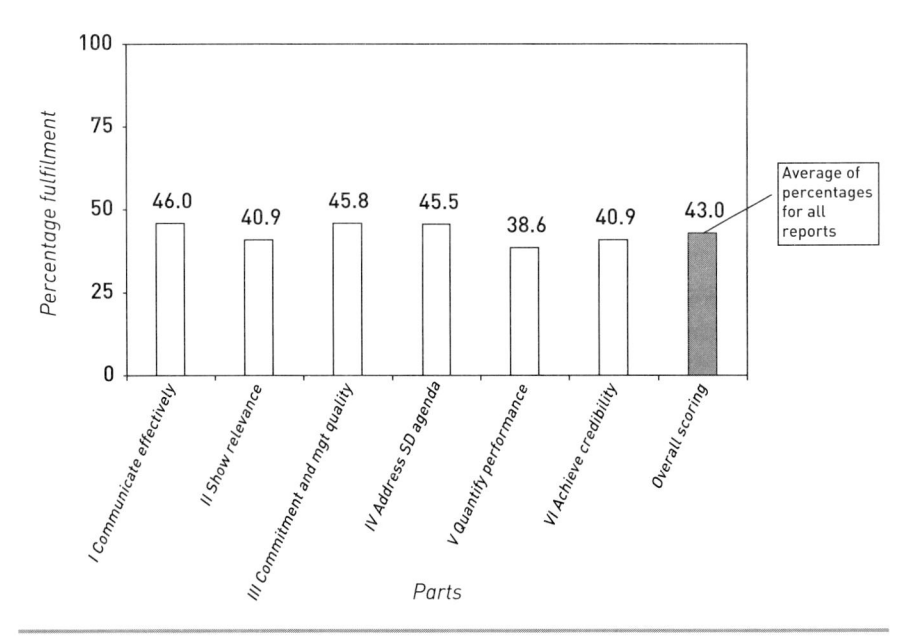

```
                            100
    Percentage fulfilment    75                                                              ┌─────────────┐
                                                                                             │ Average of  │
                                                                                             │ percentages │
                             50   46.0              45.8   45.5                   43.0       │ for all     │
                                         40.9                      38.6    40.9              │ reports     │
                                                                                             └─────────────┘
                             25

                              0
                                    I         II         III        IV         V       VI      Overall
                                 Communicate  Show    Commitment  Address  Quantify  Achieve    scoring
                                 effectively relevance and mgt    SD agenda performance credibility
                                                      quality
                                                         Parts
```

Figure 10.4 Summary chart

Source: Deloitte Touche Tohmatsu

The scorecard chart (Fig. 10.5) with a bar for each of the 30 criteria shows the average scores, as well as averages for bottom quartile (bottom 25% of the reports), top quartile (top 25%) and for the 50% of the reports in the middle. Findings from these charts are reflected in the observations and strengths/weaknesses sections above.

Recommendations on some emerging questions

Do automotive companies report what their readers want to know? There is some concern that the automotive companies' communication does not reach the relevant readership. For many users, the reports might be too thick and too technical. Engaging with stakeholders to identify what is of relevance to them, involving them in the development of the reports, and addressing specified target audiences, are suitable measures that help make sure reports tell the right story and are read and considered by interested readers.

What are the relevant issues? The reports do not provide compelling analyses of the relevant sustainability issues related to their business. While addressing many things, the reports do not capture how the automotive companies intend to help mobility become sustainable overall. We think that it is useful to report users if the relevant sustainability issues are identified and described in the reports and if the company's management and performance reporting systems deal with those issues.

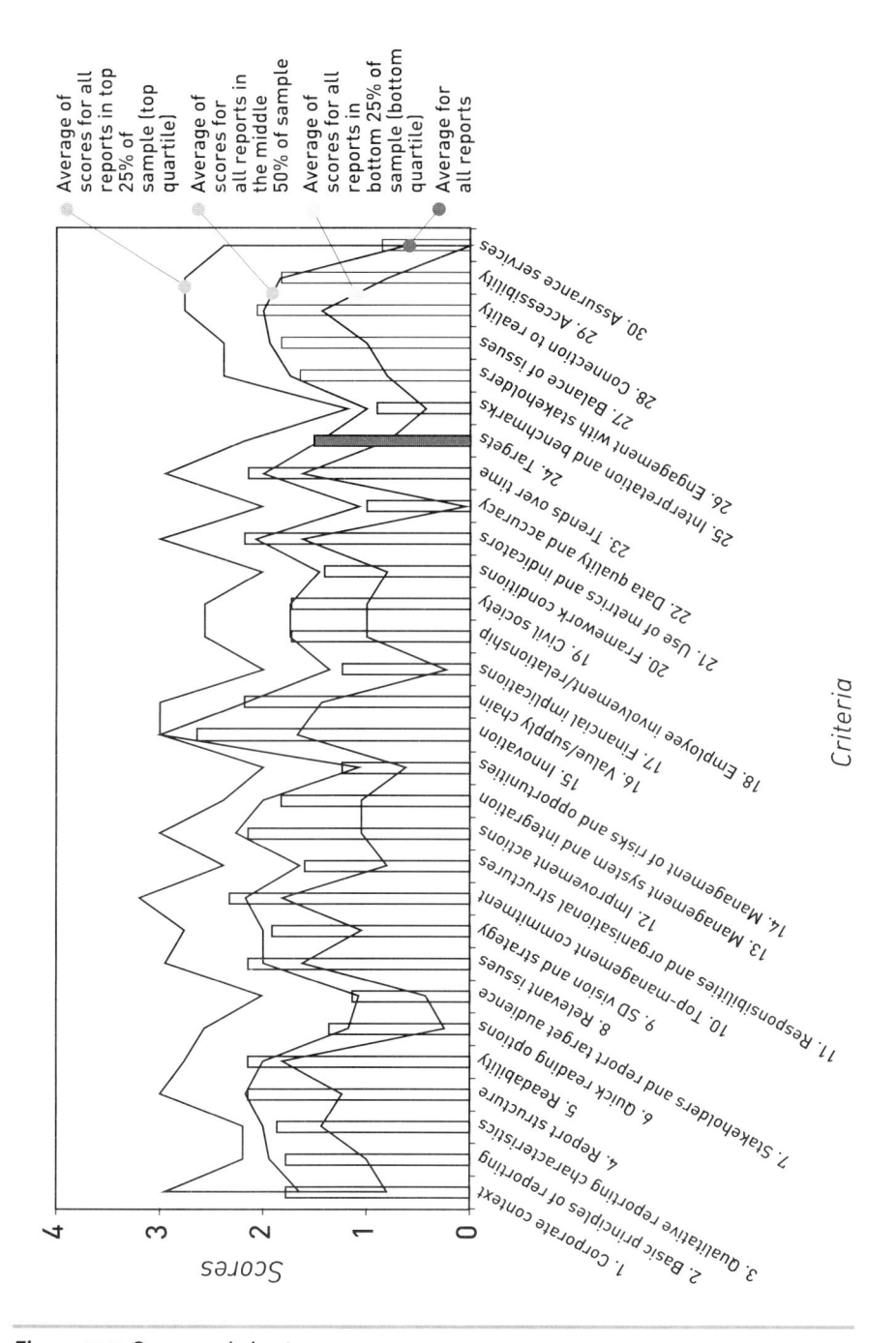

10. Deloitte Sustainability Reporting Scorecard *Lehni* 91

Figure 10.5 Scorecard chart

Source: Deloitte Touche Tohmatsu

Can the 'box on four wheels' finally become sustainable? Automotive companies appear very confident that they can design and build an all emissions- and impact-free automobile some time in the future. Several stakeholder groups may well put some question marks over this assumption, seeing a need for changed mobility and living patterns as well. Seven leading automotive companies have started engaging with stakeholders to develop a vision for 'sustainable mobility 2030'. The expectations of that process go much beyond the 'box' of the automobile, including all modes of transport and not only technological but also behavioural innovation. Such expectations also include creative business solutions from the automotive industry.

How well do the reports build trust and credibility? Automotive companies need to continue engaging with their stakeholders and demonstrating their commitment to accountability and honest and transparent communication. The reports could also be better in telling a credible story with a 'red thread' from identifying the relevant issues all the way to concrete actions for change, quantified targets, and achieved performance. Additional essential means to achieve more credibility are assuring that the information presented in the report is realistic, complete and balanced, and that the information presented and the reporting procedures used are verified.

11
Sustainability management? Don't bother!
Practical steps for bringing sustainability into core management practice

Peter Zollinger
SustainAbility, UK

The development of our triple-bottom-line thinking on corporate sustainability reflects a few key assumptions about the future nature of global economic development; the drive for increased accountability underlying the corporate pursuit of sustainability; and some specific definitions of the key dimensions of sustainable development (Elkington 1997).

Our first premise is that the early decades of the new millennium will be characterised by market-based capitalism. While we hope for new, more inclusive, democratic and participatory forms of capitalism, we see an irreversible shift of power to markets and market-makers. This has major implications for the business community, particularly the multinational business community. If capitalism is to be the engine of economic growth, then corporations will be the vehicle. As a result, we see the corporate sector as a vital and central agent of change in the transition toward sustainability.

Second, the sustainable development agenda is rooted, for most involved in the debate, in the rise of environmental concerns and movements of the 1970s and 1980s. Indeed, environmental concerns were at the heart of the Brundtland Report on and defining sustainable development—a platform that, with its subsequent translation into the balancing of economic, environmental and social priorities, we fully endorse (WCED 1987).

We believe, however, that in parallel with (and no doubt in part spurred on by) the focus on environmental degradation, there has been a profound shift in society's values and expectations of business; this has been reinforced by a sustained decline in trust in governments and institutions more generally. We judge this shift in values, expectations and accountability to be at least as great a consideration for business as the specific environmental drivers that have alerted progressive (or threatened) businesses to the need to understand and engage the sustainable development agenda.

And, third, SustainAbility's particular focus on the corporate sector has led us to see sustainability for business as the commitment to contribute to three linked sets of societal objectives (Fig. 11.1):

- Economic prosperity, through, for example, employment creation and distribution of wealth
- Social responsibility reflected in, for example, commitment to using skills, power and influence to make a positive contribution to society
- Environmental protection, by preventing any further damage, and where possible reversing past damage

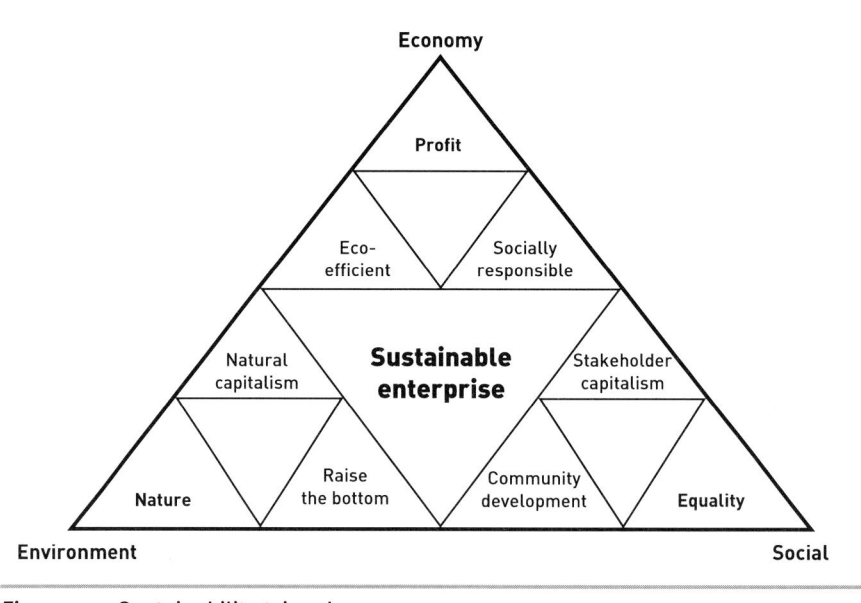

Figure 11.1 Sustainability triangle

Source: adapted by Stuart Hart from McDonough & Partners

The stakes have risen

A few decades ago, the aim of most companies was relatively simple: to provide safe products or services together with a reasonable return to shareholders in accordance with their legal obligations. But in a world dominated by multinational corporations a rising tide of public opinion demands greater accountability. Since the mid-1990s companies have started to feel the impact of their (lack of) social understanding in the business arena. The well-documented cases of Shell, Nike and BP have brought issues such as human rights into corporate boardrooms.

Key drivers in this wave of change toward social accountability and equity have included:

- The rising influence of pressure groups and NGOs that track the activities of corporations worldwide
- The 'global village', in which near instantaneous global media coverage ensures that a company can be 'caught out' anywhere, any time
- The blurring of boundaries between the respective social responsibilities of government and business. The role of the state has been reduced through, for example, privatisation, deregulation and reduction of subsidies, placing greater responsibility on the individual and business.

From 'trust me' to 'engage me'

In the past business leaders and, to a degree, politicians could rely on a culture where there was a greater degree of trust in traditional institutions. Shell (1998) notes that the world is moving from a 'trust me' culture (where companies can rely on society's broad acceptance that they act in good faith), through a 'tell me' culture (where society wants to be told what is going on) and a 'show me' culture (in which companies have to demonstrate their serious intent to change for the better) to an 'engage me' culture (in which involving key stakeholders in learning and decision-making leads to better strategies).

Obviously, different parts of the world still operate along different lines. Until the recent focus on 'crony capitalism' in countries such as Indonesia and Malaysia, for example, most of Asia was still very much in 'trust me' mode. But the globalisation of the media, leading to the creation of what some dub a 'CNN world', means that all major international companies will increasingly be exposed to 'tell me' and 'show me' requirements.

So what does this greater accountability imply? For many companies it means turning the concept of a 'show me' world into a reality—and a starting point is to listen to stakeholders and respond to their views. The degree of trust between a corporation or industry and their external stakeholders is likely to be a key factor in determining their long-term sustainability and their licence to operate. The traditional definition of 'licence to operate'—compliance with local, national and international regulations and legislation—has therefore become earning the trust and respect of diverse stakeholders.

The business case

Concern is sometimes expressed that sustainability has no clear business benefits and could destroy shareholder value by diverting resources from core commercial activities. Many in business are worried that businesses will be persuaded to take on social responsibilities that should be handled by governments and individuals.

In fact, to survive and prosper companies have to accommodate changes in what the public expects of business. Currently, the pressure on business is to demonstrate that it can behave ethically and responsibly. Maintaining such a reputation is essential for retaining society's 'licence to operate'.

The challenge is to deliver sustainable value to markets and society. Recent research by SustainAbility strengthens the business case for sustainability. It shows that the impact of sustainable development performance on shareholder value is neutral at worst, and in some instances has been shown to add considerable value (SustainAbility 2001).

The SustainAbility Business Value© matrix[1] identifies those dimensions of sustainable development that show a strong correlation between greater social responsibility and improved business performance, as illustrated in the three examples below.

Socioeconomic development—the degree to which a company actively and constructively uses its resources to support the social and economic development of communities—has a strong positive impact on brand value and reputation. A Cone-Roper study found that 86% of consumers have a more positive image of a company if they see it doing something to make the world a better place (Creyer and Ross 1997).

Human rights—the degree to which a company actively and constructively contributes to the protection of human rights (for its employees, its neighbours and indeed all host-country residents, in the regions in which it does business and even potentially areas where it does not do business)—has a strong positive impact on licence to operate. Overall, the short-term regional advantages of co-operating with governments that abuse human rights are being shown to pale against the loss of international licence to operate.

Workplace conditions—the degree to which a company proactively strives to foster a high-quality work environment and work–life balance for its employees—have a strong positive impact on company revenue and human and intellectual capital. Employee-friendly work practices strongly contribute to increased revenue, as motivated employees are more productive and willing to go 'the extra mile' for their employer. A ten-year comparison between six 'employers of choice' and a control group found that employers of choice substantially outperformed their peers in revenue growth and net income, both in absolute terms and when measured per employee (Catlette and Hadden 1998).

---

1 See www.sustainability.co.uk/business-case. The business case is still evolving, and we encourage practitioners to participate in this 'open source' learning process.

Integration of sustainability into core business thinking and processes

In this section, we build a framework for assessing the ways in which companies can move toward greater sustainability in their operations and products.

Strategies for sustainability are in a sense no different from any other business strategy designed to cope with a changed external environment. Business responses to change range from short-term coping strategies to long-term shifts in direction. For the purpose of this chapter, we divide potential sustainability strategies into four basic types:

- **Realignment**: a short-term response to change through adjustments in present operations to meet external conditions (e.g. short-term cost cutting)
- **Re-emphasis**: a short- to medium-term response to change through juggling current activities, products, or departments
- **Replication**: a longer-term response to change, by bringing external expertise (e.g. strategies, technologies) in-house
- **Reinvention**: a pioneering company shows the longest-term response to change by reconsidering its fundamental mission, policies, practices and portfolio

One can also classify sustainability strategies according to the level at which they are aimed within the company. For example, there are

- Corporate strategies that define the direction and composition of the core business
- Business/functional strategies directed at internal systems and processes at existing businesses
- Operational strategies

These levels need to work in harmony; changes in corporate strategy must be translated into business and operational strategies to be effective.

Table 11.1 illustrates the two dimensions of strategy identified above by plotting real-life business responses to various elements of the sustainable development agenda.

The following examples underline the positive potential of and need for integration into existing, central business processes:

Internal

- Better employee motivation through open communication and integration of sustainability aspects into core business principles and non-financial objectives

98   Eco-efficiency and Beyond

Strategic response	Realignment	Re-emphasis	Replication	Reinvention
Strategy levels				
Corporate	UK retailers' avoidance of genetically modified food	Re-emphasis in portfolio from product-based to service-based (e.g. Xerox)	Manufacturer purchasing servicing facility (e.g. Ford and Kwik Fit)	The concept of a 'restorative' company or the 'stakeholder' corporation
Business/ functional	1980s 'green' marketing	Environment, health and safety promoted to board responsibility	Certification to ISO 14000/ EMAS environmental standards/ biomimetics	Developments in new environmental or sustainability indicators (e.g. Shell KPIs)
Operational	Basic environmental efficiency initiatives	'Incentivising' environmental performance	Industrial ecology	Virtual stakeholder engagement

Table 11.1 Responses to the sustainable development agenda

- Improvement of management information systems through closing of information gaps and introduction of complementary non-financial key performance indicators that cover relevant sustainability aspects
- Strengthening of internal risk management systems and strategic planning through early and systematic identification of emerging non-traditional opportunities and risks

External

- Preparation of objective facts and figures to facilitate meaningful engagement with key stakeholders
- Creation of reputational and brand value through alignment of all channels of external communication (e.g. investor relations, marketing, public affairs)
- Reduction of pressure for regulatory measures through effective voluntary actions with measurable positive sustainability impacts

The future

The long-term changes will go deep. We have entered an era of intense economic metamorphosis, an era we are calling the 'chrysalis economy' (Elkington 2001). One key driver is the non-sustainability of current patterns of wealth creation.

Ours is a 'caterpillar economy', often highly destructive of natural, social and other forms of capital. And the events of 11 September 2001 served notice on the rich world that both absolute and relative poverty will be major issues for a long time to come.

The notion of reinvention will be brought to new levels in this period of metamorphosis. We will see the emergence of truly regenerative business models. 'Corporate honeybees' will be the domain into which growing numbers of innovators, entrepreneurs and investors will head in the coming decades.

The key characteristics of the corporate honeybee include:

- A sustainable business model based on constant innovation
- A clear, and appropriate, set of ethics-based business principles
- Strategic, sustainable management of natural resources
- Sociability and the evolution of powerful, symbiotic partnerships
- The sustainable production of natural, human, social, institutional and cultural capital

Today, sustainability and corporate responsibility are already at the top of the business agenda for the early years of the 21st century. The development of appropriate governance frameworks (global and corporate) (SustainAbility and IBLF 2001) that set parameters for acceptable corporate behaviour is crucial, both nationally and internationally.

Ways to manage, measure and report on sustainability are essential if the issues are to be integrated into the general management of corporations. No new, add-on management systems are needed. Making sustainable development one of the core values of a company leads to its integration into planning and decision-making processes.

12
Sustainable accounting initiatives in Japan
Pilot projects of material flow cost accounting

Katsuhiko Kokubu
Kobe University, Japan

Michiyasu Nakajima
Kansai University, Japan

Environmental management in Japanese companies has rapidly developed during the last decade. The number of sites that have ISO 14001 certification was 8,169 in January 2002. This is the largest number in the world. Many environmental management tools, such as LCA, eco-labelling, design for the environment, environmental reporting and so on, are also becoming popular in Japan. Among these methods environmental accounting has seen the most remarkable development and spread in this country.

Kokubu and Nashioka (2002) surveyed environmental reports published by companies listed in the first section of the Tokyo Stock Exchange Market and found that out of 1,430 companies (the total number of all listed companies) 257 published environmental reports in 2000 and 184 disclosed environmental accounting information in the reports. This figure is rather higher than in other industrialised countries, mainly because of the Ministry of the Environment (MOE) initiatives on this issue. MOE released draft guidelines in 1999 (MOE 1999) and published a final version in 2000 (MOE 2000). The guidelines recommend that companies disclose environmental accounting information (environmental conservation costs and benefits) in their environmental reports. According to Kokubu and Nashioka (2002), 106 companies (58% of those disclosing environmental accounting information) conformed their environmental accounting formats to the guidelines. They concluded that the influence of the guidelines on corporate environmental accounting practices was quite strong.

The MOE guidelines attached much more importance to external disclosure of environmental accounting information than internal management. This makes Japanese corporate practices of environmental accounting oriented to external disclosure purposes. The Japanese external environmental accounting goes ahead of US and European practices (see Kokubu and Kurasaka 2002; Kokubu 2001) but the internal function of environmental accounting lags behind them. The big issue in Japan is to develop internal environmental management accounting practices that match the external environmental accounting system. In order to improve this situation the Ministry of Economy, Trade and Industry (METI) formed a committee for environmental accounting in 1999, which consists of academia and industry representatives. This is a three-year research project. These METI initiatives focused exclusively on the internal function of environmental accounting within a company.

The METI committee is studying various areas of environmental management accounting, including environmental capital investment appraisal, environmental quality costing, environmental target costing, material flow cost accounting and life-cycle costing. Among these, the project of material flow cost accounting is particularly important because the committee implemented some pilot tests to introduce this new environmental accounting system into Japanese companies. As far as the experience of the committee is concerned, these pilot projects were a great success. In this chapter, these pilot projects will be discussed as sustainable accounting initiatives in Japan. Before examining case studies, the outline of the METI initiatives and the basic idea of material flow cost accounting (MFCA) will be briefly explained.

METI initiatives on environmental accounting

METI formed an environmental accounting committee in 1999, the secretariat of which was the Japan Environmental Management Association for Industry (JEMAI). This was a three-year research project. It was completed in March 2002 and a new project started for dissemination of environmental accounting tools, developed by the committee. Each year the committee published an interim report (JEMAI 2000, 2001). The final report was published by METI (2002) The purpose of the METI initiatives is to develop environmental management accounting tools fitted to Japanese companies. This is an information-based policy instrument.

The METI committee is studying various areas of environmental management accounting. In the first year the committee studied environmental management accounting practices and governmental initiatives in North America and Europe. The committee then established the following five working groups for the second year:

- Working Group 1: environmental capital investment appraisal
- Working Group 2: environmental cost management

- Working Group 3: material flow cost accounting
- Working Group 4: environmental corporate performance evaluation
- Working Group 5: life-cycle costing

Working Groups 1, 2, 3 and 4 were formed in the second year, 2000. While Working Group 4 completed its research by the end of the second year, the other three continued their research projects into 2001, when Working Group 5 was also inaugurated.

The purpose of Working Group 1 was to develop a method of environmental capital investment appraisal. These methods have been studied for many years, especially in the USA. This group not only introduced US-based appraisal tools into the Japanese context but also tried to add some new functions to evaluate the effectiveness of environmental investments. Working Group 2 has two aims: environmental quality costing and environmental target costing. For environmental quality costing the group developed a new format of environmental costing based on the MOE environmental accounting guidelines. For environmental target costing, while this was quite a tough issue to be tackled because there have been few previous studies and practices in this area, the group proposed a framework for constructing methods. Working Group 4 investigated corporate practices that introduced an environmental performance index into their corporate performance evaluation system. While this is quite a new practice, it has been gradually becoming popular in Japanese companies. The group completed its case studies, including Sony, Ricoh, Canon and Osaka Gas. These companies have already introduced some environmental performance index into their corporate performance evaluation schemes. Working Group 5 proposed a method of life-cycle costing that integrates cost information of product usage and disposal with LCA information.

The purpose of Working Group 3 was to introduce MFCA into some Japanese companies and to evaluate its effectiveness. The group sent some members to Germany to investigate MFCA theory and practice, after which a pilot project was implemented in the second year. Nitto Denko, a manufacturer of electric insulation materials, participated in this first pilot project. In the third year the number of companies participating in the project was increased. While Nitto Denko continued to take part in the project, Tanabe Seiyaku, Takiron and Canon were new participants. Tanabe is a pharmaceutical company, Takiron is a manufacturer of vinyl chloride resin and Canon is an electrical equipment manufacturer. The group has implemented five pilot surveys in total (twice for Nitto Denko and once for the other three).

While each case study has some interesting points, we do not have enough space to discuss all of them in detail. Therefore, we will focus on two of them: namely, the cases of Nitto Denko and Tanabe. Nitto Denko is the only company that has had two years' experience with the pilot project and Tanabe used an enterprise resource planning (ERP) system when introducing MFCA. Before discussing these two case studies in detail, the basic idea of material flow cost accounting will be briefly explained.

What is material flow cost accounting?

Material flow cost accounting (MFCA) was developed by Institut für Management und Umwelt (IMU), which was founded by B. Wagner and M. Strobel in Germany. The METI environmental accounting committee based its ideas on IMU's theory and somewhat modified those methods when introducing them into Japanese companies. The basic idea of MFA is explained here according to Strobel and Redmann (2001), which has been referred to by the METI committee.

MFCA is an essential instrument of flow management. Strobel and Redmann (2001: 1) defined flow management as an effort 'to organise production companies beginning-to-end in terms of their flows of materials and information—all structured in an efficient, objective-oriented manner'. In MFCA systems materials are traced in production processes either as quantities (physical units) or costs (monetary units), and materials here not only consist of the final products but also resulting losses are calculated for each material item. Existing conventional cost accounting methods are not able to provide sufficiently precise data concerning the cost of materials as well as material losses. MFCA eliminates this shortcoming by closely linking quantitative data to material flows. In other words, the purpose of MFCA is to render production more transparent than conventional cost accounting can.

Strobel and Redmann (2001: 8) outlined the merits of MFCA as follows:

> The decisive factor in harmonising economic and ecological objectives is the reduced or more efficient use of materials and energy. Flow cost accounting with realising comprehensive and flow-specific beginning-to-end transparency (in physical and monetary terms) is thus not only an answer to criticisms of costing methods in ecological terms but also less to criticisms in economic terms.

The values and costs of MFCA are divided up into the following three categories:

1. Material
2. System
3. Delivery and disposal

All items of material are calculated by quantity as well as by monetary units at the quantity centre. The quantity centre is a spatial and functional unit at which material is transformed physically or exists through time (e.g. stored, tested or sorted). The basic idea of MFCA is shown in Figure 12.1. A square cell in the figure is a quantity centre. Materials are calculated by the actual flow of the quantity, and system values and costs, main items of which are depreciation and personnel costs, are allocated to each quantity centre by employing material flows as cost drivers.

Introducing MFCA into the production process, management is able to get more transparency in terms of figures and costs in the process. Strobel and Redmann (2001: 7) suggest this transparency has the effect of encouraging

- The development of products that require fewer materials
- The development of product packaging that requires fewer materials

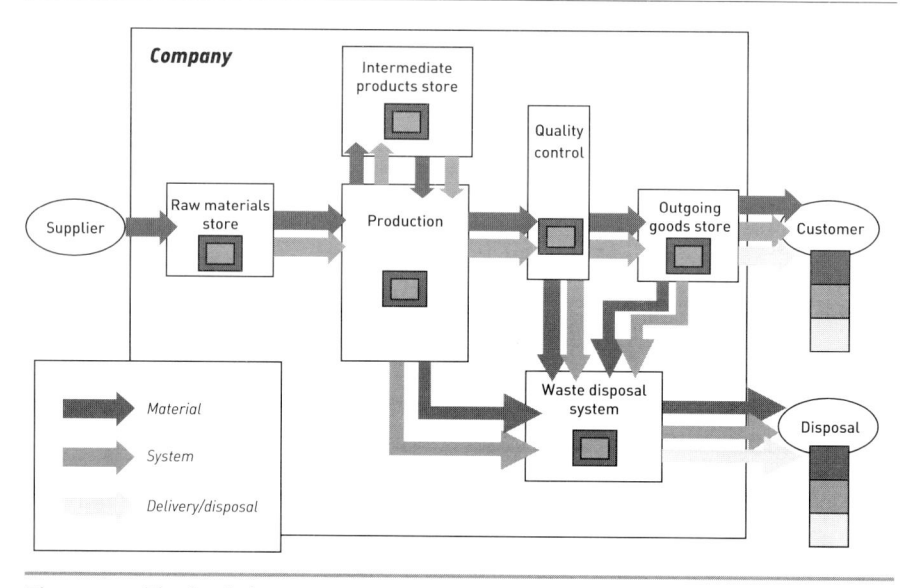

Figure 12.1 **The basic idea of material flow cost accounting**
Source: Strobel and Redmann 2001: 12

- The reduction of material losses (e.g. rejects, scrap, cut-offs) and, as a result of this, reduction of waste (i.e. solid waste, effluent exhaust)

The MFCA approach has already been successfully tried and tested in a number of production companies in Germany of varying size and in different sectors. The aim of the METI committee was to examine the practical relevance of MFCA for Japanese companies. Four case studies have already been conducted. Two of them will be discussed in the following two sections.

Case study 1: Nitto Denko Co.

The METI environmental accounting committee formed a working group on MFCA in the second year, 2000. Nitto Denko participated in this working group in that year, and underwent the pilot project of MFCA trial introduction twice, in 2000 (the second year) and 2001 (the third year). Both pilot projects were implemented in the same manufacturing line for adhesive tapes for electronics applications in the Toyohashi Plant.

Nitto Denko was established in 1918 as a manufacturing company for electric insulation materials. The company is a comprehensive functional materials manufacturer in the fields of chemistry, electronics and medical treatment. The amount of total assets and sales at consolidated base is JPY357,653 million and

JPY365.697 million respectively in March 2001 (annual figures). The number of employees is 8,585. The company currently handles 13,500 types of product.[1]

Nitto Denko annually publishes an environmental report that discloses environmental accounting information. The statement of environmental accounting in 2000 is shown in Table 12.1. The company divided environmental costs into environmental conservation costs and environmental impact costs. The former conforms to the MOE guidelines, but the latter was originally defined by the company. Among the environmental impact costs, the figures for industrial waste were the biggest. While the calculation of industrial waste is different from the MFCA approach, it is clear that reducing waste is vital for the company.

Unit: JPY 1 million/year

Categories	Fiscal 2000 budget	Fiscal 2000 results
Total sales	17,995.0	18,534.2
Sales value of own products	16,594.6	17,093.3
Environmental conservation costs		
General and administrative overhead	66.9	80.0
Treatment for industrial waste	68.7	79.1
External services for environmental management	20.2	19.2
Personnel	43.1	43.5
Depreciation	58.3	93.2
R&D&E	118.3	92.9
Total	375.5	407.9
Environmental impact costs		
Value of industrial waste	2,645.1	2,913.9
Energy	309.7	326.3
Organic solvents	150.0	141.1
Water	21.7	18.9
Total	3,126.5	3,400.2
Ratio of environmental impact costs	17.4%	18.3%

Applicable range of totalling: Nitto Denko only, April 2000–March 2001

Table 12.1 Environmental cost

Source: Nitto Denko, Environmental Report 2001: 12

MFCA includes three types of cost: (1) material costs, including energy costs; (2) system costs, including personnel and depreciation costs; and (3) delivery and disposal costs. In the first pilot project, only material costs, excluding energy costs,

1 See www.nitto.com.

were calculated and the scope was extended to include energy costs as well as the other two costs, system and delivery/disposal costs, in the second pilot project. Energy costs were calculated in the whole plant, but were not allocated to each quantity centre. The term of calculation of the first project was one month.

MFCA traces the flow and storage of material in the targeted process. At the quantity centre all sorts of material are calculated in physical and monetary units. The flow of materials through the quantity centre, excluding stock at the centre, is separated into two channels: one for the product and the other for the material loss as wastes. The stock is the balance between the input and the output of the centre. The quantity of materials is counted by each item of material at the quantity centre. The unit cost of each material is then multiplied by the quantity to get the monetary value. In this way the quantity and cost of materials at each quantity centre was calculated in the pilot project at Nitto Denko.

The results are shown in Figure 12.2. The figures in the chart are somewhat modified, but not far from the actual data. There are seven quantity centres: dissolution, batch blend, coating and drying, store, slitting, inspection and packing, and warehouse. Three groups of material are put into the line: adhesive, which is produced by five kinds of material in the first two quantity centres in the plant, backing film and separator. Both quantity and costs of these three materials were calculated at the seven quantity centres but because of corporate confidentiality only the cost information was indicated. These results show that material losses at the slitting centre were the largest. The company had already realised this, but the value of losses had not been identified. Clear monetary information about the material losses makes decision-making more accurate when it comes to choosing alternatives for improvements.

In the second year of the working group project—the third year of the METI project—the targeted cost was expanded to cover energy costs, system costs and delivery/disposal costs. The pilot project was implemented in the same line. The purpose of the second-year project was to provide more accurate information of the material losses in order to improve management decision-making toward cost reduction and eco-efficiency. The term of the data calculation was also extended to five months. The scope of material costs was the same as in the previous project. System costs consisted of corporate personnel costs, consignment labour costs and depreciation. Energy costs included electricity and fuel costs. Delivery/disposal costs included waste disposal costs and delivery/transport costs. A corporate financial data system was used to collect this information.

From the results of the second-year project the problems at the plant's slitting centre were more clearly identified. The results of MFCA with only material costs calculated in the previous project proved to hold on a more general level. However, the amount of losses in the slitting centre was about 20% larger than previous results because the scope of costs was enlarged. Such information is more accurate and useful for management decision-making. Nitto Denko proposed two measures to solve the problems. At the slitting centre, a test was conducted to improve material loss resulting from the separator, and the width of the loss was minimised. Because of this improvement, material losses decreased by around 7%. Activities for material loss reduction at the coating and drying centres were also under consideration. The company started to re-examine the material of backing films carefully because the production and usage of this material was critically important for the material losses identified.

Since this type of decision-making, including decisions on new investment, is handled at top-management level, the MFCA information should be compiled into a report for top management to advance improvements. Nitto Denko developed a chart to list physical units and monetary values in one sheet. This can be extremely effective in reporting to top management. Space limitations prevent us from showing the chart, but its basic framework is similar to Figure 12.2.

The results of these pilot projects suggested that MFCA was useful for material and parts manufacturing companies such as Nitto Denko. In the next section we will examine the case of the pharmaceutical company.

Case study 2: Tanabe Seiyaku Co.

Tanabe Seiyaku Co.[2] is a pharmaceutical company and participated in the MFCA project of METI in 2001. Tanabe provides medicines such as treatments for high blood pressure and cardiac patients for the global market. The amount of total assets and sales of consolidated base is JPY496,590 million and JPY194,027 million respectively calculated in March 2001 (annual figures). The company has 9,579 employees.

A pilot project of MFCA was implemented in a manufacturing line of one product type in the Onoda Plant. In the manufacturing process, several raw materials are synthesised and then purified. After that the refined product is put into the next processing stage and manufactured into a bulk pharmaceutical. The bulk is then weighed. After a preparation process packaging is carried out according to various dosages and packages. The material losses generated at the processing stages are either recycled/re-used or disposed of as wastes. Ten quantity centres were created including recycling processes.

The relationship between the corporate information system and the MFCA system is very important and another purpose of this pilot project was to examine the relationship between ERP and MFCA systems. In most case studies carried out by IMU in Germany, the MFCA system was grafted onto the existing corporate ERP system: for example, SAP R/3 and Oracle. In the case of Nitto Denko, in contrast, no ERP system was available and hence the MFCA system was introduced independently of the existing corporate information system. However, in the case of Tanabe, the company was preparing to introduce SAP R/3 by April 2002, so it was possible to introduce the MFCA system within the company's ERP system.

The costs to be measured by this MFCA project included all cost items: material, system and delivery/wastes costs. Manufacturing costs for the product were broken down and categorised under these three cost items. The data collection term was one year from April 2000 to March 2001. Since a centralised database had been installed for the ERP system, it was much easier to get information of material flows

2 See www.tanabe.co.jp/english/index.html.

108 Eco-efficiency and Beyond

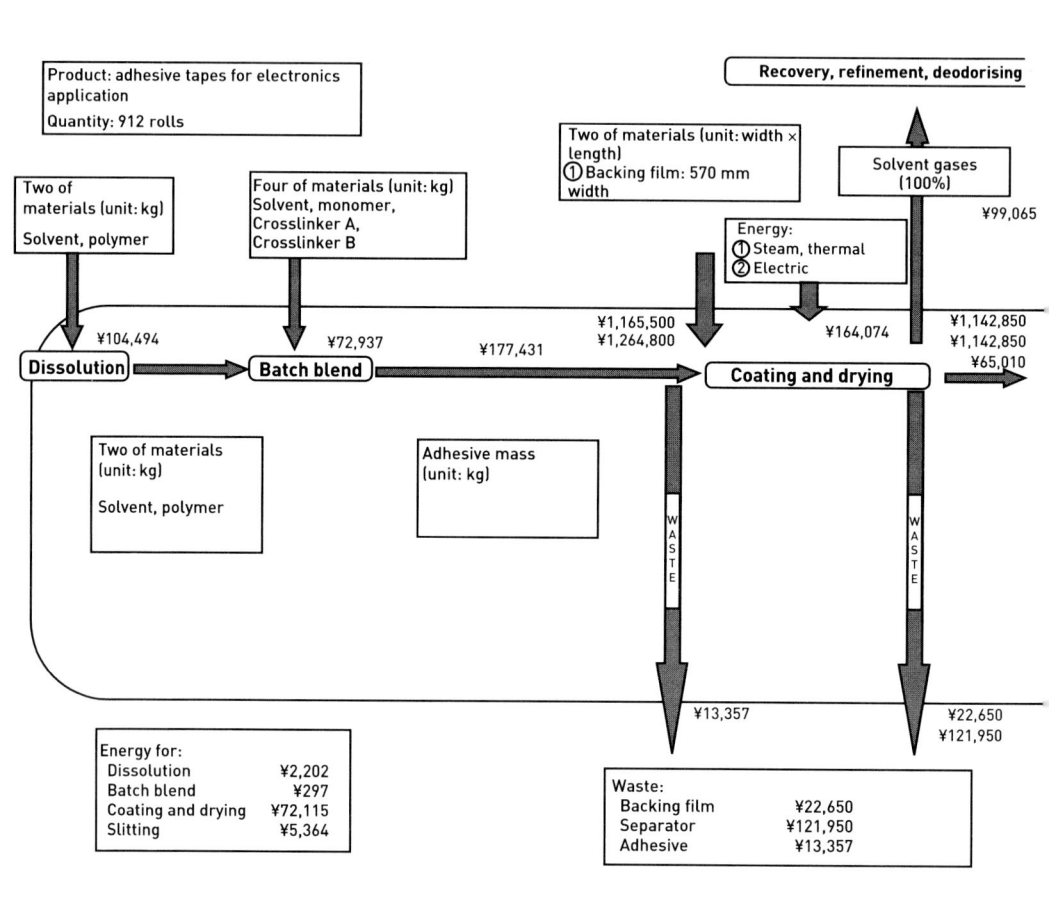

Figure 12.2 Flow chart of Nitto Denko

Source: METI 2002: 94

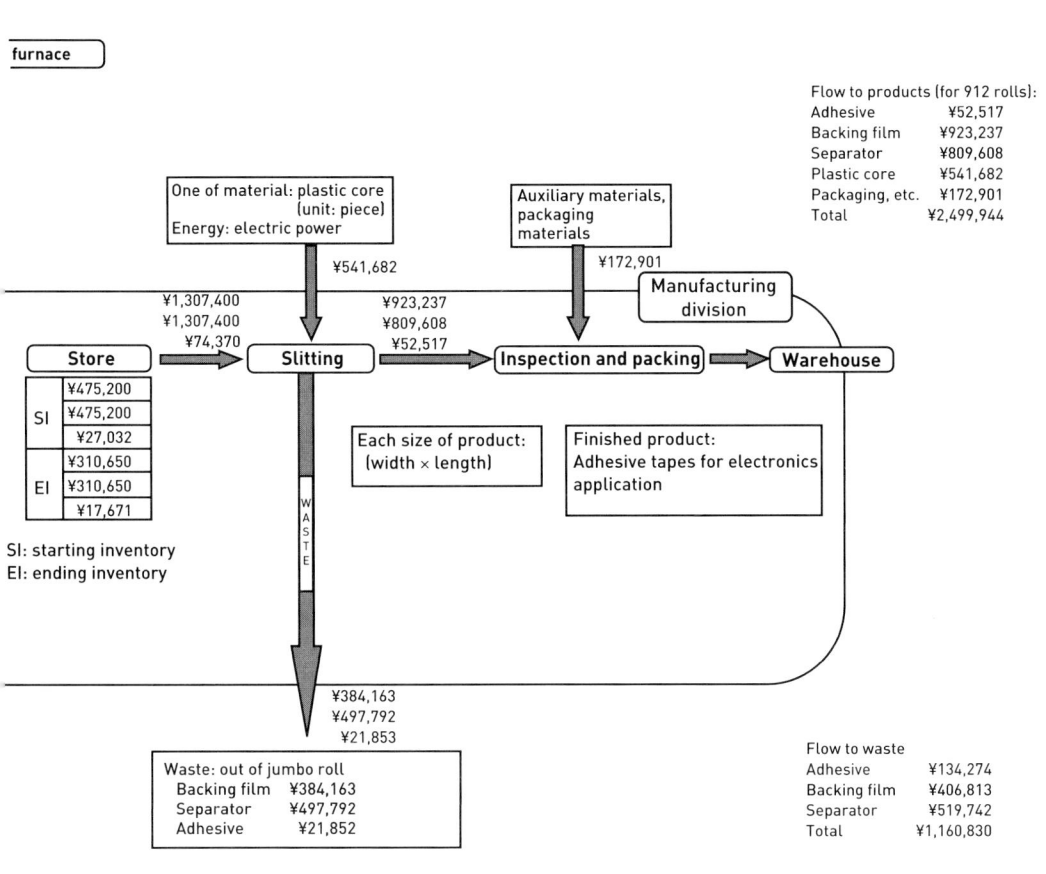

12. Sustainable accounting initiatives in Japan Kokubu and Nakajima 109

```
furnace
```

Flow to products (for 912 rolls):
Adhesive	¥52,517
Backing film	¥923,237
Separator	¥809,608
Plastic core	¥541,682
Packaging, etc.	¥172,901
Total	¥2,499,944

One of material: plastic core (unit: piece)
Energy: electric power

Auxiliary materials, packaging materials

¥541,682   ¥172,901

Manufacturing division

¥1,307,400   ¥923,237
¥1,307,400   ¥809,608
¥74,370   ¥52,517

Store → **Slitting** → **Inspection and packing** → **Warehouse**

	Store	
SI	¥475,200	
	¥475,200	
	¥27,032	
EI	¥310,650	
	¥310,650	
	¥17,671	

Each size of product: (width × length)

Finished product: Adhesive tapes for electronics application

SI: starting inventory
EI: ending inventory

WASTE

¥384,163
¥497,792
¥21,853

Waste: out of jumbo roll
Backing film	¥384,163
Separator	¥497,792
Adhesive	¥21,852

Flow to waste
Adhesive	¥134,274
Backing film	¥406,813
Separator	¥519,742
Total	¥1,160,830

for a one-year period than doing it by hand. If the ERP system and MFCA are introduced at the same time, the ERP system should be designed to cover MFCA information as well. However, it is necessary to examine just how to integrate MFCA into the ERP system. For example, if MFCA is integrated directly, the system has to be customised. This requires time and money. Consequently, it is necessary to consider developing a secondary system where data is extracted from the ERP system and arranged for MFCA. Moreover, it will be necessary to determine what data is required for MFCA. Tanabe considered how to redesign the ERP system so that it would get such data. However, at this stage concrete design plans have not been settled yet.

The data on material (raw material) costs, labour costs and physical quantities was collected by Tanabe's manufacturing cost simulation system. Other cost data was taken from the company's financial data base. Tanabe developed theoretical value, standard value and actual value for materials (raw materials) used in each manufacturing process. These three values were applied to the calculation of material losses. In this project the material loss was determined as the difference between theoretical value and actual value. However, where the whole value resulted in a loss, the amount was measured on an individual basis. Energy costs, such as electricity, fuel and water costs, are allocated by machine hour based on usage to the quantity centre (Machine hour equals per lot standard machine hour multiplied by number of production lots. The use of machine hour is for the purpose of comparison with data after the introduction of the SAP R/3 in April 2002. Compared to the previous allocation of machine hours, the current allocation of machine hours is more accurate.)

The results of the pilot project of Tanabe are shown in Table 12.2. Because the whole picture of the flows in the plant is very complicated, the cost information of the main quantity centre, excluding some minor quantity centres such as recycling centres, is only presented as a cost matrix. The figures in the chart are not modified actual data as in the case of Nitto Denko. The results of the pilot project in the Onoda plant point to two problems. First, in the synthesis process, the waste disposal cost related to the use of chlorine-based solvents for the purpose of chemical reaction is critically significant. The solution was to implement research and development, manufacturing process management and some capital investment in order to reduce the waste disposal cost of chlorine-based solvents. These activities would promote an increase in re-use and recycling and reduce waste. In addition the fuel and labour costs related to disposing of the chlorine-based medium would be reduced. The economic benefits due to these improvements are estimated to be around JPY30 million per year. Second, material losses in the synthesis and purification centres are significant during the manufacturing process. The solution has not been settled, but it gave a new target to research and development activities as well as considering a new investment.

The pilot project of MFCA in Tanabe suggested that the construction of MFCA systems within ERP systems was very effective for corporate management. The ERP system makes the introduction of the MFCA system much easier. Furthermore, the MFCA system enabled Tanabe to identify precise cost data for some very significant inefficiency in the plant. Because the information from the MFCA system was very

(Unit: thousand yen)

Quantity Centre	Synthesis	Purification	Bulk drug substances	Weighting	Preparation	Packaging
Input						
Material cost	303,967	279,603	223,263	732,175	712,992	958,509
System cost	161,886	360,382	727,671	1,018,524	1,234,074	1,921,328
Cost of electricity	12,930	11,359	28,657	941	2,817	3,151
Total	478,783	651,344	979,591	1,751,640	1,949,813	2,882,988
Material loss						
Material cost	242,949	207,996	27,589	20,334	23,737	40,778
(for recycling)	(125,510)	(88,762)	(2,116)	(19,592)	(3,038)	(1,535)
(for waste)	(117,440)	(119,234)	(25,474)	(743)	(20,699)	(39,243)
System cost	92,810	33,535	90,213	14,218	113,228	213,744
Cost of electricity	3,899	806	2,876	1	81	167
Disposal cost	126,048	2,100	17,065	0	1,941	3,879
Total	465,706	244,437	137,743	34,553	138,987	258,568

Table 12.2 Flow cost matrix: Tanabe Seiyaku Co.

Source: METI 2002: 120

accurate, management could propose much more precise proposals to settle the problems.

Conclusion

Environmental accounting practices in Japan have been more oriented to external reporting because the MOE guidelines, which stress this function, strongly influence Japanese companies. The MOE guidelines encourage Japanese companies to disclose environmental accounting information in environmental reports. The number of companies disclosing such information is increasing. On the other hand, environmental accounting for internal usage—that is, environmental management accounting—has not been as much developed as external environmental accounting. The METI committee on environmental accounting was formed to develop environmental management accounting practices in Japan.

The METI initiatives were concerned with several kinds of environmental management accounting tools. Among them the project on MFCA was of particular importance because some pilot projects were implemented in Japanese companies. Most existing tools of environmental management accounting have been developed outside Japan and there was no evidence that such tools were effective in Japanese companies as well. For example, when we explained MFCA in Japan, we often encountered negative comments: for example, that Japanese companies do not need a tool such as MFCA because the Japanese style of production management based on total quality management (TQM) or *kaizen* activities does not leave room for further MFCA improvements. However, the pilot projects of MFCA in Japan proved such criticisms incorrect.

The five pilot projects, including the two case studies discussed in this chapter, suggested that, as an environmental management tool for reducing waste and cost at the same time, MFCA is sufficiently effective for use in corporate business practices. In particular, MFCA makes the data systematically collected within a company useful for corporate management and offers various alternatives. In addition, it allows companies to consider specific directions for improvement and allows for economic improvement through the reduction of waste.

MFCA is not an environmental accounting tool promoted only by an environmental protection division. The scope of MFCA is beyond the environmental division. If a company wants to introduce it, at least production and accounting divisions must take part in the initiative. In both cases of Nitto Denko and Tanabe, staff from various divisions participated in the project team. Corporate sustainable initiatives are not the exclusive tasks of the environmental division and they should be organised as a part of a whole corporate strategy. The pilot studies of MFCA in Japan suggested that an introduction of MFCA into companies must be arranged as a whole corporate project.

13
The BASF eco-efficiency method as a sustainable decision-making tool

Andreas Kicherer
BASF AG, Germany

The general public has an ambivalent attitude to the chemical industry. On the one hand, it is obvious to just about everybody that life without chemistry would be inconceivable while, on the other hand, the potential risks and polluting effects on the environment associated with chemical production and chemical products are viewed critically. BASF as the largest chemical company in the world has long been aware of its responsibility to humanity and the environment. Thus from a very early stage we have professed our support for the global initiatives of sustainable development and responsible care. Moreover, BASF is a member of the WBCSD and of the Global Compact initiative of the UN.

To meet these commitments and obligations we have to be verifiable and accountable in our actions. Accordingly, in the mid-1990s we started to examine our products with regard to their sustainability. The questions 'What must the products of the future look like for them to be sustainably successful?' or 'How can sustainability be measured and presented in a simple manner?' were to be investigated by means of a readily communicable method.

Up to that time environmental protection had been directed primarily at end-of-pipe production technology. Today, however, the products themselves are increasingly being evaluated with regard to their impact on the environment. To arrive at quantified assertions and to document the innovative progress of our products, BASF, together with an external partner, Roland Berger, started in 1995 to develop the instrument of eco-efficiency analysis. Eco-efficiency analysis considers the economic and ecological effects of a product, giving both aspects equal weight, so in addition to its relevance to the environment the costs of a product are taken into account.

114   Eco-efficiency and Beyond

The pivotal point of an eco-efficiency analysis is specific customer benefit. Examples of the questions to be asked, therefore, are 'What is the most eco-efficient method for packaging dairy products?' or 'How can an end-user most eco-efficiently whitewash a wall?' or 'Which methods of tanning leather are best?' To answer such concrete questions alternative approaches to a solution are drawn up and their effects on the environment and their costs to the end-user are determined. The entire life-cycle of the products—the extraction of crude oil or gas via production, distribution, the usage phase and recycling—is taken into consideration (see Fig. 13.1).

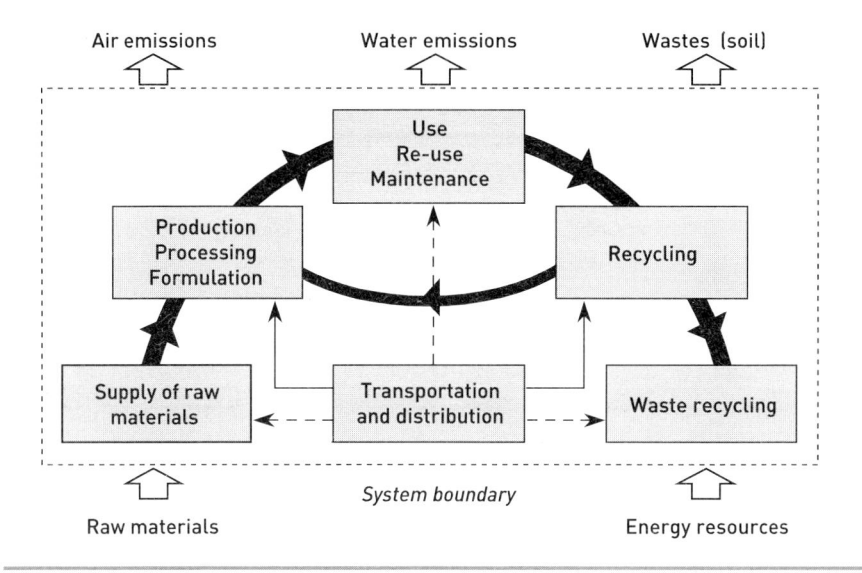

Figure 13.1 Review of a product's entire life-cycle

Objectives for the development of eco-efficiency analysis

Implementing the concept of sustainability in a large company requires identifying an instrument that finds widespread acceptance. Only in this way can it be ensured that, on the one hand, analyses are conducted and hence strategies for sustainability are developed and that, on the other hand, these strategies are actually implemented. To that effect a methodical approach must meet the following set of requirements:

- Criteria for sustainability should be quantified as far as possible and not be presented just in qualitative terms.

- The results must be easy to understand and allow the development of scenarios.

- A pragmatic approach must be chosen that allows adaptation to the special conditions of specific products and processes.

- Direct links to customers and/or suppliers ensure the interest of the marketing departments in the results. This frequently leads to rapid implementation of the outcome.

- A modular structure helps to achieve short project times and hence low project costs. This is a fundamental requirement for widespread application of the method.

- Despite the pragmatic approach the analysis should have a well-founded scientific basis so that the results are rendered reproducible. This should provide stimuli for discussion and for expanding the point of view.

- To spread the philosophy of sustainability it must be possible for a high number of staff to communicate the results of the analyses.

- Since a company has to maintain a presence in the marketplace and adapt to political conditions, there should also be opportunities for marketing and politics as well as possibilities for taking strategic decisions.

Eco-efficiency analysis as developed by BASF covers the major part of this set of requirements.

Principles

The first aim is to establish the total costs of each alternative. These include the costs of production, purchase, use (e.g. maintenance, repair and operating costs) and those for disposing of or recycling the product. At the same time the burdens on the environment are determined by means of a life-cycle assessment (LCA) conducted in accordance with ISO 14040–14043. These ecological burdens are grouped into six principal categories: energy consumption, consumption of raw materials and resources, emissions, toxicity potential, land use (included since 2002), and hazard potential (what is known as residual hazard). Many individual categories are combined in these principal categories. In the case of emissions, for example, water emissions, wastes, global-warming potential, ozone-depletion potential, photochemical ozone-creation potential and acidification potential are included (Fig. 13.2).

The numerous individual criteria in an LCA are related to each other and to the costs. This makes it possible to present the results in a transparent and readily communicable manner in what is known as the eco-efficiency portfolio. By this means an analysis can be carried out with little expenditure of time and resources and scenarios can be calculated easily. At the same time the underlying methods

116 Eco-efficiency and Beyond

```
Quantitative energy
consumption (20%)

Quantitative consumption      Air emissions         Greenhouse gas
of materials (20%)              (50%)                  potential
                                                         (50%)
Quantitative
emissions (20%)

Quantitative                   Water                 Ozone-depletion
land use (10%)               emissions              potential (20%)
                               (35%)
                                                     Photochemical
Qualitative                                          ozone-creation
toxicity (20%)                                       potential (20%)
                              Wastes
                               (15%)                  Acidification
Qualitative hazard                                   potential (10%)
potential (10%)
```

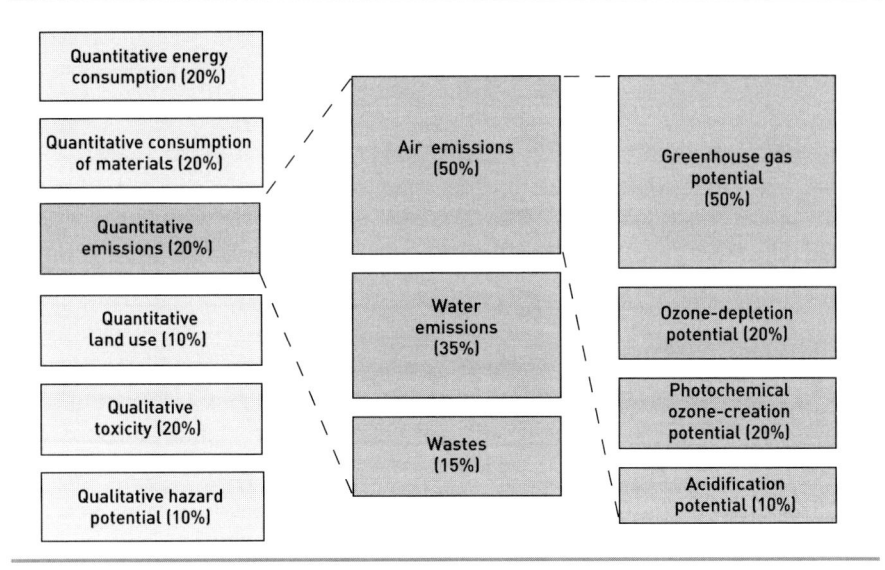

Figure 13.2 Society-related evaluation factors for emissions

have a sound scientific basis. Such a procedure opens up the possibility of providing a sheet anchor for the idea of sustainability in a large company. Management philosophies change accordingly and product development gains more innovative drive.

Status of eco-efficiency analysis

Since 1996 more than 190 analyses have been carried out in key fields at BASF (paints and dyes, plastics, life science, oil and gas, and chemicals). Eco-efficiency analysis has been applied in four divisions.

In **strategic decisions** it is possible for the application investigated to distinguish products with a promising future from products with a less promising future. Even in investment decisions eco-efficiency analysis provides valuable pointers.

The second field of application relates to **research and product development**. Promising products are identified at an early stage, thus facilitating decision-making about the primary thrust of the development.

The third field of application is the drawing-up of position papers for **discussions with opinion-formers**. Eco-efficiency analysis makes it possible to present the complex, holistic interconnections in industrial production and product use in a graphic and readily communicable form. This allows the conduct of quantitative discussions, with politicians for instance, about the effects of planned legislation.

Eco-efficiency analysis is even used in **marketing**. Since the entire life-cycle of a product is considered, the effects for our customers are integrated into the analysis. As a result the total vision inherent in our products can be communicated to our customers.

Two specific examples will illustrate our procedure.

Shock absorbers in automobiles

Suspension systems in automobiles are basically composed of three components: the actual steel spring, the lower elastic support for the steel spring and an auxiliary spring made of an elastic material (Fig. 13.3).

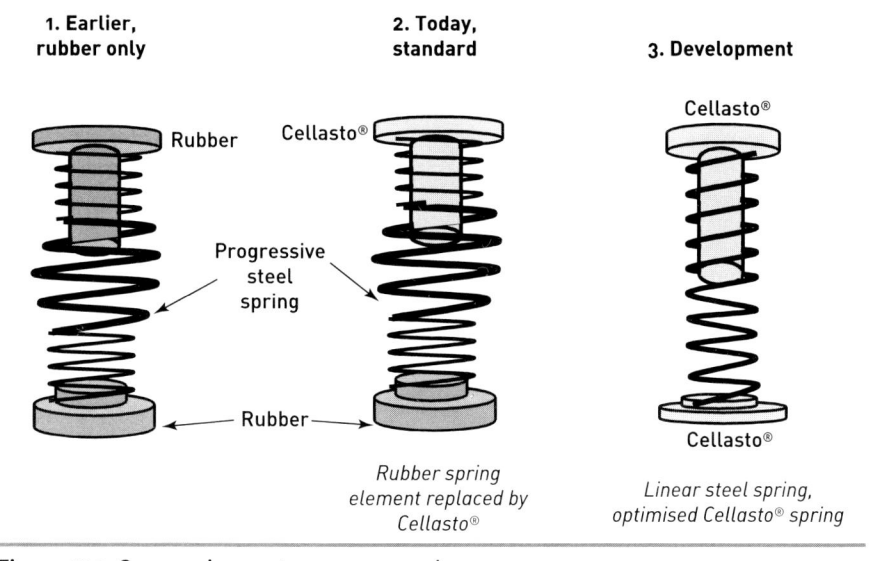

Figure 13.3 Suspension systems compared

Formerly, a progressive steel spring was used and the support and the auxiliary spring were each made of rubber. In today's mass-produced vehicles a progressive steel spring is often still used, the lower support is also made of rubber but the auxiliary spring is produced from Cellasto®, which means a distinctly higher level of comfort. Cellasto® is a polyurethane foam. A third alternative is at the development stage. Here the Cellasto® auxiliary spring can assume springing properties so that instead of the heavy progressive steel spring a lighter linear steel spring can be used. In addition the spring support can also be produced from Cellasto®.

For these three systems both the total costs from the point of view of the end-user (the automobile driver) and the environmental impact over the entire life-cycle were determined. The results of this analysis are plotted in what is known as the eco-efficiency portfolio (Fig. 13.4).

118 Eco-efficiency and Beyond

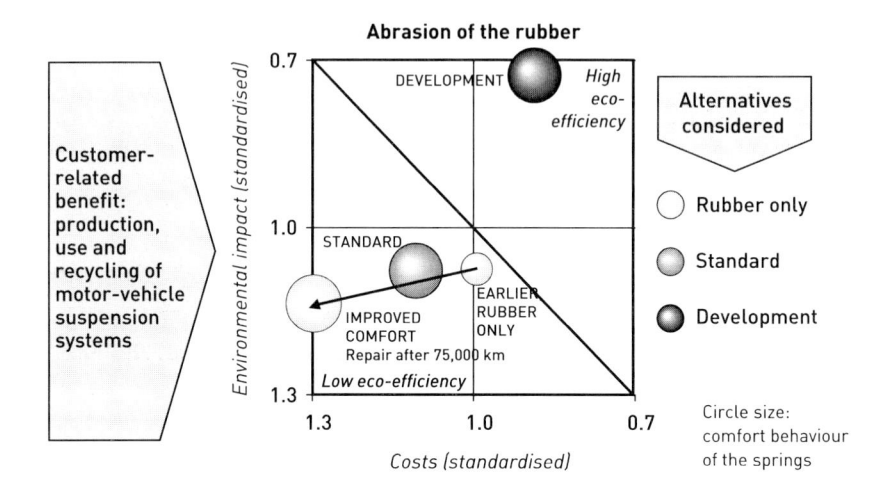

Figure 13.4 The reduced lifetime of the rubber option reduces the eco-efficiency significantly

In this case the x axis shows the total costs (low costs on the right; high costs on the left) and the y axis reflects total environmental pollution (high environmental impact at the bottom; low environmental impact at the top). This results in a graph with four quadrants. Eco-efficient products are found in the upper right quadrant: these are products that simultaneously have low costs for the end-user and cause low environmental impact. Less eco-efficient products are found in the lower left quadrant. These products generate high costs and high environmental impact. The spring systems are plotted onto this portfolio.

In this analysis the circle sizes reflect the comfort properties of the suspension. In contrast to earlier systems today's series, although generating slightly higher costs, has distinctly higher comfort characteristics.

Another possibility is making the rubber-only variant more flexible to achieve a similar level of comfort. However, this solution would significantly increase wear on the rubber buffer, which would have to be changed after 75,000 km or so, and substantially raise costs.

The new development can, however, achieve a great eco-efficient leap forward. Because of its low weight, the linear steel spring, which is based on the assumption of damping properties by the Cellasto® spring member, allows distinct savings in costs and environmental pollution during the usage phase. Obviously, lighter motor vehicles consume less fuel, so the development project offers by far the most eco-efficient suspension system. The excellent physical properties of Cellasto® allow optimisation of the steel spring. This optimisation of the total system with a marked reduction of material consumed significantly increases eco-efficiency.

This analysis demonstrates the advantages of BASF materials to customers in a total system review. Naturally, comparisons must always be carried out on the basis of customer benefit and the total system. Simple comparisons of materials are inconclusive.

Sizing materials in the weaving of cotton fabrics

In modern looms the weft threads reach speeds of up to 200 km/h. To prevent weaving faults due to minute protruding fibres the weft and warp threads are surrounded by a coating known as size. Usually this protective jacket is made from natural materials such as corn or potato starch. In addition, however, there are synthetic sizes based in acrylate developed by BASF.

The sizing and desizing of 1,000 m² of cotton fabric for workwear twill was investigated in an eco-efficiency analysis. In this case, in addition to the starch size, there are two other variants, a CE™/PVA size and a CO™-starch size (Fig. 13.5).

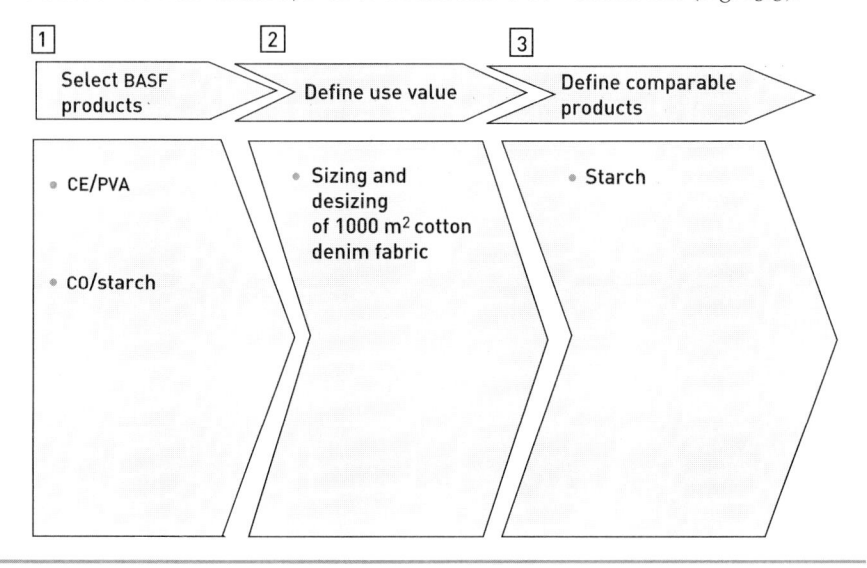

Figure 13.5 Comparison of sizing agents

The system limits (Fig. 13.6) encompass the production of the size, its use—that is, the actual sizing process—together with desizing and the possible recycling of size materials. The results of the calculation of levels of environmental impact are reproduced in what is known as the ecological fingerprint (Fig. 13.7).

The five principal categories of energy consumption, materials consumption, hazard potential, toxicity and emissions are plotted along the axes of a five-pointed star. The worst option in each case is assigned the value 1.0. The other options are plotted relative to this. In this way the strengths and weaknesses of the individual products can be quickly identified. These environmental categories are weighted by means of statistical factors and by means of the results of public opinion surveys and plotted together with the costs in the portfolio (Fig. 13.8). Improving the ultrafiltration recovery rate to 80% increased the eco-efficiency of CE/PVA; omitting ultrafiltration reduced it

Sizes based on renewable raw materials cause the highest environmental pollution. The purely synthetic size CE/PVA has the lowest environmental impact

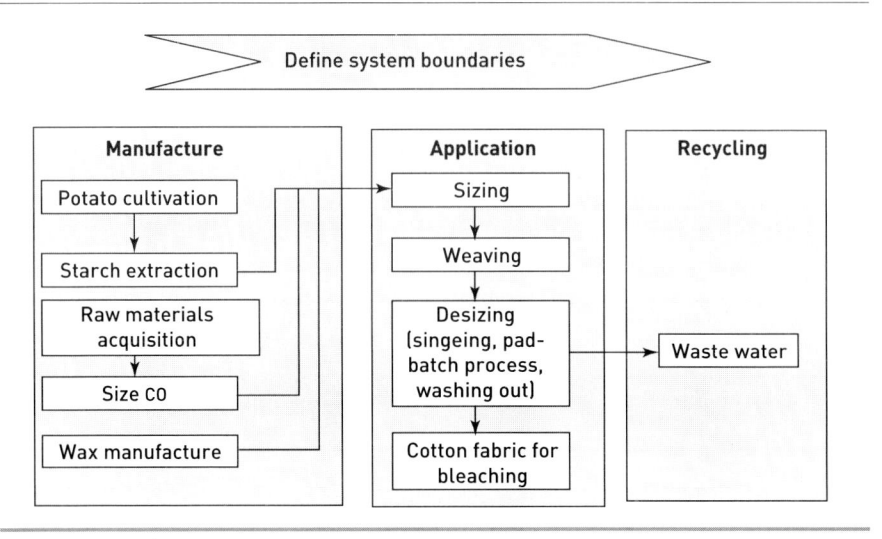

Figure 13.6 CO/starch

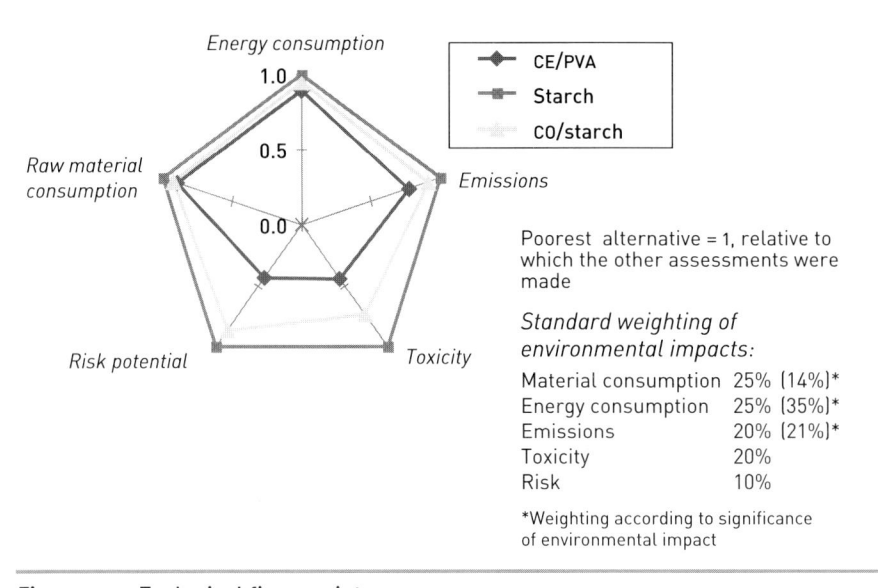

Figure 13.7 Ecological fingerprint

because synthetic starch can be recycled after desizing. A customer in whose plant the fibres are both sized and desized derives significant advantages from synthetic sizes.

If only the process step of sizing is considered—that is, not the entire life-cycle of the product—no advantages emerge for CE/PVA, so this example also shows that identifying the most eco-efficient variant requires the assessment of the entire life-

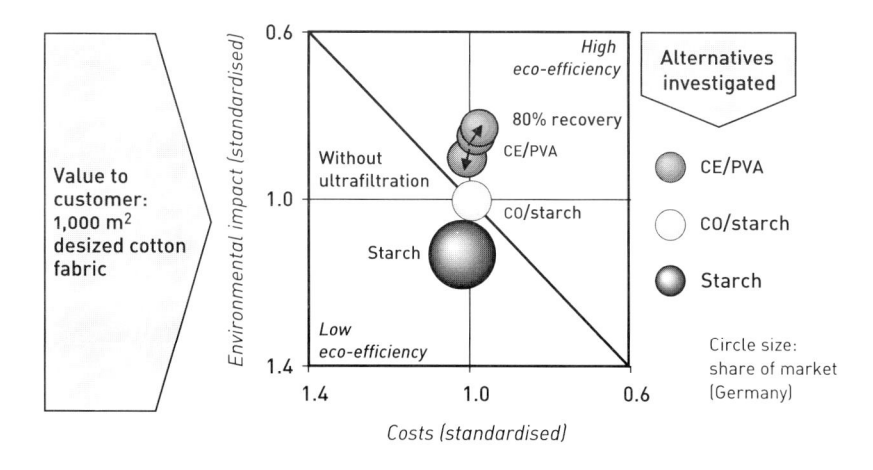

Figure 13.8 **Improving the ultrafiltration recovery rate to 80% increased the eco-efficiency of CE/PVA; omitting ultrafiltration reduced it**

cycle. The advantages of CE/PVA emerge in weaving (higher beneficial effect in weaving) and in desizing (no enzymes needed, lower requirement for washing chemicals and the possibility of ultrafiltration).

Depending on the scenarios considered, eco-efficiency analysis can yield highly different answers. It adapts well to different customer demands and is oriented on workable solutions.

Methodology

How are the various environmental categories evaluated? Two different evaluation factors come into play. On the one hand, there is a society factor. Public opinion surveys shed a light on the value society attaches to the reduction of individual potentials. This is a qualitative method. On the other hand, what are known as relevance or normalisation factors are introduced: for example, to determine the share of the emission or energy consumption under consideration in the total emissions of that type or energy consumption in Germany. The data calculated for the alternatives is compared with statistical values for Germany. This is a quantitative method. Both values are incorporated with equal weights in the calculation of environmental burdens.

The relevance factors also allow the relation of environmental pollution to total costs. Here the total costs from the point of view of the end-user are considered in relation to the total GDP of the country. In this way eco-efficiency analysis makes a highly effective contribution to obtaining answers to many questions of environmental policy: for example, 'Do specified environmental advantages justify the extra costs caused by this?' In addition, environmental conservation projects are evaluated with regard to their economic effectiveness. Eco-efficiency analysis graphically and persuasively shows which environmental conservation projects are to be preferred, and where most relief to the environment is achieved for the financial resources employed.

Summary

BASF has developed eco-efficiency analysis into a central and important instrument for optimising our portfolio with regard to ecological aspects and acquiring competitive advantages. Seminars and symposia, but primarily specific co-operative ventures with different partners, make the method and knowledge of eco-efficiency analysis available to other parties.[1]

---

[1] Further information about the details of the method and actual projects can be found at www.oekoeffizienzanalyse.de

14
Toward sustainable products and services

Christa Liedtke
Wuppertal Institute, Germany

Eco-efficient economic activity can be combined with a profit-oriented and competitive business and consumption strategy. It has often been proved that enterprises can consider both ecology and economy in a win–win strategy, as shown in Figure 14.1. Still, the true potentials have not been fully used, and what services exactly the consumer requires are rarely considered.

At present, practice focuses on short-term product cycles (cf. IT products) and high sales margins. But it seems that the limit is slowly being reached as increasingly short product cycles overtax management and product development, profit margins are getting smaller and clients are becoming more and more dissatisfied. An individualisation of products or services seems to be unavoidable, and made-to-measure rather than made-to-mass production is a possible model for the future. This makes sense, not only for the national economy but also for the individual economy as resources—human and natural —are used more efficiently and the creation of wealth is oriented to human needs. Within such an economy, enterprises gain their profits from intelligent, innovative services, from the use phase and reintegration, re-use, recycling, treatment and further use of resources or product parts.

14.1 What is eco-efficiency?

In a nutshell, eco-efficiency means increasing value while using fewer resources with less environmental impact. Less is more. Eco-efficiency strategies and concepts maximise the economic value of a product while at the same time minimising negative environmental impacts (Ayres and van Leynseele 1997; Hawken 1997).

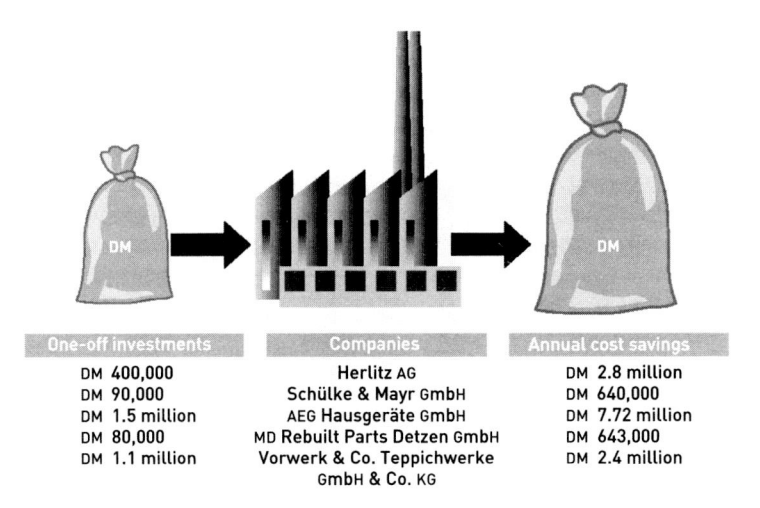

One-off investments	Companies	Annual cost savings
DM 400,000	Herlitz AG	DM 2.8 million
DM 90,000	Schülke & Mayr GmbH	DM 640,000
DM 1.5 million	AEG Hausgeräte GmbH	DM 7.72 million
DM 80,000	MD Rebuilt Parts Detzen GmbH	DM 643,000
DM 1.1 million	Vorwerk & Co. Teppichwerke GmbH & Co. KG	DM 2.4 million

Figure 14.1 Companies save money
Source: Gege 1997

The fewer resources used in generating equal performance or equal customer benefits, the less needs to be invested in

- Purchasing the resources
- Process management
- Waste disposal

Product lines and accompanying production processes are optimised along the whole life-cycle: that is, from cradle to cradle. The optimisation of the use phase toward eco-efficiency is another focus (eco-efficient product design, closing of material cycles, need orientation, risk minimisation for health and environment, etc.). The company earns on the whole life-cycle of a product: for example, leasing or other concepts. Therefore, it not only sells 'end products' but also earns on the use phase, optimising it in such a way that investments in consumption are hardly necessary, thus preserving valuable part components and resources. Most eco-efficiency concepts (Schmidt-Bleek 1993; Fussler 1996; Liedtke *et al.* 1998; Lehni 1998; Wirth 1999) therefore also mean, from cradle to cradle,

- Minimisation of material intensity of the offered service
- Minimisation of energy intensity of the offered service
- Increase of the use value of products and the resulting services

Why eco-efficiency? Why resource productivity?

The dimension of global environmental impacts caused by human activities mainly depends on the amount of material turnover. A definite decrease in current total resource consumption (of material, energy and land) therefore is a prerequisite for ecologically sustainable development. Instruments of material flow analyses can be applied for planning and monitoring adequate improvement measures on a national and corporate level. In most cases it is not possible to determine the effects single substances and the immense turnovers have on ecosystems. Neither the destruction of the ozone layer nor the causes of the extinction of biodiversity have so far been predictable. Nor is it possible to determine timescales for potential cause–effect mechanisms. It is completely unclear at what point specific substances and materials develop damaging effects, on their own or in combination with other emissions: now, or much later? Is it at once, in one year, in five or in twenty to a hundred years, when we can expect certain risks to occur? As long as consequences and effects cannot be sufficiently determined, it would seem sensible to take precautions to avoid them (Factor 10 Club 1997–2000).

Eco-efficiency, eco-effectiveness and measurability

The examples described in the following—partly target-oriented, partly state of the art (e.g. ISO 14000)—show that such strategies make economic and ecological sense. Eco-effectiveness (product design, material cycles, etc.) is a sub-area of eco-efficiency that needs special attention, a fact that specialist literature on eco-efficiency took into account right from the beginning (von Weizsäcker *et al.* 1997; Klostermann and Tukker 1998; Schmidt-Bleek 1993). For example, the indicator MIPS (material input per service unit)—the concept of the ecological rucksack and measurable resource productivity—calculates and evaluates the closing of material cycles as well as an appropriately optimised design of products and services, service orientation and service performance. This concept as one of the indicators proposed by the European Environment Agency (EEA) makes eco-efficiency (including eco-effectiveness) measurable. Many of the examples described so far represent outstanding corporate performances. However, as long as the increase in resource and capital productivity and the decrease in environmental impacts cannot be proved—that is, verified by numbers—such optimisation activities may take a wrong direction in view of the single and total economy. For example, it has not been scientifically proved that material cycles designed to be biodegradable or relying exclusively on renewable resources are conclusively the most ecological or most eco-efficient cycles. Still, it is undisputed that toxic substances should not be part of the product as such, for the sake of humankind and the environment. It is important, though, to look at land and water use, consumption of abiotic and biotic resources, and global warming potential in an integrated manner. Consumption is measurable and manageable with regard to necessary amounts and application (cf. Chapter 13).

The result of our research so far is that only what is measurable, what can be experienced and what is understandable can help every relevant actor in the enterprise to make targeted decisions to optimise products and services in a marketable and profitable way.

It is important for decision-making in product and service development to have information on relevant factors and how to evaluate them. This information facilitates the possible implementation and transparency of win–win situations. Ecological and economic performance must be measurable if it is to work and contribute to sustainable development. This is especially true if not only global players but also small and medium-sized enterprises are to be integrated into such development.[1] These are the supporting pillars for the reduction of resource consumption, for product and technology development and consequently innovation, employment, service and customer orientation, and often also for progressive regional development (Schmidheiny 1992; Efa and Wuppertal Institute 2001; de Simone and Popoff 1997; GRI 1999; Eurostat 1997).

From eco-efficiency to sustainable development

Sustainable development is often defined by the three-pillar model: ecological, social and economic aims, and effects of societal and economic activities should be optimised in an integrated approach (Elkington 1997). Risks that are beyond control in one sub-system endanger the whole system. Precautionary and sustainable risk minimisation therefore requires the evaluation of risk-intensive factors in an integrative manner.

But does the three-pillar model really meet human needs and prevent risks worldwide? And does not each of the three pillars support different qualitative levels of systems and sub-systems? Nature or rather ecosystems live and develop independently from humankind. The economy does not. It is man-made and a sub-system of total societal activities. From an anthropological and sociological view, sustainability can be defined by those functions that are a prerequisite for protecting human dignity. Only when sustainable development leads to a socially, individually and environmentally sound design of the environment of each individual and each sub-system is it a true target definition. An intact environment is crucial for sustainable societal activities such as wealth generation by the economic system. It is necessary to balance these three formulated aims if we want to increase wealth, support humans in their individual development and at the same time preserve the environment.

Economy as a sub-system of society is a service provider for the fulfilment of human needs and, in this sense, humans have the possibility to influence and optimise it. Economy as a sub-system of the social system can take the economic–political guidelines into account and thus optimise production factors. Competition would then serve—provided sustainability-oriented, economic–political frame-

1 See www.wupperinst.org/safe; www.eco-efficiency.de.

works exist—to offer optimal service, making profit while using few resources, taking advantage of innovation potentials and supporting sustainable technologies. Politics and also society are responsible for reforming and organising the social, education, financial and economic systems accordingly. The German parliament's Commission of Enquiry on Globalisation has defined several urgent areas for action in this direction.

Eco-services and sustainable development

Eco-services play a key role. They use and integrate products and new technologies to fulfil the social needs of the individual and the community while preserving resources. By definition, eco-services are tenders that aim at the eco-efficient use of a good through services. These services provide at least the same if not higher benefits for the customer while using fewer resources (material, energy and land) than a corresponding product. Eco-services combine higher quality of living with the achievement of corporate competitive advantages. Here, dematerialisation and generation of wealth go hand in hand with what is called 'servicealisation' of our economy and way of living (Ax 1999). This necessitates more and better customer-oriented services instead of additional sales of material-intensive goods (made-to-measure instead of made-to-mass).

As eco-efficient services are directly influenced by the wishes and expectations of customers, it is necessary to individualise products. In future, customers will not buy mobile phones but a service package that meets exactly their demand for information transfer—and this is exactly what they pay for. Customers no longer need to pay for thousands of additional functions provided by the product that they do not use. Nor will it be necessary to read complex and extensive operating instructions. Instead, the product will explain the functions based on a comprehensive didactic concept. This orientation on individual and at the same time common needs of our daily life makes it reasonable that the highest potential for such services lies in the household (living, nutrition) and 'on the road' (mobility). But also in the areas of clothing and free time we can expect corresponding made-to-measure solutions and services. Even in the health sector we already speak of 'individualised therapy', and education increasingly promotes individual abilities as supporting factors for societal development. Approaches and concepts such as life-long learning promote and integrate both social and individual competence for the benefit and progress of society and the economy.

Let us consider some businesses that offer services for households.

Pay per wash

Electrolux wants to lead the development of environmentally sound products and processes and seeks to accelerate the demand for eco-products. A proactive environmental strategy aims to make customers pay more attention to the life-cycle of a product than to the mere product costs when buying it.

The idea of the Electrolux tender 'pay per wash' or 'pay as you use' is that no longer the product (the washing machine) but the function of the product and the related benefit (clean clothing) is sold. The customer borrows the washing machine free of cost and pays only SEK495 for installation. The Internet links the washing machine with a centralised databank and an 'intelligent electricity meter' calculates electricity consumption per wash. The customer pays about SEK10 per wash. These costs add to the electricity bill. The washing machine stays the property of Electrolux, which takes care of maintenance, and after about 1,000 washes (every four to five years) replaces or technically renews it.[2]

SPECIAL EDITION

Siemens's lending service SPECIAL EDITION offers the use of a household appliance without buying it. This initiative is an association of selected, medium-sized appliance dealers that came together in the association 'SPECIAL EDITION by Siemens' founded in 1995. The main criteria for membership in this certified community are **consistent service and customer orientation, commitment to continuous improvement** and the **economic prosperity of the enterprise**.

Siemens provides an exclusive product programme that can be obtained only by SPECIAL EDITION dealers. These products represent the state of the art in technology, fabrication, quality control and operational safety and therefore offer an above-average life-span. Should an appliance be faulty, it will be repaired free of charge or replaced by a new appliance.[3]

Outlook: where are we going?

As observed above, the term 'eco-efficiency' comprises the two areas 'ecology' and 'economy'. Still, meeting the challenge of sustainable development not only requires technological changes and innovations but also social innovations. The social aspects of sustainable development play an increasingly important role. Nowadays, it is acknowledged that sustainable development requires involving citizens. Corporate and production processes have to be transparent and comprehensive to lead to practicable eco-efficiency strategies. Otherwise, eco-efficiency remains lip service and implementation impossible.

However, sustainability cannot be dictated to enterprises or customers. Sustainability is a process of learning and searching that demands reliable instruments which can at least give direction to future-oriented development. In order to meet this challenge various instruments have already been developed (CEFIC 1998, 2002; Kuhndt and Liedtke 1999; AG PVC 1999; Nattrass and Altomare 1999; ICC 1991; Weaver *et al.* 2000). The aim is to question, analyse and optimise, if neces-

---

2 You can find further information at www.corporate.electrolux.com.
3 You can find further information at www.siemens.at.

sary, single processes, process chains, products and also services. Here, we consider economic, social and ecological aspects to arrive at a sustainable fulfilment of needs. In this way, sustainability can be applied and experienced.

Sustainability calls for equal support of ecological and economic development, right from the beginning of the economic cycle, where aims and policies are defined, and not at the end, where society has to carry the cost of damage caused by unsustainable patterns of production and consumption. Dematerialisation creates synergetic effects toward a change in society's values, especially in Western countries. Indeed, eco-efficiency in itself can give fresh and important impetus, and at the same time offers a valuable base for structural changes required for a more innovative and service-oriented economy. Moreover, eco-efficiency can also contribute to more sustainable consumption patterns by providing clear and understandable information: for example, for the purchase of eco-efficient products and services. Therefore, eco-efficiency represents a key component in future-oriented and sustainable development.[4]

'To make planet Earth a secure place for future generations, we have to tackle the essential mistakes within the economic and societal systems—and this, at the same time with those of the ecological crisis' (Steilmann Commission 2000).

---

4 International links are:
Integrated Product Policy of the EU at
www.europa.eu.int/comm/environment/ipp/home.htm;
European Environmental Agency at www.eea.eu.int;
Factor 10 Innovation Network at www.faktor10.at;
Factor 10 Institute at www.factor10.de;
WBCSD at www.wbcsd.org;
EEEI at www.epe.be/menutexts/documents/epenewsletter.pdf;
Product Service Systems at the SERI website: www.seri.at/pss;
www.sustainability-index.com;
BASF at www.basf.de/de/corporate/sustainability/oekoeffizienz;
www.efficient-entrepreneur.net;
GRI at www.globalreporting.org;
www.cleaner-production.de;
OECD at www.oecd.org/topic;
UNCTAD at www.unctad.org;
UNEP at www.uneptie.org/pc/cp.

15
Climatex® LifeguardFR™ upholstery fabrics
Chronicle of a sustainable product redesign

Albin Kälin
Rohner Textil AG, Switzerland

Alain Rivière and Ralf Ketelhut
EPEA Internationale Umweltforschung GmbH, Germany

Michael Braungart
EPEA Internationale Umweltforschung GmbH, Germany, and McDonough Braungart Design Chemistry, LLC, USA

There are several good reasons why, at the beginning of the 1990s, the situation of the small Swiss textile mill Rohner Textil AG was somewhat challenging. The company was located in a building that was constructed in 1911 and was under conservation orders. The building was situated in a residential and small-business district. The firm anticipated increasingly strict noise regulations which, if violated, would result in having night shifts banned. These noise restrictions also hampered efforts at improving productivity because newer, higher-capacity looms generated more vibrations, which would be transmitted throughout the neighbourhood through the air and, more importantly, through the clay on which the mill and residential structures were built. Relocating the firm was not an economically acceptable option.

Moreover, the city of Heerbrugg is located in the Rhine Valley near Lake Constance, a major drinking-water reservoir. The more stringent environmental regulations and costs for emissions to air, waste-water management and noise reduction had to be faced at a very early point.

Even the economic situation looked threatening. At the beginning of the 1990s, the European textile industry suffered an enormous decline. A large number of companies closed their businesses because severe competition drove selling prices downward. At the time, the business community focused on profit, market positioning, quality, return on investment, just-in-time delivery, inventory management, competitiveness and globalisation.

Severe market conditions in the early 1990s forced companies to boost investments in new equipment to increase productivity. Consequently, there were only small margins left providing resources for investments to offset increasing governmental regulations (Steger and Alikhan 1999a).

Ten years ago, Rohner Textil, like other firms, was facing an increasingly difficult and complex situation involving local, economic and environmental issues. Today Rohner Textil is manufacturing high-end upholstery fabric designs. It is still located in the historical building in Heerbrugg and employs 30 people. The firm creates new designs in-house and also works with outside designers. It dyes yarns in its dye facility and it produces textiles in its weaving mill. Many of Rohner Textil's customers, such as DesignTex, Herman Miller, Giroflex, Girsberger, Sitag, JAB Anstoetz, Wellmann and Carnegie, bestow the company with international recognition.

In 2002 Rohner Textil is still successfully operating because it identified tangible targets and then promptly implemented necessary measures to develop and improve new product qualities leading to success beyond the factory gate. Today Rohner Textil has qualitatively outstanding products, but this development has not yet come to an end. With regard to the goals we have set, there are still steps to take.

This chapter retrospectively describes the development with a special focus on Rohner Textil's latest innovation, Climatex® LifeguardFR™, and the corresponding network structure of the supply chain. Furthermore, it presents an Index of Sustainability™, an instrument for measuring progress toward sustainability. The Index has been developed by McDonough Braungart Design Chemistry (MBDC) and the Environmental Protection Encouragement Agency (EPEA), the companies that have accompanied the development of Rohner Textil and strongly influenced the environmental quality of Rohner Textil's products for more than eight years.

Shift to proactive environmental management

By the end of the 1980s, Rohner Textil had decided to eliminate the use of cotton from its product line because cotton dyes would have required it to install additional, expensive waste-water treatment equipment.

In 1992 the company set out on a new path to shift from reactive to proactive environmental management. The first step involved subjecting all of Rohner Textil's products to tests to obtain the eco-label Oeko-Tex Standard 100. Though Rohner Textil's products passed these tests, this did not resolve all environmental issues related to dyeing and other manufacturing processes, because only the chemical compounds remaining in finished products were analysed.

This led Rohner Textil to develop a strategy to balance the values in economy and ecology that would enable us to survive as a company. Rohner Textil articulated this strategy in its internal management document system, Eco-Eco Concept 1993–2000 (1). At the heart of the challenge was the quest for a way of allocating funds for investments in ecological efforts while simultaneously investing in new equipment for productivity gains. Over 10% of Rohner Textil's turnover had to be invested in new equipment to increase competitiveness, which left few resources to spare for ecological initiatives. Noise pollution and historic building restrictions also had to be addressed.

The management at Rohner Textil struggled with a number of questions: How could it convince the company board to accept investments in environmental projects in addition to the productivity investments of over 10% annually over the next eight years? Was it management's job to change the board's thinking so that it endorsed the environmental idea? Would it be better to make special agreements with governmental institutions? What responsible actions should the board take? The answer, in common business language, was that economic advantage is the key (Riess 1998; Steger and Alikhan 1999; Gorman and Mehalik 1998; Gorman et al. 2000).

Use of tax policy opportunities

Rohner Textil's tax consultant realised that the region of St Gallen provided special tax breaks for the depreciation of capital related to environmental investments. This tax incentive provided Rohner Textil's management with a justification for environmental investments that the board of directors could agree with. Investments had to be planned ahead of time.

Beginning in 1993 Rohner Textil included environmental investments in its annual budgets. The investment amounted to 1% of the total budget. In addition, an environmental cost was included in calculating the cost of producing the product. The existing accounting systems were modified to incorporate these two measures. The first environmental investments were implemented in 1995 (Bosshard 1997; Mehalik et al. 1997).

First steps

Very soon the management recognised the necessity to achieve a clear understanding of the environmental situation for improved decisions and management tools (Mehalik 2000). The company conducted an inventory and analysis of its environmental factors, and each department measured and catalogued its environmental problems. Each department also proposed solutions and set priorities for implementation. This process resulted in the certification of Rohner Textil's quality management according to ISO 9001 in 1994 and its environmental management system according to ISO 14001 (Hillary 2000). It was the first Swiss company to establish an environmental management system according to EMAS in 1996.

Having efficiently installed these management systems, the company realised there was a need to understand the interactions of its systems to make its solutions really effective. More transparency was required to know exactly what the products were made of.

Rohner Textil developed eco-controlling, a quantitative assessment of each product's overall environmental impact on all its products to promote a long-term ecological product development focus for their entire product line. The goal was to enable the R&D department to focus more strongly on potential environmental quality improvement of products.

Synergies with customers, design and science

Customer reactions followed these initiatives. The process was largely sustained by a close co-operation with designer Susan Lyons from DesignTex, architect William McDonough and chemical engineer Michael Braungart, as well as MBDC and EPEA.

Susan Lyons, Design Director at DesignTex, Inc., a subsidiary of the New York-based Steelcase, Inc., approached Rohner Textil in the autumn of 1993. She had investigated innovative suppliers and discovered the proactive activities of Rohner Textil. Rohner Textil's efforts toward environmentally optimised production were almost unique at that time.

Susan Lyons proposed that the team develop an 'environmentally intelligent' line of textiles, focusing on the product itself and not only on the production process. In order to provide optimal synergies she requested that Rohner Textil collaborate with DesignTex and the American William McDonough and his friend and partner Michael Braungart, a chemical engineer and former founder of the German Greenpeace Chemical Division. The goal was to make a vision for a new industrial revolution—the clean revolution—a reality.

The paradigm for an industrial revolution

When McDonough and Braungart met for the first time in 1991 they realised that they had found congenial partners in each other. Based on Braungart's 'intelligent product system' they consequently developed their eco-effective agenda (Braungart and Engelfried 1992). They understood that current approaches failed to describe the devaluation of material and energy flows, and felt the necessity of putting the environmental aspects of industrial activities in positive, attractive terms rather than seeing them as costly disturbances at the end of the pipe. They understood that the latter approach would be misleading and only delay the issues. Integrating environmental aspects as an inherent part of quality provides a huge variety of opportunities to be identified and developed as the result of a positive approach.

Three principles for an industrial revolution

Using nature as a model, they derived principles for eco-effective design of products and their corresponding material flows:

- Waste equals food
- Use current solar income
- Respect diversity

In nature, all materials that organisms take from the environment are combined and transformed without accumulation of waste as we understand it. Everything is cycled continuously with all waste equalling food for other living systems. McDonough and Braungart believe the word 'waste' should be removed from our vocabulary and the word 'nutrient' used instead (McDonough and Braungart 2002; McDonough et al. 1992). If waste equals food, it is the result of an intention for another purpose. Materials are moved and transformed with energy. In nature, the energy is provided by the sun. An industrial revolution will be characterised by the ability to provide energy with environmentally neutral material flows. This implies the domestication of the solar income.

In nature, it is diversity that allows waste to equal food. Complex ecosystems accommodate functional hierarchies of organisms capable of constructing and degrading materials and combining them in new and adapted forms. The integration of biodiversity, as well as cultural and know-how diversity, will be the motor of the industrial revolution, too.

The typology of products

The intelligent product system is based on the understanding that integration of material flows to closed-loop systems will provide the most efficient and effective use of resources. It differentiates two strategies for closing material loops.

Products of consumption—biological nutrients

Products of consumption are returned to biological cycles. Typically, they are based on renewable agricultural or forestry resources and may break down during or after their period of use. After degradation, materials are biological nutrients for further agricultural, forestry or biotechnological production without negatively impacting exposed organisms, food chains and generational successions.

Products of service—technical nutrients

Products that cannot be effectively transformed by nature are returned to technical cycles. Raw materials are combined and designed for disassembly, remanufacture, and continuous re-use as technical nutrients in the industrial metabolism. Products of service are embedded in a material flow management system that ensures effective use of materials.

Products that are not compatible with this system will still remain waste after use. Thus adopting the eco-effective agenda inherently eliminates the entire concept of waste.

Beyond limits: product redesign for safety— Climatex® LifeguardFR™

Rohner Textil adopted the eco-effective agenda. Climatex®Lifecycle™ Redesigned for Nature upholstery fabrics were designed as a product of consumption: that is, they are degradable to environmentally sound biological nutrients.

This development was begun by the end of 1993 and reached market maturity in 1995. It has been honoured with more than a dozen awards.[1] Worldwide recog-

---

1 Climatex®Lifecycle™ and Rohner Textil have been awarded several design prizes and awards:
    - 1995: Gold of Neocon for DesignTex, Chicago, USA
    - 1996: Arge Alp (Community Alpine Countries) Environmental Award
    - 1997: Support from the NGO 'Deutsche Umwelthilfe'
    - 1998: 1st prize in Austria's eco-design contest
    - 1999: Gold of Neocon for Carnegie, Chicago, USA
    - 1999: iF Ecology Design Award, Best of Category, Industrial Forum, Hannover, Germany
    - 1999: Best Environmental Report, ÖBU, Switzerland
    - 1999: Registration as one of the 450 'worldwide international projects' for the World Expo 2000, Hannover, Germany
    - 2000: Silver Innovation Award, Rhine Valley
    - 2000: Millennium Award for Environmental Achievement, International Chamber of Commerce (ICC)/UNEP
    - 2000: 1st prize, GBP40,000, Design Sense Award, Design Museum, London, UK
    - 2001: Nomination, Swiss Marketing Trophy
    - 2001: Nomination, iF Ecology Design Award, Industrial Forum, Hannover, Germany
    - 2001: 1st prize, Design Resources Award
    - 2001: UBS Key Trophy to Albin Kälin, Entrepreneur of the Year, Rhine Valley, Switzerland
    - 2001: Award, Special Efforts for the Environment, Switzerland
    - 2001: Sustainability Award, Conference, Lake Constance *(continued over)*

nition highlights the originality of design, the innovative character of combining environmental soundness with superior functional 'climate-control seating', and traditional aspects of quality such as aesthetic performance. Climatex® Lifecycle™ has been the subject of case studies in academic institutions for sustainable design, production, services and management around the world.

Climatex®Lifecycle™ upholstery fabrics, made from wool and ramie, are safe for biological cycles, humans and the environment and, at the same time, adhere to all traditional industrial quality standards. However, Climatex® Lifecycle™ passes only a few fire regulations.

Rohner Textil has opened a new dimension in ecological product innovation with the development of Climatex® LifeguardFR™ Redesigned for Safety upholstery fabrics as an extension of its earlier Climatex® Lifecycle™ series.

Fire regulations for hotels, airports, restaurants, theatres, sport arenas, offices and residential areas are becoming more complex in the contract furniture business. These regulations often vary from country to country and especially in transportation applications, such as aircraft, trains and buses. Most products are optimised to comply with fire safety standards; however, flame-retarded products usually contain chemicals that are in some ways the least compatible with environmental soundness. Regulations are increasingly dictating the necessity of buying materials according to ecological criteria, so the need to resolve this incompatibility was also increasing.

In 1996 the design team at Rohner Textil set out to address this difficult question and to search for possibilities for meeting all fire standards without restrictions on safety on a product line designed to return to biological cycles. The Rohner Textil team accomplished the redesign over a period of four years with the co-operation of those involved in the original design: first and foremost the environmental institute EPEA in Hamburg, Germany (Rivière et al. 1997).

The story of this development illustrates how sustainable product redesign may be integrated into the business context.

The fibre raw materials

The prototype of an upholstery textile was developed to determine whether substituting the ramie fibre from Climatex® Lifecycle™ with man-made cellulose fibre

> Internationally acclaimed museums and exhibitions including Climatex®Lifecycle™ in their displays:
> - 1995: Solomon Guggenheim Museum, New York, launching of 'The William McDonough Collection' of Climatex®Lifecycle™ by DesignTex
> - 1999: iF Forum Design, Hannover, Germany
> - 2000: World Exhibition 2000, Hannover, Germany, Living Lakes Concept and iF Forum Design
> - 2000–2001: Design Museum, London, UK—Winner of Design Sense Award 2000
> - 2001–2005: Re(f)use—exhibition travelling around the world
> - 2001: iF Forum Design, Hannover, Germany
> - 2001: 'Swiss Made' Museum für angewandte Kunst, Cologne, Germany
> - 2001–2002: Design Resources Award, Seattle/Japan/Australia
> - 2001: 'Gut in Form 1950 + 2000' Museum für Gestaltung Zürich, Switzerland
> - 2002: Quality label 'Naturpark' for the location of the Rohner Textil facility

(viscose) containing flame retardant would provide flame-retardant properties while maintaining all other valuable technical properties of Climatex® Lifecycle™, especially climate-control seating and environmental soundness. The very positive outcome encouraged us to deepen the assessment of environmental quality.

The viscose fibre used in the prototype was the only new element. It was therefore assessed with respect to its environmental quality before the final decision was made to integrate it into the new product development. The assessment showed high-level environmental quality of resource origin (beech wood from sustainable Central European forestry) and processing in this fibre, but one weak point was identified. After negotiations, the possibility of an increase in sales of this fibre motivated the renowned Austrian fibre manufacturer Lenzing AG to address the problem and to test a recommended environmentally superior sub-process alternative. Again the results satisfied the expectations of Rohner Textil, opening the way to the environmentally optimised flame-retarded fibre Redesigned LenzingFR™ and the environmentally optimised upholstery textile Climatex® Lifecycle™ containing it.

The flame-retardant chemical

However, at that level of investigation, the flame retardant itself remained an area that lacked definition. Filling this gap and developing a consistent environmental message on Climatex® LifeguardFR™ required involving the entire supply chain in the process.

The flame-retardant chemical integrated into the mass of the viscose fibre is supplied by Clariant AG, a leading chemical manufacturer. Clariant was asked to provide the deep chemistry of this chemical for assessment by the EPEA. In spite of initial reservations, and after a number of talks, Clariant finally agreed in 1999. However, not all questions raised by the EPEA for understanding the impact of the flame retardant on environment and health could be answered at that time.

Clariant, Rohner Textil and the EPEA then agreed to solve remaining questions in extensive laboratory trials. Rohner Textil and Clariant shared the financial cost of the project. Early in 2000 the results documented the product's superior environmental quality.

Dyes and textile auxiliary chemicals

A positive list of 16 dye chemicals from Ciba had been developed under the guidance of the EPEA for Climatex®Lifecycle™ products (Kälin and Mehalik 2000; Kälin 2001). The change of fibre in Climatex® LifeguardFR™ resulted in the revision of dyeing recipes. The new recipes, however, are still based on the positive list used for Climatex® Lifecycle™.

The manufacturing process

Most processes for manufacturing Climatex® Lifecycle™ remained the same for the redesigned product Climatex® LifeguardFR™. The EPEA conducted comprehensive assessments and initiatives for environmental optimisation in the processing chain at all levels, from production and early processing of fibre raw materials to spinning and twisting mill processes, yarn dyeing, weaving and textile finishing processes.

The final product

The result is Climatex® LifeguardFR™ Redesigned for Safety, which is made from wool and the man-made cellulose fibre Redesigned LenzingFR™ based on the renewable resource beech wood.

The final product complies with all industrial standards and passes the most severe flame-retardant tests worldwide, even for aircraft. The patented function of climate-control seating remains intact. The ecologically optimised production processes previously developed for the product line Climatex® Lifecycle™ remain unchanged. The positive list of textile chemicals and 16 dyes from Ciba SC developed with the EPEA also remained. The choices for colours and designs are nearly unlimited, except for brilliant colours and pure black. The prices are comparable to wool products. The EPEA confirms the high health and environmental quality of Climatex® LifeguardFR™ and its compatibility with biological cycles. Rohner Textil owns the exclusive rights for the modified fibre Redesigned LenzingFR™ which replaces the ramie fibre used in previous Climatex® Lifecycle™ products.

Secondary products

Even with the environmental optimisations of Climatex® LifeguardFR™, the production process still generates adjacent materials flows in the form of trimmings during weaving. The technical and environmental features of the textile remain an inherent part of these materials. They are suitable for a differentiated strategy that uses the flame-retardant benefits in secondary products rather than regarding them as waste. Alternative secondary products could be, for example, felt liners for panels or walls, flame-retarded insulation material, woven flame-retarded blankets for private use or in public transportation (trains, aeroplanes, buses).

Anticipating the successful development of secondary products with Climatex® LifeguardFR™ quality, Rohner Textil already takes back residual materials of seat-covering cutting from clients, especially furniture manufacturers. This strategy was already adopted with Climatex® Lifecycle™: felt is manufactured from trimmings from our own production and clients return cuttings. The felt finds application in gardening, in slippers or even coasters.

The 'eco smart licensing' concept

Rohner Textil got ahead of tremendous market opportunities in different market segments. However, the company's location as described in the introduction limits possibilities of growing on-site.

Lists of positively defined materials and positively defined supply chains behind Climatex® Lifecycle™ and Climatex® LifeguardFR™ have built a know-how platform. Despite supply chain complexity, it is transferable as a whole in the framework of licences (*Green@work* 2000).

This combination of specific location limits and opportunities provided by a solid know-how platform led Rohner Textil to adopt licensing as its growth strategy. The procedure—encompassing production and marketing—allows for market differentiation. Though itself a small company, Rohner Textil could win global market leaders as licensees in different business segments while retaining the market segment for residential home interiors and contract furniture. By 2002, three licence agreements had been contracted:

- Lantal Textiles with Climatex® LifeguardFR™ for transportation, including exclusive rights for aircraft upholstery fabrics
- Victor-Innovatex with Climatex® LifeguardFR™ piece-dyed upholstery and panel fabrics for the original equipment manufacturer for office furniture market in North America
- Lady Brazil with the original Climatex® for office seating in South America, with the option to integrate Climatex® LifeguardFR™ technology in the future;

The process of licensing itself acts as an environmental quality control that aims at ensuring equivalence of products as outputs of different production contexts. The EPEA monitors the process from the scientific point of view. The structure of the licensing network is shown in Figure 15.1.

Instruments for the environmental evaluation of products, product developments and optimisation measures

Sustainability in the balance

William McDonough and Michael Braungart and their collaborators have developed principles that foster an ecologically, socially and economically effective approach to design. Focusing on any single component creates an imbalance that is not sustainable. For example, focusing solely on the economics of a product's manufacture and distribution excludes crucial environmental and social concerns.

Designing with solely ecological aspects or social equity in mind is not the answer, either. Thinking in this way does not guarantee that people will buy a product or that it will be affordable, accessible and profitable to manufacture. The condition for sustainable development is an appropriate balance of the three components, ecology, economy and equity, in the process of product design as shown in Figure 15.2.

Rohner Textil AG—Switzerland
Licenser

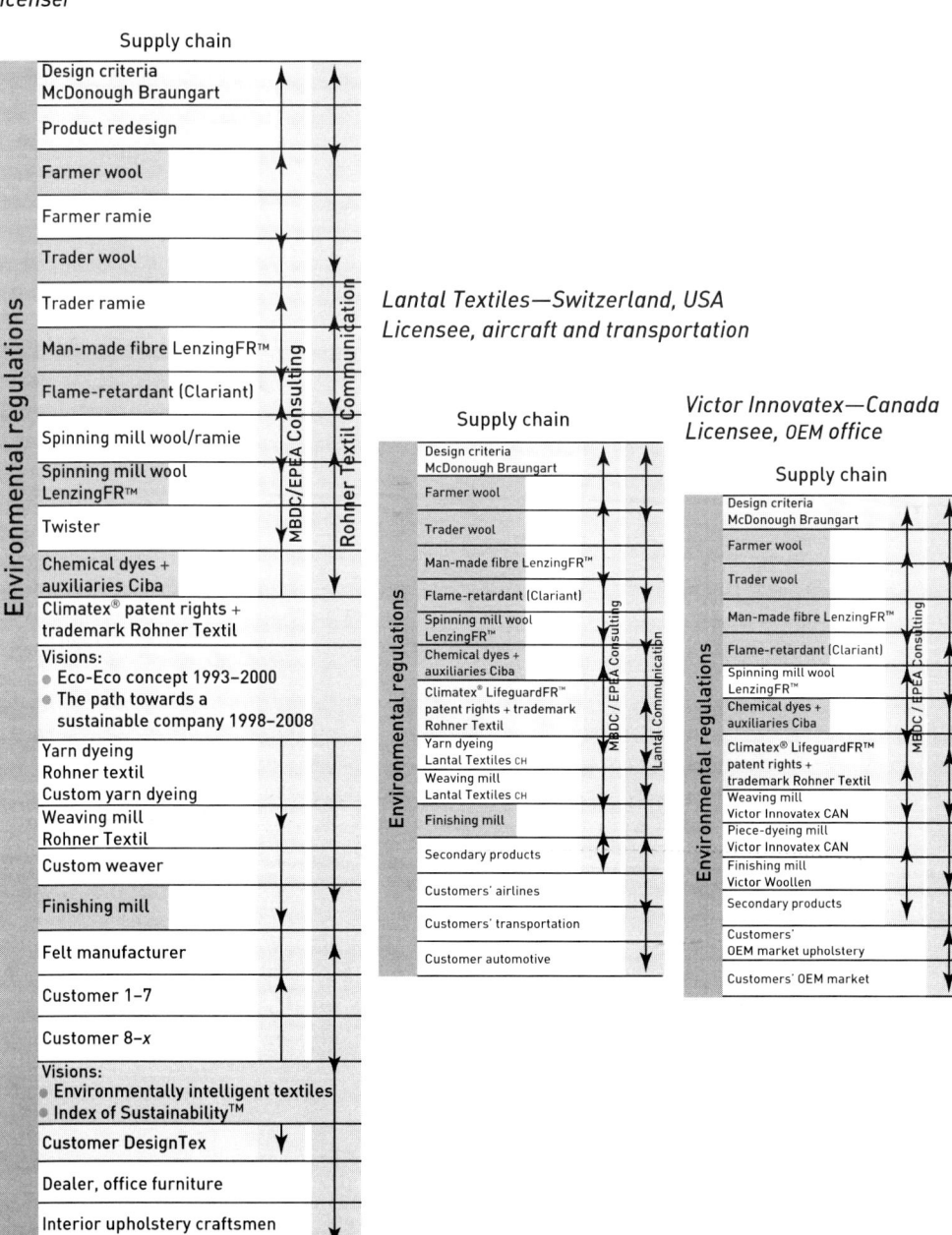

Supply chain
Design criteria McDonough Braungart
Product redesign
Farmer wool
Farmer ramie
Trader wool
Trader ramie
Man-made fibre LenzingFR™
Flame-retardant (Clariant)
Spinning mill wool/ramie
Spinning mill wool LenzingFR™
Twister
Chemical dyes + auxiliaries Ciba
Climatex® patent rights + trademark Rohner Textil
Visions: • Eco-Eco concept 1993–2000 • The path towards a sustainable company 1998–2008
Yarn dyeing Rohner textil Custom yarn dyeing
Weaving mill Rohner Textil
Custom weaver
Finishing mill
Felt manufacturer
Customer 1–7
Customer 8–x
Visions: • Environmentally intelligent textiles • Index of Sustainability™
Customer DesignTex
Dealer, office furniture
Interior upholstery craftsmen
Garden centres
Consumers
Consumers

(Environmental regulations; MBDC/EPEA Consulting; Rohner Textil Communication)

Lantal Textiles—Switzerland, USA
Licensee, aircraft and transportation

Supply chain
Design criteria McDonough Braungart
Farmer wool
Trader wool
Man-made fibre LenzingFR™
Flame-retardant (Clariant)
Spinning mill wool LenzingFR™
Chemical dyes + auxiliaries Ciba
Climatex® LifeguardFR™ patent rights + trademark Rohner Textil
Yarn dyeing Lantal Textiles CH
Weaving mill Lantal Textiles CH
Finishing mill
Secondary products
Customers' airlines
Customers' transportation
Customer automotive

(Environmental regulations; MBDC/EPEA Consulting; Lantal Communication)

Victor Innovatex—Canada
Licensee, OEM office

Supply chain
Design criteria McDonough Braungart
Farmer wool
Trader wool
Man-made fibre LenzingFR™
Flame-retardant (Clariant)
Spinning mill wool LenzingFR™
Chemical dyes + auxiliaries Ciba
Climatex® LifeguardFR™ patent rights + trademark Rohner Textil
Weaving mill Victor Innovatex CAN
Piece-dyeing mill Victor Innovatex CAN
Finishing mill Victor Woollen
Secondary products
Customers' OEM market upholstery
Customers' OEM market

(Environmental regulations; MBDC/EPEA Consulting; Victor Communication)

Climatex® Lifeguard FR™ are patent rights and trademark of Rohner Textil AG
OEM = original equipment manufacturer

Figure 15.1 Network structure of the Climatex LifeguardFR™ project

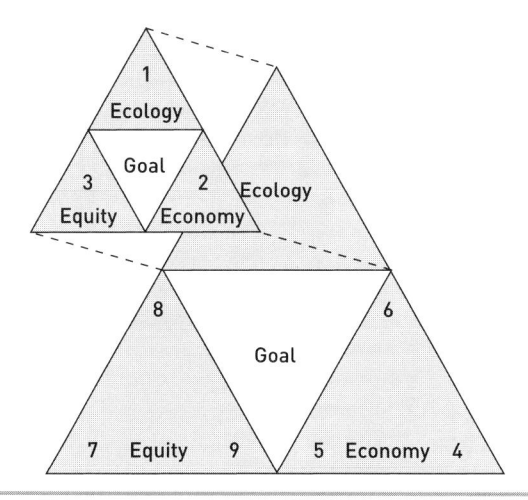

Figure 15.2 Balancing ecology, economy and equity in product design

The introduction of the first collection in 1995 and co-operation among participants resulted in a successful product. But it was clear that the development had not reached an end. The Index of Sustainability™ was therefore established to measure the status of product sustainability as well as further improvements (Rohner Textil 2001).

DesignTex financed the development of the index performed jointly by MBDC and the EPEA (Version 1.0). It was first presented in Rohner Textil's environmental statement in 1998 and applied to Climatex® Lifecycle™.

The Index of Sustainability™ (Version 1.1)

Product users and industry can use the Index of Sustainability™ as a guide to better understand the product design's progress in the context of sustainability. Like Version 1.0 of the Index of Sustainability™, Version 1.1 implements McDonough and Braungart's eco-effective design criteria to evaluate environmental aspects of product and process design. Similar criteria for the assessment of social and economic aspects of product development will be integrated in a later version of the Index of Sustainability™.

Evaluation of potential toxicological and eco-toxicological impacts, as well as aspects of resource renewal, encompasses all material flows at all process levels along the production chain. Each material and chemical that is used during production, distribution or resource recovery is defined as an input with corresponding material flow and then evaluated. This also includes material flows associated with energy supply.

As in the former version, indexing a product or a service implies that material inputs pass a knockout filter. Table 15.1 presents the set of criteria used for a product of consumption.

Knockout criteria	Differentiation criteria
• Carcinogenicity • Reproductive and developmental toxicity • Mutagenicity • Bioaccumulation with acute toxicity • Endocrine disruption	• Definition level of composition (molecular and elemental level) • Origin of resources (materials and fuel/genetic engineering) *Bioaccumulation potential* • Biodegradation/metabolism/persistency • Toxicity for water and soil organisms • Chronic toxicity (including immunotoxicity) • Potentials of epithelia irritation

Table 15.1 Parameters of eco-effectiveness

Climatex® Lifecycle™ and Climatex® LifeguardFR™

Rohner Textil's *Environmental Statement 2001* optimises the Index of Sustainability™. Aspects of impacts to environment and human health often coincide, so Version 1.1 evaluates them in an integrated way. Moreover, the graphic presentation of evaluation results is modified to make the distance to the target clearer.

The Index of Sustainability™ (Version 1.1) is applied to Climatex® Lifecycle™ at the 2001 state of production and retrospectively to the 1998 state, tracing the development and optimisation of environmental quality. Climatex® Lifecycle™ was developed as a Product for Consumption™ oriented on the compatibility of materials with biological cycles. Evaluation results are presented in Figure 15.3.

The application of the Index of Sustainability™ has been extended to the new development Climatex® LifeguardFR™, and application to Rohner Textil polyester products is also planned. This implies, however, that suppliers take an active part in the process of product definition, evaluation and eventual optimisation.

Despite the high level of environmental quality already reached in 1998, Climatex® Lifecycle™ has been improved further in the meantime. The definition of the environmental quality of the used wool was extended. Rohner Textil is currently establishing a direct commercial relationship with wool producers, which will allow the involvement of a defined reproducible and improved environmental wool quality.

A systematic inventory and evaluation of production water flows has indicated that the current cycle-closing strategy over the waste-water treatment plant is more meaningful under the perspective of environmental quality than an internal closing strategy at Rohner Textil. The waste-water load does not represent an ecotoxicological problem, so Rohner Textil is benefiting from its targeted selection of defined chemicals.

[Radar chart with axes: Wool, Ramie, Dyestuffs, Other production auxiliaries, Transport, Packaging, Process energy, Water, Closing of material flows. Two series shown: Climatex® Lifecycle™ 2001 and Climatex® Lifecycle™ 1998.]

Key:
1. Acceptable. Very much improvement needed.
2. Good. Much improvement needed.
3. Very good. Some improvement needed.
4. Excellent. Little need for further improvement.
5. Perfectly sustainable. No need for further improvement.

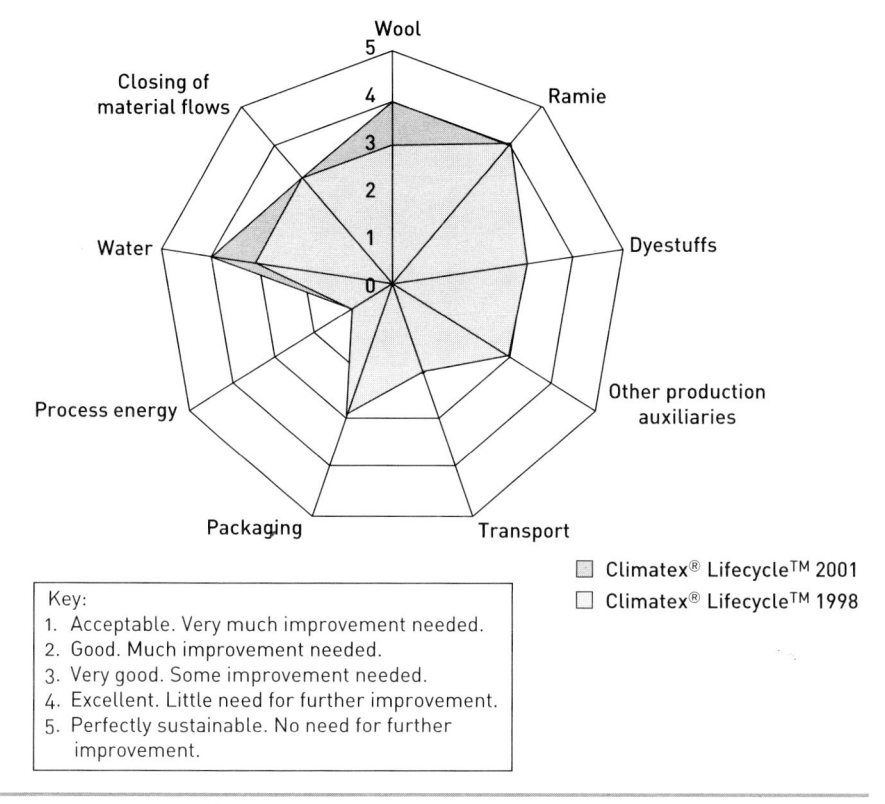

Figure 15.3 Climatex® Lifecycle™

Source: Rohner Textil 2001

Further optimisation of textile chemical flows is currently under investigation. It is based on the re-use of spent dyeing baths without previous separation of water from textile chemicals.

Even Climatex® LifeguardFR™ was developed as a Product for Consumption™, targeting compatibility of materials with biological cycles. Figure 15.4 shows the results.

Climatex® LifeguardFR™ already achieves a very high environmental quality. This is because Climatex® LifeguardFR™ is based on Climatex® Lifecycle™. The substitution of the ramie fibre with Redesigned LenzingFR™ alone enables the resulting Climatex® LifeguardFR™ to match high flame-retardant requirements. Its composition is compatible with a biological strategy for closing material flows. Technological and logistic developments that Rohner Textil has already embarked on will emulate this potential.

The most important drawbacks of both products are the source of energy used in production and transport. Both are largely out of reach for Rohner Textil, so that average standards cannot be surpassed. Transport and energy supply for production are based mostly on open material flows such as the incineration of fossil fuels.

144 Eco-efficiency and Beyond

Figure 15.4 Climatex® LifeguardFR™

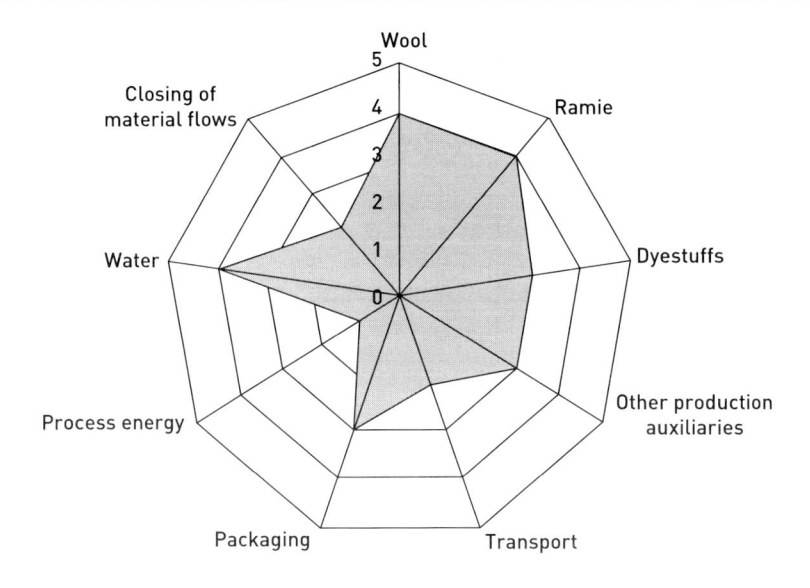

Source: Rohner Textil 2001

Key:
1. Acceptable. Very much improvement needed.
2. Good. Much improvement needed.
3. Very good. Some improvement needed.
4. Excellent. Little need for further improvement.
5. Perfectly sustainable. No need for further improvement.

Conclusion

The first collection of Climatex® LifeguardFR™ was presented in 2000 on the contract market for office seating. The marketing concept was very well received by the customers. In autumn 2000 the first customers launched Climatex® LifeguardFR™ upholstery fabrics at the world's largest office furniture exhibition, Orgatec, in Cologne, Germany. The German Central Bank Deutsche Bundesbank specified Climatex® LifeguardFR™ fabrics for their office seating.

On the residential market for interior fabrics, the Johannes Wellmann Textilverlag—with the concept 'aesthetics for the future'—made a major launch of Climatex® LifeguardFR™ at the Heimtex exhibition in Frankfurt in January 2001. Johannes Wellmann is one of the leading editors of interior textiles in Europe. The design team at Rohner Textil developed aesthetics that successfully competed with the highest design standards, implementing the most advanced technical and environmental safety rules to manufacture and market a sustainable fabric.

The first licensed products were launched in June 2001 at the Paris Air Show and at Chicago's Neocon.

Eco-effective product design implies new ways of thinking and initiates unusual partnerships. Chemical companies, environmental institutions, fibre manufacturers, processing suppliers, NGOs, universities, media, direct customers and last but not least the end consumer, all these interacting actors in the extended textile network become active participants in a project of effective environmental optimisation.

Enlarging the network even more and implementing patented and environmental know-how in manufacturing and marketing together with MBDC and the EPEA lead to an even larger complexity of the project. However, Rohner Textil and its original partners in the project have demonstrated their ability to welcome the right initiative and to bring the right people together to turn the eco-effective design idea into a marketed product innovation—Climatex® LifeguardFR™.

Rohner Textil's aim of developing a defined, environmentally optimised textile represented a risk, especially for suppliers. However, after numerous negotiations, they all recognised the opportunity to stimulate products by realising a pre-existing environmental quality even if they had not been developed under these premises. An increasing number of companies in the chain recognise that positively defined material quality leads to innovations that benefit all of them and contribute funds for development.

Lantal Textiles acquired Rohner Textil on 1 December 1999 as an independently operating subsidiary 'in order to ensure its future and strong innovative spirit'. Lantal Textiles is holding true to the motto: 'Never change a winning team'. The company has guaranteed the Rohner Textil team the retention of their independence, their brand, patent and licensing rights, as well as their headquarters in Heerbrugg, Switzerland.

The international market strategy is based on core competencies: Lantal Textiles deals exclusively with ground transport and aviation fields, while Rohner Textil is responsible for its traditional market segments of objects and furnishings for home and office.

The success of the project gave the EPEA and MBDC an opportunity to draft an Index of Sustainability™. The Index of Sustainability™ was necessary to further structure the growing process of eco-effective product and material flow design and to communicate results. Its application to other eco-effective design projects will allow the refinement of its methodology and especially the integration of the social, economic and environmental aspects of product quality development.

The first industrial revolution began with the textile industry and the introduction of Jacquard looms. It is again the textile industry that triggers change—the clean industrial revolution.[2]

---

2 Climatex®, Climatex® Lifecycle™, Climatex® LifeguardFR™ are patent rights and trademarks of Rohner Textil AG.

16

Eco-effective design of products and production systems
Eight theses on methodological and institutional prerequisites

Michael Braungart
EPEA Internationale Umweltforschung GmbH, Germany and
McDonough Braungart Design Chemistry, LLC, USA

Alain Rivière and Ralf Ketelhut
EPEA Internationale Umweltforschung GmbH, Germany

This chapter focuses on the central role that product and services design plays in the environmental optimisation of economic activities, and suggests making environmental quality an integral part of total product quality.

The ideas presented here reflect the experience that EPEA Internationale Umweltforschung GmbH, Hamburg, Germany, and McDonough Braungart Design Chemistry, LLC, Charlottesville, Virginia, USA, acquired during the past years in the environmental redesign of products and services at numerous different companies, including Ford Motor Company Inc., Nike Inc., Herrman Miller Inc. and Rohner Textil AG[1] (see also Chapter 15). The eight theses to be discussed here are most indebted to our involvement in developing the furniture textiles Climatex® Lifecycle™ and Climatex® LifeguardFR™ at Rohner Textil AG. The eight theses are:

1. Eco-efficiency makes environmental sense if it works toward closing material flow cycles (eco-effectiveness).

---

1 Rohner Textil at www.climatex.com.

2. Products and services are the core of eco-effectiveness.
3. Eco-effective product or services design is a positive definition for closing material flow systems.
4. Integrated systems of production and use focused on products or services can solve environmental issues.
5. The overview of material flows is embodied in a 'bank' for physical resources.
6. Environmental optimisation generates economic opportunities.
7. The method of choice is life-cycle development.
8. Environmental quality offers new scope for sensible innovation.

Eco-efficiency makes environmental sense if it works toward closing material flows (eco-effectiveness)

Generally, the term efficiency means 'doing things right', whereas effectiveness focuses on 'doing the right things'. Slimming down material flows per product or service unit (eco-efficiency) is sustainable only if the goal of closing material flows (eco-effectiveness) has first been established. From an eco-effective perspective, there is no need to reduce material flows if appropriate materials are chosen and combined appropriately and as long as the availability of materials (resources) is maintained after use (Braungart and McDonough 1998, 2000b). The demand for slimming down material flows per unit may not result from environmental but from social imperatives, such as making products or services available for as many users as possible without irreversible damage to resources or the overall environment.

Products and services are the core of eco-effectiveness

The interplay of supply and demand for products and services moves financial and material resources. Wrong decisions in product design lead to deficits. The loss of valuable resources in the form of waste (including liquid or gaseous) and the resulting impacts on the environment are consequences of improvable design of material flows (Braungart 2000). Approaches to environmental issues that do not primarily focus on products or services may be eco-efficient while still failing to be eco-effective.

Eco-effective product or services design is a positive definition for closing material flow systems

The aim of solving environmental issues implies an understanding of materials (resources, pre-products, products and residues) as elements in a continuous material flow system. In an optimised, eco-effective system material flows tend to be closed. Products are designed to remain resources for next generations of products. This conception of design is called 'cradle to cradle' instead of 'cradle to grave'.

The transition to eco-effective product and services design implies a metabolic approach to materials and material flows (Braungart and McDonough 2000a). Eco-effective design addresses the composition of materials, processing and aspects of material flow tracing. Materials are defined positively with respect to resource origin and toxicological and eco-toxicological properties.

Processes are positively defined for their impact on resource recovery after materials have fulfilled their function:

- In **technical** material flow strategies, processes are characterised by and optimised for reversibility (dismantling, physical or chemical recycling).

- In **biological** material flow strategies, processes are characterised by and optimised for materials to reach the state necessary for biological productions (agriculture, forestry, biotechnology).

Material flows are traced in two directions:

- Backwards, to obtain materials originating as far as possible from recovered resources

- Forwards, to recover materials as resources after they have fulfilled their function

Quality is a positive characteristic of products. Communication within the system is structured positively (for example, 'made for composting') and not negatively (for example, 'free of cadmium'). Articulating environmental product properties in a positive way makes environmental quality an integral part of total product quality.

Integrated systems of production and use focused on products or services can solve environmental issues

Individual companies cannot solve environmental issues on their own as they control only a certain portion of material flows, while buyers of their products or services are basically beyond their reach.

Transforming the 'polluter pays' principle into a true 'responsible care' principle implies strategic alliances for environmentally coherent material flows. The environmental intelligence of the resulting system is embodied in a structure centred around a given product but outside the market, processing and resource recovery (see Fig. 16.1). This structure supports the definition of material composition, the impact of processes and the status of material flows with respect to their closure. It also manages continuous improvement and delivers environmental quality declarations to companies for their marketing. As a supplier of a service to the product system, it is financially carried by its actors.

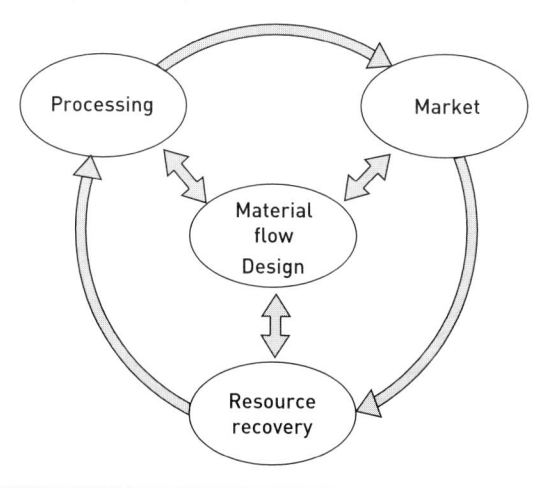

Figure 16.1 System integration for eco-effectiveness

Living organisms are structured along similar lines: individual cells have little intelligence; it is the integration of cells in an organism that enables the specialisation of an intelligent brain. The brain supplies a service to the whole organism and is nourished by it. Recently, McDonough and Braungart (2003) developed the concept of 'Intelligent Materials Pooling' as a strategy for the integration of product or service systems.

The overview on material flows is embodied in a 'bank' for physical resources

The cycle of production, use and resource recovery is enabled by a traditional bank for financial resources. This bank gives the system the mission of creating return on investment that exceeds investment.

The material flow design structure (described in the previous chapter) views physical resources the way a bank views money, though the mission to the system differs slightly as it is subjected to the law of mass conservation: the return of resources strives to recover the original resource quality.

Environmental optimisation generates economic opportunities

Local problems are increasingly determined by global reasons. This is especially so for environmental aspects. An increasing number of persons and institutions therefore begin to see themselves as global citizens with new needs.

Product systems that close material flows add value to products, a feature that can be used aggressively in marketing. In the perspective of global citizenship, ambitious environmental quality statements attached to products will open new opportunities.

In open product systems, costs arise from waste management and from resource replacement. Closed product systems have a competitive advantage over open product systems when costs for resource recovery are lower than costs for final resource destruction plus costs for their replacement for new products (see Fig. 16.2).

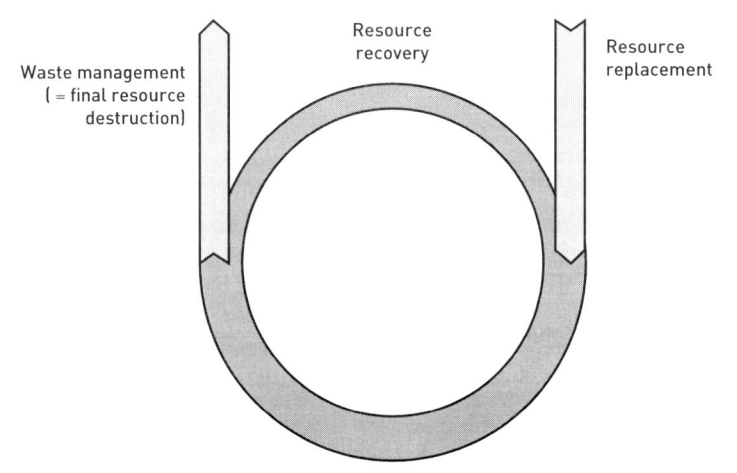

Figure 16.2 Competition between linear and cyclical strategies for the management of material flows

An economic threshold of environmental effectiveness can be transcended with prices concomitantly increasing for resource replacement and waste management. Above this threshold, environmental optimisation leads to the reduction of prices for products or services. The issues of resource availability and pollution put evolutionary pressure on the development of environmentally intelligent systems.

The method of choice is life-cycle development

Life-cycle development (LCD) is a method targeting closed-product-associated material flows (Rivière *et al.* 1997). Open material flows are seen as deficits to be compensated by material, process or information flow optimisation.

The frame of LCD resembles that of life-cycle assessment (LCA): both contain an inventory of material flows, impact assessment and optimisation. LCD, however, differs from LCA because of the emphasis put on closing material flows (eco-effectiveness) instead of simply reducing them (eco-efficiency approach of LCA). Basically, by asking what prevents the recovery of resources for next generations at the highest level of quality in this product, LCD is a method for

- Identifying optimisation impasses without detailed assessment
- Setting optimisation priorities

The iterative LCD procedure leads to

- Clearly defined optimisation steps to be used in marketing claims
- An early return on investment for financing more profound and comprehensive optimisation

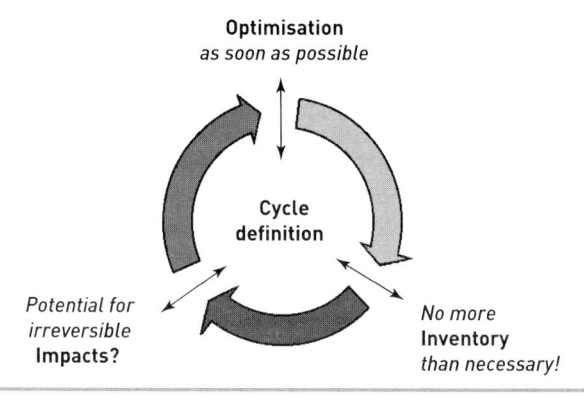

Figure 16.3 Life-cycle development: progressive establishment of eco-effectiveness

Environmental quality offers new scope for sensible innovation

Eco-effective products developed with the LCD method are available on the market. Biodegradable upholstery textiles by the Swiss company Rohner Textil AG are the most progressive example (see Chapter 15). But this is just one of the many companies that have committed to a positive approach to eco-effective products and services. Which materials can be used? How can they be combined in an environmentally intelligent way? How does one organise resource recovery? These are the questions now being addressed.

17
Efforts in the electronics industry toward creating a recycling-based society

Nobuhisa Itoh
Matsushita Electric Industrial Co. Ltd, Japan

In response to the growing risk of depletion of natural resources caused by mass production and mass consumption and the deteriorating quality of the environment due to increasing waste production and emissions, many countries are enacting laws and crafting long-term plans for attaining sustainable development.

There are three main environmental challenges that must be dealt with:

- Arresting global warming through reductions in energy consumption and other efforts
- Managing environmental risks posed by the generation or use of hazardous materials
- Achieving more efficient use of limited resources

These challenges can be summed up in three terms: 'save', 'clean', and '3Rs' (reduce, re-use, recycle).

Response from the electronics industry

Environmental considerations have become a fundamental part of most companies' business strategies. Companies have been moving from simply responding to specific environmental problems to paying attention to overall environmental conservation and to establishing total green management. In the electronics industry, as well, makers are under growing pressure to take greater environmental responsibility by cleaning up the entire life-cycle of their products, which consists of securing resources, production and sales in the 'venous phase', use by consumers in the 'consumption phase', and disposal and recycling in the 'artery phase'. Green management controls products 'from cradle to cradle'.

The establishment of an effective environmental management system is essential to running companies in a more ecologically aware manner. A growing number of local governments and businesses are adopting this type of set-up. The Matsushita Group has been making serious efforts to reduce the environmental impact of its business operations and to realise 'co-existence with the global environment' under our own Environmental Charter, which is based on a management philosophy that calls for 'the progress and development of society and the well-being of people throughout the world'. The Group's environmental strategies and policies are decided by an Environment Conference, which is chaired by the president of Matsushita Electric Industrial and is composed of the presidents and other executives of Group companies. All-company committees and other appropriate organisations within the Group address particularly important issues. All the 221 Matsushita Group manufacturing sites around the world had received ISO 14001 certification by the end of March 1999. Currently, major sales companies, research labs and other important non-manufacturing sites are seeking this certification. The number of Matsushita Group business sites qualifying for the ISO 14001 certificate reached 280 by the end of 2001. The principal objectives of our current efforts are the development of green products, the creation of clean factories and recycling of end-of-life products. We are also mounting a ' "Love the Earth" citizens' campaign' designed to boost our employees' environmental awareness as part of our efforts to become an environmentally advanced company on the cutting edge of industrial ecology.

In the following sections, the challenges the electronics industry must tackle to help realise a recycling-based society and the technologies available for these efforts will be described for each of the three phases of the product life-cycle—the venous phase, the consumption phase and the artery phase. The Matsushita Group's efforts in terms of 'save', 'clean' and '3Rs' will also be discussed in detail (Matsushita 2000).

Challenges and technologies in the venous phase

'Save': energy saving

The main production-related challenge to manufacturers concerning efforts to stop global warming is to cut emissions of the six greenhouse gases (CO_2, methane [CH_4], nitrous oxide [N_2O], HFCs, perfluorocarbons [PFCs] and sulphur hexafluoride [SF_6]) designated as reduction targets at the UNFCCC Conference of the Parties 3 (UNFCCC–COP3) in 1997. A particularly important goal is to cut CO_2 emissions, which account for 90% of all greenhouse emissions. The burning of fossil fuels to generate electricity and other forms of energy generates carbon dioxide. Slashing CO_2 emissions is a major task for the electronics industry because the manufacturing process for products such as computer chips, liquid-crystal displays and secondary batteries consumes huge amounts of energy. Companies are developing technologies and making investments with the aim of achieving higher energy efficiency. For other greenhouse gases used only for limited purposes—for example, PFCs used in the manufacturing process for computer chips—research and development is exploring alternative materials and processes (EIAJ 1999: 7-11).

In spite of Matsushita Group having consumed 31% more energy (in crude oil equivalent terms) in 2000 than it did in 1990, our CO_2 emissions were only 9% higher than the 1990 level despite rapid growth in device operations. This can be credited to the Group's strategic energy-saving efforts, including the introduction of co-generation systems, switching to natural gas, and energy-saving assessments. We are now pursuing a comprehensive approach based on an energy-saving management system.

'Clean': cleaner processes

Previously, the biggest challenge on the path toward cleaner processes was to develop alternatives to CFCs and other materials that cause ozone-layer depletion. We have eliminated all these materials. What is important now is comprehensive management of the growing range of chemicals that are used in increasing quantities because of expansion in device-related operations. We are trying to reduce pollution risks by such efforts as compliance with the Pollutant Release and Transfer Register (PRTR) law and replacement and adequate management of materials with a large environmental impact such as lead solder.

Our comprehensive management of chemical substances is applied to a group of materials including those designated in the PRTR law, our own products designated for product assessment and endocrine disrupters. These materials are ranked by environmental impact into three groups, and subjected to prohibition, reduction or adequate management, respectively. Under our green procurement campaign, launched in April 1999, we ask our suppliers to take steps to guarantee the proper management of chemicals according to our environmental impact rankings and to inform us of the chemicals included in the materials and components they make.

'3Rs': reduce, re-use and recycle

In our efforts to reduce, re-use and recycle materials, we need to improve our response to the greater responsibilities imposed on manufacturers by legislation to promote recycling. The Container and Package Recycling Law, which covers Styrofoam and paper used for packaging consumer electronics and information products, has made it mandatory for manufacturers to indicate on the packages the materials used and to cover the costs of their collection and recycling. Makers are making various efforts, through a 3R approach, to reduce the total amount of industrial waste discharged from their plants and offices and to achieve 'zero emissions' processes that create no landfill waste. We are also striving to achieve zero landfill waste, with an eye to effecting a recycling rate of 98% or higher in 2002. We have already achieved the 2000 target of reducing the per-sales amount of waste by 75% from the 1991 level.

Environmental communications

Environmental communications have become an important part of any company's responsibility for communication with society. A growing number of firms use environmental reporting and accounting to provide stakeholders with more information about their environmental policies and performance. There are not yet any widely accepted standards for these practices, so companies are working on them individually. In recent years, increasing numbers of investors have shown an interest in ecofunds, a type of mutual fund that limits investment alternatives to securities in companies with superior environmental performance. The selection of securities for investment is based on disclosed information and publications such as environmental reports, questionnaires and interviews with executives in charge of environmental issues. The popularity of ecofunds underscores the importance of environmental communications. We have been publishing environmental reports since 1997 and started publishing environmental accounting in 1998. We also supply information about our ecological efforts on our websites and at exhibitions in response to requests by stakeholders. Environmental accounting is designed to calculate the costs and effects of environmental investment. Companies are studying various related issues such as estimated effects, environmental performance evaluation and environmental risk avoidance costs for the purpose of developing a system with which to evaluate the overall eco-efficiency of management.

Challenges and technologies in the consumption and artery phases

Next, I will discuss the challenges to be addressed and technologies available for use in the consumption and artery phases, from the separate viewpoints of 'save', 'clean', and '3Rs'.

'Save': energy saving

Efforts for saving energy consumed by products should focus on improvement in energy efficiency. Consumer products accounted for 26% of Japan's total energy consumption in 1999, according to the Japan Energy Conservation Centre. Under the Revised Energy Conservation Law (the Law Concerning the Rational Use of Energy), the amount of energy consumed by the most energy-efficient products available is used as the energy-efficiency standard in a 'top-runner method' (i.e. at a leading level of the industry) for assessing all products in the same category. This approach is applied to about a dozen widely used, energy-hungry home electric appliances, such as air conditioners, lighting equipment, televisions (TVs) and refrigerators. Makers are required to fulfil the energy-efficiency standards by the designated year on a weighted-average basis. The law stipulates penalties for companies that fail to meet the standards, including the publication of their names. The law has prompted major product strategy reviews among manufacturers, leading them to step up efforts to develop energy-efficient models and stop marketing low-priced models with low energy efficiency. The number of product categories subject to this requirement was increased in 2000 to include gas and oil equipment. Implementation details, including the actual target figures designated by the top-runner method, were worked out by the end of 2001.

The two most important steps for improving the energy efficiency of products are boosting the efficiency of energy conversion and reducing the losses that occur during signal processing and switching. The former involves the use of new technologies to achieve high efficiency in the basic process of converting electricity into force, heat or light, and is used most commonly for white goods. The latter approach is used mainly for reducing standby power consumption by products such as audio-visual and information appliances.

We have received the Partner of the Year Award from Energy Star Home Electronics of the US Environmental Protection Agency, an award to endorse energy-saving achievements in the area of home electronics, for three years running since 1999. We received praise for our efforts to develop and market a wide range of energy-saving consumer products and for our active co-operation with and support for the programme. By April 2001, most of our products eligible for the programme, including TVs, met the standards.

In addition to the product-specific efforts mentioned above, system solutions form an important part of our energy-saving drive. We have proposed an integrated energy management system using the mains power supply called Home Information Infrastructure for all the products and equipment used in homes, such as air conditioners, lighting and power supplies. We are also conducting research on fuel cells for home use, high-efficiency solar batteries and wind power systems for local power generation systems.

'Clean': cleaner processes

The main area in efforts for cleaner processes is the replacement or reduction of hazardous materials to minimise environmental risks and disposal costs after useful life. The principal targets for reduction are lead and halogen compounds in solder.

Lead-free solder

Soldering, used for attaching electronic parts to circuit boards, is one of the most basic manufacturing techniques. Lead solder for joining metals has a long history that dates back to the 3rd century BCE, when it was used for decorating bronze objects (Osawa 1985: 9-11). In particular, eutectic solder consisting of tin (63%) and lead (37%) has been widely used because of its excellent usability and low cost. When exposed to acid rain, however, lead in solder can be eluted from discarded electronic equipment that has been shredded and then buried, polluting soil and groundwater. This environmental hazard has provoked international attention and policy responses. The EU's draft directive on Waste Electrical and Electronic Equipment (WEEE), for instance, calls for a ban on the use of five materials in products: lead, mercury, cadmium, hexavalent chromium, and specific bromine-based flame retardants such as polybrominated biphenyl oxides. In Japan shredder dust must be buried in risk-managed disposal facilities. These developments have spurred the electronics industry to embark on the development of lead-free solder, which has become a major issue in industrial ecology.

The characteristics required of solder are wettability, low melting temperature, good tensile strength, safety and low cost. Companies have proposed various types of Sn-based lead-free solders that contain materials such as silver, copper or zinc, and efforts to commercialise them are under way (*Electronics Journal* 2000).

We have developed new solder materials jointly with materials makers and are now trying to develop the necessary mounting technology while attempting to exclude lead from component electrodes. Our goal is to eliminate lead completely from solder in all our products manufactured worldwide by the end of 2002.

In October 1998, we launched the world's first portable minidisc (MD) player using lead-free solder. The material was a tin–silver compound with bismuth (3%) added to lower the melting temperature to 210°C. We started mass production of lead-free solder in January 1999 for the main boards (330 mm × 250 mm) of non-portable videocassette recorders (VCRs). Total shipments reached 1.74 million units by June 2001. The material is a tin–copper–nickel compound. We have also developed lead-free solder for practical use in TVs, vacuum cleaners and electric foot-warmers. Achieving higher heat resistance and eliminating lead from electrode metal plating are major challenges concerning parts and devices. We are tackling these problems over a wide variety of devices, including various computer chips, electronic parts and button-type batteries.

The key to commercialisation of lead-free solder is a total approach involving all aspects of mounting technologies, including the production process, a review of the conditions corresponding to circuit boards, configuration of parts and heat resistance.

Reduction in the use of halogen compounds

Flame retardants based on compounds containing bromine, chlorine and other halogens are widely used for making plastics used in armouring materials, mechanical parts and circuit boards in electrical and electronic products. Cable sheaths are usually made of polyvinyl chloride resins, which have good electrical insulation and heat resistance. However, these materials can produce halogen gases and dioxins when heat-treated for recycling or disposed of by incineration. The recycling processes and steps involved when using waste plastics for fuel differ greatly, and depend on whether polyvinyl chloride and other halogen compounds must be removed or not (Nakano 1999).

We are making major efforts to eliminate halogen compounds from such products, including cable sheaths, to reduce environmental risk as well as to reduce the environmental impact and costs of recycling. We developed a cable sheath free from polyvinyl chloride jointly with a cable-maker in June 1999. This cable sheath, made from polyethylene mixed with magnesium hydroxide, has been adopted for widescreen TVs. This is the first TV on the market to use a cable sheath free from polyvinyl chloride. We have adopted halogen-free plastics for cabinets of TVs and personal computers (PCs) and are also switching to chemicals with lower environmental impact in line with the rankings of chemical substance management mentioned above.

'3Rs': reduce, re-use, recycle

In order to promote the 3Rs of products, it is crucial to design products to ensure they are easier to recycle and repair.

Design for '3Rs'

We have established design guidelines to step up 3R efforts and a new system to evaluate the recyclability of products to make them easier to dismantle and recycle. Besides designing products to be easy to dismantle and recycle, we have been reviewing the recyclability of the materials we use. We have, for instance, reduced the number of wires and screws used in TV sets by adopting a modular approach to design based on the division of entire units into five separate building blocks: the cathode-ray tube (CRT), the cabinet, the back cover, the speaker system and the chassis, and designed a special fabrication structure for easy dismantling. As Figure 17.1 shows, the adoption of integral mouldings has reduced the number of materials and parts. The number of circuit boards in a 21 inch (52 cm) standard TV model, for instance, has dropped from 17 to 5, while that of cables has fallen from about 120 to 37, thanks to a simplified structure.

The total number of components in a 400 litre refrigerator decreased by about 40%, from 1,620 in 1994 to 970 in 1999, resulting in a 13 kg drop in the weight of the product. A combination of modularisation, one-direction assembly and design improvements to allow dismantling and the removal of hazardous materials without tools has provided for more-efficient recycling of materials.

Plastic materials

To ensure efficient recycling of plastic materials, plastics of the same kind and same grade must be collected together. However, plastic materials come in a wide range of grades for different uses. In 1994, there were in Japan some 9,000 grades of polypropylene, one of the commonest general-purpose resins, about 30 times more than in the USA. This explosion of grades was hindering recycling (Kodera 2000).

We have reduced the number of grades for the top ten plastic materials in the amount used through integration and standardisation. We now use only nine grades of polypropylene, for instance: down from about 120.

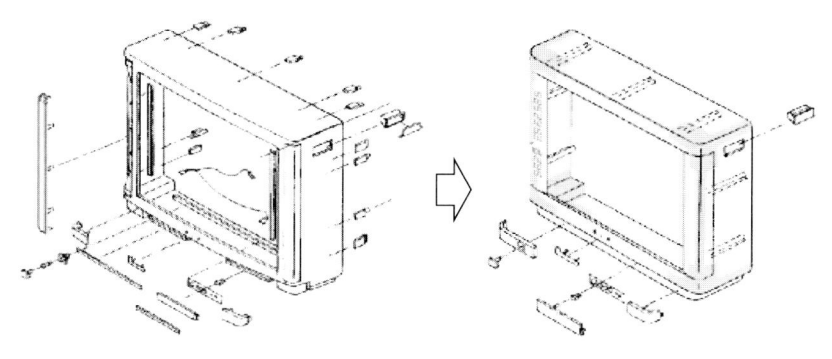

17. Efforts in the electronics industry toward a recycling-based society *Itoh*   159

- Number of components reduced from 39 to 8
- Number of types of resin reduced from 13 to 2
- Amount of resin used reduced by 26%

Figure 17.1 '3R' improvement of a TV front cabinet

Source: Matsushita Group

Magnesium alloys

Since plastics still represent a major recycling challenge, home electronics makers are taking a new look at metals, mainly as armouring and jacket materials. Magnesium alloys are increasingly being employed as materials for products that are getting smaller and lighter, such as notebook computers and cell phones, thanks to new processing techniques such as injection thixomoulding and press forging.

With a specific gravity of about 1.8, magnesium is lighter than both aluminium (2.7) and titanium (4.5). It especially excels in specific strength, heat dissipation, electromagnetic shielding and attenuation, and has an attractive texture. Its environmental impact is relatively small because of its abundance and high recyclability. Magnesium is the eighth most abundant metal on earth, following iron, aluminium and other common metals. Magnesium accounts for 2.1% of the weight of the Earth's crust and every litre of sea water contains 1.3 grams of magnesium. Recycling magnesium requires only 4% of the energy needed to cast a magnesium ingot (Mizuno 1998: 1).

We have developed a thixomoulding method jointly with the Japan Steel Works Ltd. This process was used for the first time in September 1998 for making cabinets for 21 inch TV sets. We also started using this method for the exterior of Broadcasting Satellite (BS) digital TV sets in 2000.

In thixomoulding, in a process similar to injection-moulding plastics, magnesium alloy chips are heated in a cylinder until they become a mixture of solid and liquid. This mixture is then converted into thixotropic form using turning screws for high-speed injection into metal moulds. Thixotropy is a property of certain gels (and ketchup), which liquefy when shaken and then resolidify if left standing. In the case of magnesium alloy, a shear force is applied to the half-melted alloy. Its solid phase becomes granulated, causing it to become less viscous.

Applying this process to the production of home electronics required the development of a new technology for large-scale moulding of thin walls. A high mould-clamping force of 1,600 tons is needed to ensure rapid solidification—within several hundred milliseconds—in the mould. There are still some problems with the current process, such as too many process steps. To make the technique applicable to a wider range of products, it is essential to reduce the number of process steps and material costs and improve yields by developing new processing technologies (Nishikawa *et al.* 1999).

Challenges and technologies in the recycling of packaging materials

I will now present more details of our efforts to promote the reduction and recycling of packaging materials. Makers are trying hard to reduce the total amount of packaging materials they use, both to save energy consumption during packaging processes, and to switch to materials with higher recyclability. Efforts are mainly focused on eliminating or reducing packaging, re-using the materials repeatedly and then recycling them back to raw materials for re-use.

As a result of these efforts, we have been able to develop a special packing process for air conditioners that uses 100% recycled paper. We also use soybean oil ink, which contains fewer volatile organic solvents, for printing shipping boxes, instruction manuals and catalogues (Kameda 1999). There are plans in the industry to minimise the printing of instruction manuals by posting detailed information via the Internet.

Product assessment

As described above, we are making a wide range of efforts to lower the environmental impact of our products. In the development of green products, it is important to reduce the environmental impact of products over their entire lifetimes, starting at the planning and designing stage. In 1991, when the Recycling Law was put into effect, we issued the first 'Matsushita Product Assessment' before any other manufacturers in the industry took this step. We have applied this assessment to all the products we manufacture and sell, including home electric appliances. The assessment was conducted on a total of 2,530 products in 1999. We are making constant efforts to improve and upgrade the assessment procedures we use for reducing the environmental impact of products over their entire life-cycles.

Recycling of end-of-life products

The law that regulates recycling for four large home electric appliances (TVs, air conditioners, refrigerators and washing machines) came into force in April 2001. The law requires that users return, at their own cost, end-of-life products for recycling, that retailers and designated organisations collect and hand them over to makers or importers, and that makers and importers recycle them. Manifests are used to ensure proper recycling under this Japanese system. The law requires makers to recover end-of-life products for recycling them into new products, either free of charge or for a fee. It suggests re-use rates of at least 55% for TVs, 60% for air conditioners, 50% for refrigerators and 50% for washing machines.

We started research into recycling end-of-life TVs in March 1998, ahead of other manufacturers in the industry. We have since expanded the scope of our research to cover refrigerators, air conditioners and washing machines. We opened the Matsushita Ecotechnology Centre at the end of March 2001 in Yashiro, Hyogo Prefecture. The Centre can handle up to 1 million units of the four product categories per year and is conducting research into recycling at a testing and experimenting facility under the slogan 'Product to Product'.

Some 1.5 million units of home electric appliances were recovered for recycling across the nation in the April–June quarter of 2001, according to the Ministry of Economy, Trade and Industry. Recycling the designated four products after the end of their useful life requires more than one recycling plant and numerous designated collection sites. We are working with several partners, including Toshiba Corp. and Daikin Industries Ltd, to build up a network of recycling facilities utilising the existing recycling infrastructure. Currently, we use 24 recycling plants with 190 designated collection sites.

We need to make further efforts to expand the scope of products covered, raise recycling rates and lower recycling costs. We are also studying recycling and disposal technologies for such hard-to-handle products as motors, compressors and printed circuit boards.

Environmental communications

Makers are now under growing pressure to disclose relevant information to enable consumers to choose environmentally friendly green products as part of their environmental information services. In related developments, the Japanese Industrial Standards (JIS) energy-efficiency labelling system was launched in August 2000. The Environment Ministry started operating a database on eco-friendly products, made accessible to the public in April 2001. Many more such moves are likely to be on the way. Disclosure of accurate information is a prerequisite for genuinely effective environmental protection.

Companies have established their own standards for environmentally friendly products and indicate the ecological qualifications of their products in their own ways. The trend is toward a unified disclosure system and international standards for more reliable and transparent disclosure. The main issues for debate include the definitions of related terms and indication methods.

We started attaching 'characteristic stickers', giving environmental information, to our products that fulfil the environmental assessment standards to inform consumers of the eco-friendly qualities of the products. By the end of March 2001 the stickers had been attached to some 270 products.

17.4 Conclusion

We have examined the major challenges on the path to a recycling-based society and the technologies available to make it happen, focusing on the Matsushita Group's efforts.

The enactment of the Home Appliance Recycling Law, which mandates Japanese electronics-makers to build 'reverse' plants for recycling, is an epoch-making event that truly marks the opening of the 21st century, the century of the environment.

Developing products with less environmental impact and better basic performance and quality without raising production costs poses a huge challenge to manufacturers. In spite of this, a growing number of high-performance, eco-friendly products without noticeably higher price tags are hitting the markets. To create a sustainable, recycling-based society, government, consumers and businesses all need to understand what they must do, contribute their wisdom, and take the initiative to achieve the goal in the coming years.

Manufacturers in the electronics and other areas will have to play an important role in promoting both information technology and environmental protection. Japanese makers have the ability to make greater contributions to the effort toward global sustainability by developing eco-friendly products using cutting-edge green technologies.

18
Ten years of sustainability at Henkel
Innovative products as a basis for long-term business success

Rainer Rauberger and Michaela Raupach
Henkel, Corporate Sustainability Management/Reporting and Stakeholder Dialogue, Germany

Founded in 1876, the Henkel Group today is a leader in consumer brands and technologies. In 2002, Henkel's core businesses recorded sales of EUR9.7 billion, of which 21% were generated in Germany and 79% in international markets. The controlling company is Henkel KGaA, Düsseldorf. Henkel preferred shares have been traded on the stock exchange since 1985, ordinary shares since 1996.

The company operates worldwide, with 48,600 employees and subsidiaries in more than 75 countries (Henkel 2003). Its branded business sectors—Laundry and Home Care, Cosmetics and Toiletries, and Consumer and Craftsmen Adhesives— represent 70% of Henkel sales; 30% are generated by Henkel Technologies, which comprises the three systems businesses of industrial adhesives, engineering adhesives, and surface technologies.

Ten years of sustainable development

In 1987, the Brundtland Commission set up by the UN formulated the concept of sustainable development as a guideline for the international community of nations (WCED 1987). The International Chamber of Commerce (ICC) gave form to this vision for business enterprises, defining 16 management principles for sustain-

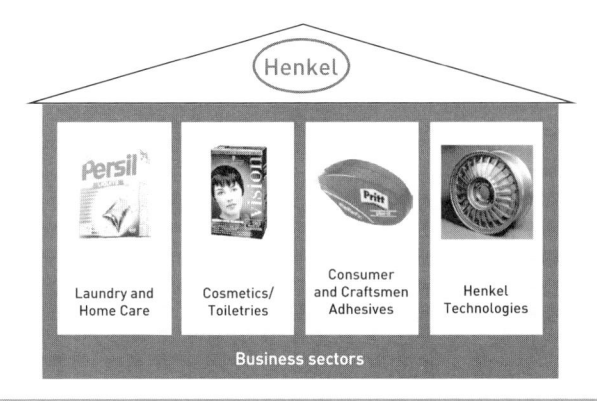

Figure 18.1 Henkel business sectors

ability in its Business Charter for Sustainable Development (ICC 1991). Henkel signed the Charter in 1991, one of the first companies to do so. This commitment launched the Henkel Group's sustainable business management process.

In 1991 the starting conditions for implementing the Charter varied widely within the company. In R&D, for example, environmental protection had already been a priority objective since the 1960s. In the late 1970s this resulted in a marketing strategy, which still holds today, of securing competitive advantages through high-performance products that combine customer benefits with ecological progress.

Until the mid-1990s, however, the instrument needed for implementing sustainable development throughout the group was not yet at hand. This instrument is the integrated management system, which adapts the company's processes to sustainability requirements. Its structure and effectiveness have been recognised on several occasions: Henkel was awarded first place in the 1999–2000 environmental competition of the Federation of German Industry (BDI) and has also received an honourable mention from the EU in the Management Award for Sustainable Development 2000.

Taking the ICC Charter for Sustainable Development as a basis, Henkel has evaluated how far it has progressed toward sustainability during the past ten years (see Fig. 18.2). This systematic review revealed strengths and weaknesses.[1] Throughout the Group, for instance, Henkel needs to focus more carefully on selecting and assessing its contractors and suppliers in accordance with sustainability requirements. Greater emphasis must also be placed on the integration of newly acquired companies. The evaluation also constituted a good basis for further building on Henkel's strategic strengths.

1 See www.henkel.com/sustainability.

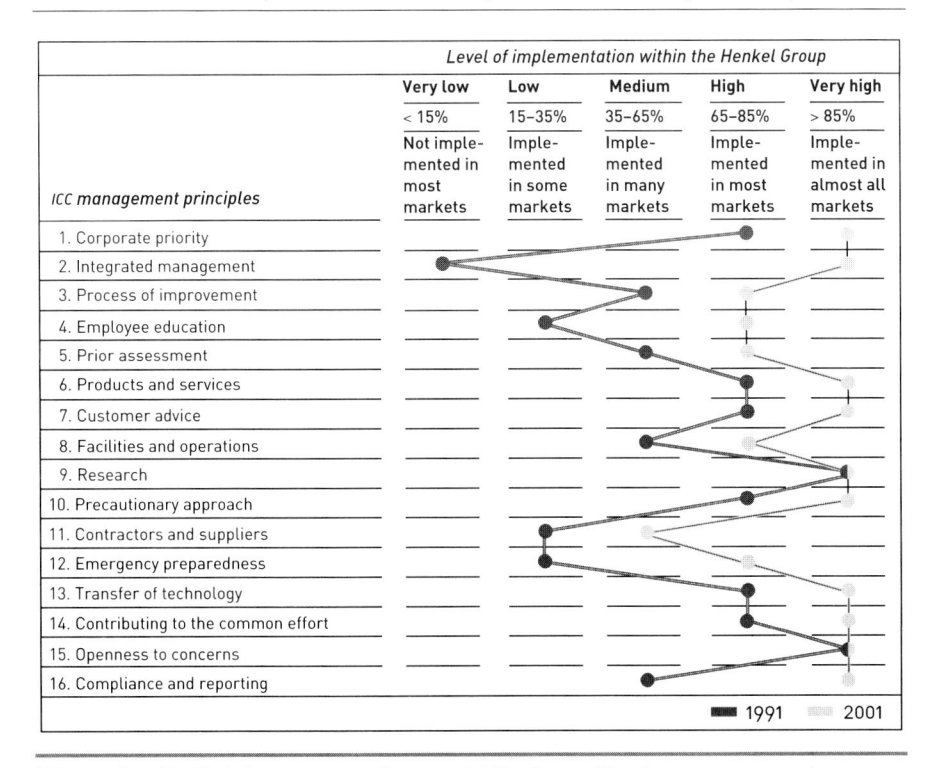

ICC management principles	Level of implementation within the Henkel Group				
	Very low	Low	Medium	High	Very high
	< 15%	15–35%	35–65%	65–85%	> 85%
	Not implemented in most markets	Implemented in some markets	Implemented in many markets	Implemented in most markets	Implemented in almost all markets
1. Corporate priority					
2. Integrated management					
3. Process of improvement					
4. Employee education					
5. Prior assessment					
6. Products and services					
7. Customer advice					
8. Facilities and operations					
9. Research					
10. Precautionary approach					
11. Contractors and suppliers					
12. Emergency preparedness					
13. Transfer of technology					
14. Contributing to the common effort					
15. Openness to concerns					
16. Compliance and reporting					

■ 1991   ▦ 2001

Figure 18.2 Henkel Corporate review on ICC Business Charter management principles, 1991 and 2001

Organising for sustainability

The Henkel management board bears overall responsibility for sustainability matters. It aligns its business policy to the opportunities and requirements of sustainable development. The heads of the business sectors are responsible for implementing this policy in the Henkel companies assigned to them. A Sustainability Council, with members from the entire group, has a global steering function and co-operates with business sectors and corporate functions (see Fig. 18.3).

The key instruments for implementing sustainability at Henkel are the integrated management systems; their worldwide introduction was completed in 2001. The systems were based on the existing quality management system and incorporate globally uniform standards for safety, health and the environment. These standards cover the entire life-cycle of products, from raw materials through product development and production to disposal after use. The integrated management systems optimise business processes and ensure that resources are used efficiently. They are complemented by a Code of Conduct, binding for all

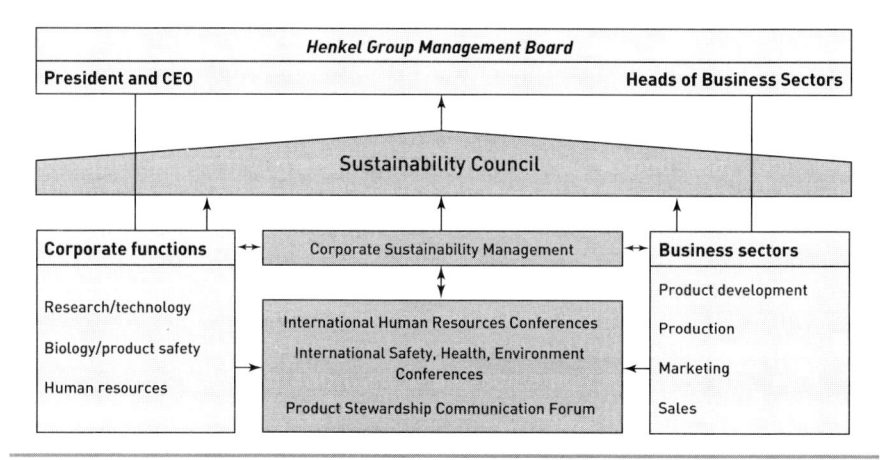

Figure 18.3 Organisational structure for sustainability

Henkel employees, in which Henkel defines the basic rules for its business practices (Henkel 2000). Implementation of group-wide requirements is regularly checked by means of internal audits as well as external certifications. Today, more than 60% of production output is certified to the international environmental management standard ISO 14001.

However, social aspects are not yet included in the existing management systems. Henkel has therefore set itself the objective of consolidating all group-wide requirements on sustainable development into corporate sustainability standards by 2004. An international working group will define standards on social responsibility and integrate them into the existing management systems for safety, health, environment and quality.

Sustainable products and services

Building on innovative strength

Henkel's strategy is to secure market advantages with high-performance, safe, and environmentally friendly products. One example is modern detergents and household cleaners, which are easy to use and help to conserve resources and reduce the burden on the environment. Henkel is also a pioneer in solvent-free adhesives and is worldwide leader in this market. The success of this product strategy relies on a high degree of innovative impetus, which Henkel achieves through knowledge of customer needs, targeted research activities and alliances, and employee creativity.

Only consistently innovative companies can enjoy long-term success and maintain their capability to meet the challenges of the future. This is why Henkel is striking out in new research directions. Parallel to expanding its existing product portfolios, the company aspires to build new business. To this end, Henkel is selectively acquiring equity in young technology and research enterprises.

One such company is SusTech (derived from 'sustainable technologies') Darmstadt, a joint venture established by Henkel, the Technical University of Darmstadt (TU Darmstadt), and prominent university professors (see Fig. 18.4). SusTech Darmstadt develops sustainable products and processes based on nanotechnology. For example, its researchers are working on 'switch-off' adhesive bonds that make it possible to separate even composite materials for recycling, and on dirt-repelling surface coatings that lead to resource-conserving cleaning technologies. Convinced by the overall benefits of the public–private partnership, the German Ministry of Education and Research (BMBF) provided financial support for SusTech Darmstadt's initial projects.[2]

Market success	SusTech Darmstadt	Location success
Sustainable products and technologies		New jobs Start-ups, spin-offs

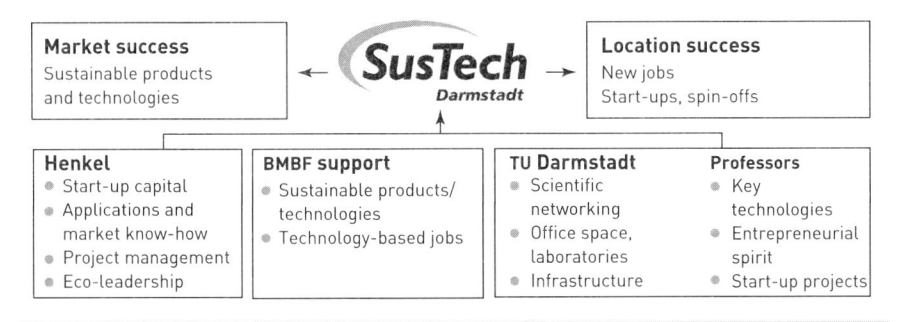

Henkel	BMBF support	TU Darmstadt	Professors
• Start-up capital • Applications and market know-how • Project management • Eco-leadership	• Sustainable products/technologies • Technology-based jobs	• Scientific networking • Office space, laboratories • Infrastructure	• Key technologies • Entrepreneurial spirit • Start-up projects

Figure 18.4 The SusTech Darmstadt co-operation model

In this way, Henkel systematically draws on external knowledge to create new market opportunities and to develop new and innovative products and technologies that contribute to sustainability.

Product stewardship

Aligning product policy to sustainability requires a systematic approach. This means that measures intended to improve the safety, health and environment (SHE) performance must concentrate on the parts of a product's life-cycle where the greatest progress can be made. Detailed life-cycle assessment data and substance evaluations provide the necessary basic information. However, sustainable products must also offer customers noticeable additional benefits, such as better performance or superior dispensing. In general, most consumers are not prepared to pay more or change their habits just because a product or a service is more environmentally friendly. In aligning their product policies to sustainability, therefore, the business sectors give due consideration to the key specific aspects of SHE as well as to customer requirements.

2 See www.sustech.de.

At Henkel, this strategy is carried out through close co-operation between the business sectors and corporate research. A risk assessment is carried out for each new product and process. It is updated as soon as relevant new SHE data becomes available. If a risk is identified, effective and proven action will be taken to ensure that the product will be safe to use. If, despite these precautions, there is still any vestige of doubt about the safety of the product, it will be withdrawn from the market.

System solutions play a key role in Henkel's industrial business. In co-operation with customers and plant manufacturers, Henkel offers problem solutions that go far beyond the 'simple' sale of products. They range from plant planning to running the processes on-site. In this way, Henkel secures long-term access to new markets and customers.

For example, Henkel Surface Technologies gained Italy's largest refinery as a customer by offering a convincing system for on-site treatment of cooling water. Henkel's advantage was that the readily biodegradable products are not only kind to the environment but also to pipes and cooling systems. This lowers overall costs. Billing is no longer done per kilogram of product but for services rendered at the customer's site—yet another incentive for the customer and Henkel to contribute toward sustainability through optimal utilisation of resources.

Based on market requirements, the business sectors align their product policies to sustainability. The following examples demonstrate how innovative solutions help to improve SHE and how Henkel uses this to secure competitive advantages. As can be seen by the examples, sustainable product optimisations are not always instantly successful on the market. In most cases, long-term market strategies are needed to achieve enduring success with customers.

Laundry and Home Care

In 1953, the Henkel ecology department began to collect data on the fate of detergent ingredients in the environment—as a basis for preventative environmental protection. Today, product life-cycle assessments are fundamental to the development of environmentally friendly detergents. A priority objective here is to combine steadily improving product performance with continuous reductions in the amount of product that has to be used.

One of Henkel's success strategies is the use of specifically tailored regional brands. A group-wide formulation information system helps to ensure that Henkel products will not pose any risk to health or the environment anywhere in the world. Only tested raw materials and approved formulations that have been cleared by headquarters in Düsseldorf may be used. Another component of Henkel's market success is its responsiveness to consumer needs. With its detergents in tablet form and with the recently launched Persil LIQUITS®, Henkel is applying an innovative concept that unites easy handling with exact dispensing.

Example 1: the right amount of detergent

Whether the detergent is liquid, powder or solid, Henkel continuously aims to improve performance, reduce the environmental burden and simplify usage of its laundry detergents. At the same time dosage per wash cycle and the amount of packaging has been reduced (see Fig. 18.5). Henkel's innovative products made it a driving force in many markets in the 1990s and strengthened its competitiveness.

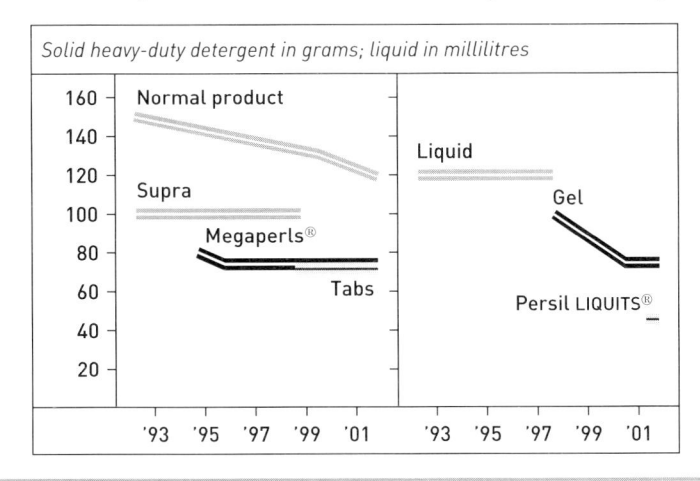

Figure 18.5 Amount of detergent per wash cycle

The development of Megaperls® and Tabs, with the resulting savings in the consumption of raw materials, was a step in this direction. In comparison to traditional washing powders, the average amount of detergent per wash cycle could be more than halved (75 g per wash cycle for Tabs and Megaperls® compared to 150 g for traditional powder detergents). But washing powders are still popular and are therefore being improved continuously. Since active agents are more concentrated and the amount of fillers has been reduced, powder can be used more sparingly. Today, 25% less detergent is needed compared to 1992. The same principle applies to concentrated liquid detergents and the recently launched Persil LIQUITS®, where considerable savings were also achieved.

Optimised product concepts and more effective ingredients mean that products can be used more sparingly and marketed in smaller packs, two factors many consumers appreciate. Moreover, improved formulations have resulted in greater washing efficiency even at lower temperatures. As a result, consumer demand for traditional powder products is decreasing. In Europe their market share has fallen from more than 80% to around 65% since 1998. An additional advantage of the tablets and Persil LIQUITS® is that they make it almost impossible to use too much product per wash cycle.

Cosmetics and Toiletries

When Henkel's cosmetics experts develop a new product, it has to be effective, but it must also satisfy two other key criteria: it must be safe to use, and it must be compatible with human beings and the environment. Only good, well-tolerated and easy-to-use cosmetics can generate long-term consumer trust. This is why developers of cosmetics assign a high priority to compatibility and ecological degradability. Every new product that is developed has to undergo a comprehensive test programme proven over a period of years and continuously updated in line with the latest technical developments.

Henkel studies skin compatibility by means of dermatological tests and *in vitro* tests on cell cultures, which do not require animal experiments. The company has worked with independent institutes since the early 1980s to develop and optimise alternative test methods. Further development of test methods that do not involve live animals will continue to be an important objective of the company.

Example 2: natural-colour cream for greying hair

In 1998, after intensive research and development, Schwarzkopf & Henkel launched Poly Re-Nature, a 'natural-colour' cream for greying hair. The product's especially gentle action principle mimics nature, restoring the hair's previous natural colour. The cream is therefore well tolerated by users who are allergic to the ingredients of conventional hair colorants. Poly Re-Nature cream has established itself firmly in the market and stands out as having the highest hair colorant repeat purchase rate. Its use was initially limited to medium blonde to dark brown hair. Through intensive research it has now become possible to launch the product in southern countries, too, where hair shades traditionally tend to be darker.

Example 3: optimised soap formulations

With annual sales amounting to around 80 million bars, hand soaps are an important product group for Schwarzkopf & Henkel. Formulations and production processes have now been subjected to a two-year study, with excellent results: the quality of the soaps has been improved and their production costs cut. The soap bars now contain alkyl polyglycoside (APG), a washing active substance that is especially well tolerated by the skin and is made exclusively from vegetable raw materials. Talcum improves the soaps' application properties, and the environment benefits from a 10% reduction in energy consumption and the smaller volume of waste-water generated during the production process.

Consumer and Craftsmen Adhesives

Henkel is number one in the global adhesives market and also holds a leading technological and ecological position. The aim is to gain competitive advantages through the business sector's leading role in consumer protection and the environmental compatibility of its products. The development and active marketing of solvent-free adhesives are crucial to this strategy, as the solvents they emit are one of the major pollutants associated with adhesives and are a significant health concern. Additionally, Henkel's adhesives developers have continued to focus on renewable resources.

An important factor in their market success is that Henkel adhesives are designed for convenient, precise and safe use by consumers and craftspeople.

Example 4: low-emission flooring adhesives

In 1997, Henkel Bautechnik, a leading supplier of flooring adhesives, joined with eight other producers to found a quality association for emission-controlled flooring adhesives, the Gemeinschaft emissionskontrollierter Verlegewerkstoffe. Its objective was to promote the use of extremely low-emission and low-odour adhesives by means of uniform labelling. Since then, planners, craftsmen and homeowners have had the assurance that the EMICODE EC1 label is the best safeguard against indoor air pollution.[3] Henkel now markets EC1 adhesives in nine European countries. At present, 70% of all Thomsit dispersion adhesives qualify for the extremely low-emission category (see Fig. 18.6). The aim is to increase this figure to 90% by 2005.

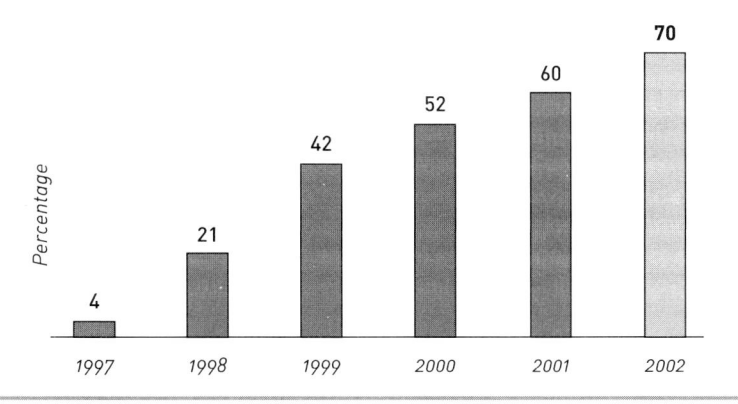

Figure 18.6 **Proportion of low-emission flooring adhesives**

Example 5: solvent-free assembly adhesives

Success in the highly competitive do-it-yourself market depends on easy-to-use, cleanly dispensable and, above all, high-performance product innovations. Henkel's water-based assembly adhesives, developed in the 1990s, are a prime example. Laborious jobs such as drilling, screwing and nailing have become superfluous; moreover, the initial tack of the water-based adhesive is definitely superior to that of solvent-based products. The special feature is that, despite the high initial tack, there is a comfortable margin of a few minutes during which the parts can be repositioned before the adhesive sets. Use of these adhesives cuts solvent consumption by about 1,500 metric tons per year. Today, Henkel's innovative assembly adhesives are firmly established in the European market, and sales in America and Asia are increasing.

---

3 See www.emicode.com.

Example 6: eco-friendly glue stick

The solvent-free Pritt Stick celebrated its 30th anniversary in 1999. With more than one billion units sold, it has been an environmental and economic success. Since 1995 it has also been available as a refill cartridge. Glue sticks are manufactured in very large quantities, thus particularly high priority is placed on ecological compatibility and the conservation of resources. A team of product developers and application engineers worked for three and a half years to achieve a significant increase in the proportion of renewable raw materials used to make the glue stick. In 1999 a formulation was introduced that is based almost entirely on renewable raw materials.

Henkel Technologies

Henkel Technologies is a provider of system solutions for industrial applications. One of this business sector's main objectives is to develop and market alternative products that offer customers the benefits of enhanced environmental and health protection coupled with economic efficiency.

As a global market leader, Henkel Technologies offers individually tailored systems, discussing the specific problems involved with its industrial customers, and jointly developing new processes with them. Work is often carried out in a team including plant manufacturers and suppliers of raw materials. A growing trend is for Henkel Technologies to offer its customers full-service on-site system solutions, allowing them to focus on their core competencies.

Example 7: solvent-free laminating adhesives

Hard-wearing, light, and aroma-sealing are typical demands made on laminated films and foils for flexible food packaging. Henkel provides the solution with its Liofol brand laminating adhesives. In the 1980s, Henkel helped to initiate the switch to solvent-free laminating adhesives. In 1998, it achieved a breakthrough with its newly developed universal laminating adhesives. Faster production times, reduced wastage and especially good processing conditions contributed to increased sales of solvent-free products. Around 60% of all laminates produced with Liofol are now solvent-free; this saves several thousand metric tons of solvent (see Fig. 18.7). As a global leader in this technology, Henkel will continue to profit from this rapidly growing business in the future.

Example 8: efficient paint shop systems

When car bodies are sprayed, around one-third of the paint misses its target. Using a US method, this residual paint is recovered by flushing it out of the spray booth with the help of organic solvents. Henkel-AWARE Technologies has developed the StayClean process and, together with Ford, brought it to market. Instead of organic solvents, it uses biodegradable, environmentally friendly polymers and surfactants. This reduces the burden on the environment while also saving between 5% and 10% of the paint.

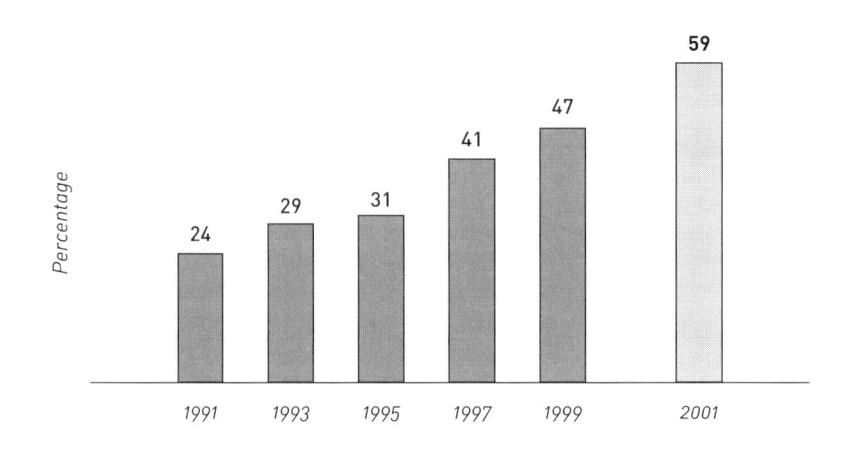

Figure 18.7 Proportion of solvent-free laminates

Nearly all resulting paint coatings are free of flaws, so there is no need for wearisome and costly touch-ups. The products developed by Henkel-AWARE Technologies and the service provided by the experts who look after the installations keep the paint shop clean longer, and prevent solvent-containing wastes. Ford already utilises these benefits on a wide front; since spring 2001 all of Ford's European production sites have been converted to the new method. Other automobile manufacturers have also expressed great interest.

Motivation and benefits

External assessments

Research institutes, sustainability analysts and business journals regularly assess how companies balance economic, ecological and social factors. Henkel welcomes these external assessments of sustainability performance, which result in greater market transparency. Cross-sectoral sustainability and ethical indices also play an increasingly important role in international capital markets.

Since the assessments are carried out according to widely varying criteria, Henkel conducts an intensive dialogue with the rating departments of these institutions. This dialogue complements the well-established exchange of views between Henkel and ecological institutions, other stakeholders and financial circles (analysts, investors and financial journalists). Furthermore, the discussions inject additional innovative ideas into the company.

In August 2001, Henkel was listed in the worldwide Dow Jones Sustainability Index for the third time and was ranked as a sustainability leader in its industry sector. Henkel's score was more than twice as high as the average of all consumer goods companies. Henkel is thus a market leader among the companies that make up the top 10% of their sector in terms of sustainability performance.[4]

Henkel was also selected for inclusion in the first FTSE4Good Index of the Financial Times Stock Exchange (FTSE), launched in June 2001. This ethical index lists quoted companies whose performance in environmental protection, observance of human rights, and acceptance of social responsibility is rated as exceptionally good.[5]

In 1999, the Henkel Group moved into first place in a comparative ecological performance study conducted by the Hamburg Environment Institute. The study examined the environmental performance of the world's 50 top chemical groups. In six out of ten categories Henkel ranked among the world leaders (see Fig. 18.8) and was the only company to be rated 'very good' in the category 'sustainability of products' (Pallas 1999).

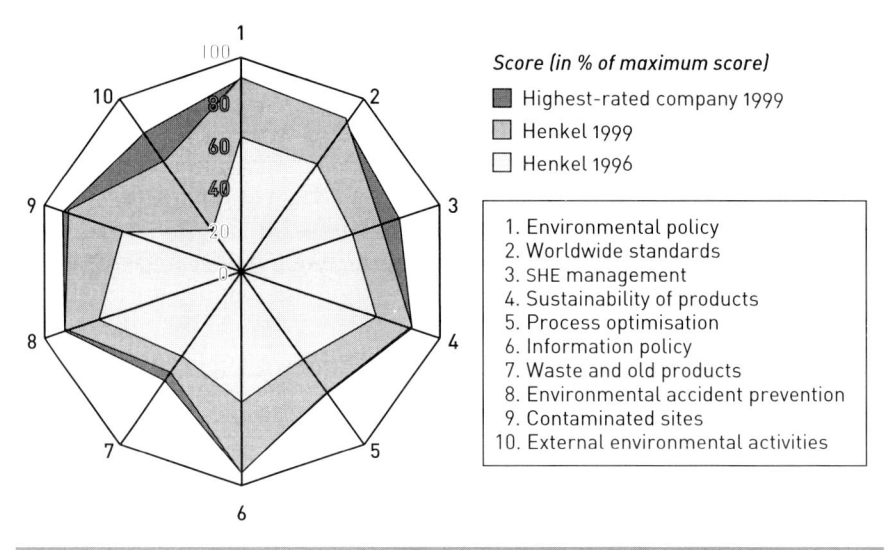

Score (in % of maximum score)
■ Highest-rated company 1999
■ Henkel 1999
☐ Henkel 1996

1. Environmental policy
2. Worldwide standards
3. SHE management
4. Sustainability of products
5. Process optimisation
6. Information policy
7. Waste and old products
8. Environmental accident prevention
9. Contaminated sites
10. External environmental activities

Figure 18.8 Ecological performance study by Hamburg Environment Institute 1999

Henkel considers these assessments to be an important external benchmark for the confidence shown in the company's future viability.

Sustainability and shareholder value

With innovative products, efficient processes and comprehensive risk management, Henkel's sustainability strategy contributes to long-term increase in the value of the company. Henkel has significantly reduced its consumption of resources and

4 See www.sustainability-indexes.com.
5 See www.ftse4good.com.

its emissions since 1992. During the same period, its sales rose by more than 80% and its profits increased to more than two and a half times the base figure (see Fig. 18.9).

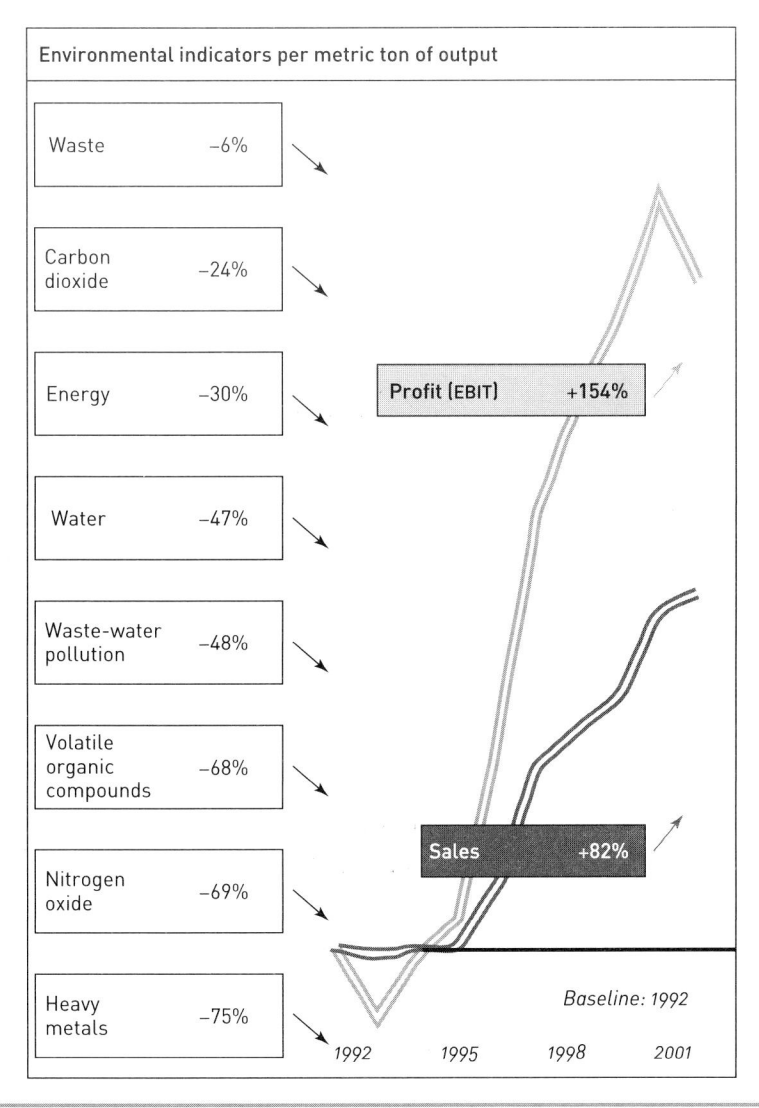

Environmental indicators per metric ton of output	
Waste	−6%
Carbon dioxide	−24%
Energy	−30%
Water	−47%
Waste-water pollution	−48%
Volatile organic compounds	−68%
Nitrogen oxide	−69%
Heavy metals	−75%

Profit (EBIT) +154%
Sales +82%
Baseline: 1992
1992　1995　1998　2001

Figure 18.9 Sustainability performance from 1992 to 2001

The experience gained within the Henkel Group demonstrates how the implementation of environmental protection measures generates savings and how sustainable development can yield competitive advantages in the market. This includes savings in the resources consumed, transport and disposal, as well as innovative products with which Henkel has been able to position itself advantageously in the marketplace. Just the same, a company must also identify, assess and minimise the risks associated with its activities.

Group-wide risk management makes an indispensable contribution to value-oriented management in the Henkel Group. It enables business opportunities to be optimally utilised and possible risks to be countered at an early stage. Independent safety, health and environment audits are an important component of this function. For example, if an operational incident endangers the neighbourhood or harms the environment, this entails more than high, unexpected costs. The company's reputation suffers as well.

Furthermore, the success of products not only depends on quality and price. Customers and stakeholders also judge manufacturers, especially globally operating companies, by the social and environmental aspects of their activities. In the case of the Henkel Group, which generates 70% of its sales with consumer brands, this constitutes yet another crucial factor. Shoppers can decide on a daily basis whether or not to buy Henkel products, thus influencing Henkel's economic success. This is yet another reason why sustainability-oriented management structures and high internal standards are of major importance for the company's future viability.

Focus on future viability

Sustainability brings new challenges. Henkel's intention is to proactively turn these challenges into competitive advantages. Maintaining an even balance between the economic, ecological and social aspects ensures that the company will remain commercially successful and attractive.

Henkel cultivates a continuous and open dialogue with the public about its progress and priorities on the path to sustainability. This is the only way to harmonise the needs of businesses and society in the long term. There are no universal answers, each separate case requiring an individual solution. The implementation of sustainable development grows out of the interplay of political conditions, social demands, and business opportunities. In a constantly changing world with largely globalised markets, a company has to adjust continuously its sustainability orientation to new developments.

No single improvement will bring about sustainable development. All relevant factors must be continually reassessed. Henkel is meeting this ongoing challenge with a market-oriented sustainability strategy and is convinced that this constitutes a clear win–win situation for the company, for society and for the environment. Sustainability means future viability.

19
Toward sustainable banks and insurance companies

Thomas Orbach and Timo Busch
Wuppertal Institute, Germany

Consider the various groups of society, their potentials and present commitments in the context of sustainable development, and you will find many areas still characterised by a lack of practically implemented sustainable strategies. This chapter takes an economy-based view of this lack. A fundamental assumption is that there is huge potential for companies and markets to enforce environmental and social improvements. A context of active forces includes political decisions, NGOs' targets or national and international laws, but we will focus on the financial services sector as one decisive stakeholder with considerable influence on companies and markets.

In the industrial world, banks, savings banks and insurance companies play a vital role in the economy as a whole and for individual entrepreneurs. Whatever form economic development takes, the financial services sector with its financing function is closely involved in the allocation of capital on the macro and micro levels. Decisions made at financial institutions are therefore crucial in determining whether an economy will succeed in following a sustainable path. Moreover, their management decisions and specific requirements give them enormous influence on individual entrepreneurs and their attitude toward the idea of sustainable development.

Until now, the entire field of sustainable finance has been little specified and hardly explored, though a number of options and potentials for new products and markets exist in the financial services sector. Risks caused by environmental or social impacts of companies' activities (in a wider sense) can be avoided by appropriately assessing sustainability-related issues. Beyond this risk-related perspective, financial institutions have the possibility of generating positive image effects by including sustainability performance in their marketing strategies.

However, the majority of financial institutions, if at all, have only started to integrate these aspects into their business strategy. The major problem is mostly related to the current lack of relevant and meaningful information. As a result, indicators are linked to profitability and fail to give a broader perspective of how effective sustainable strategies actually are. Financial markets traditionally prefer companies making immediate profits to those with future potentials (Schmidheiny and Zorraquín 1996: 8). Therefore, approaches based on a long-term ecological perspective are often underestimated in terms of their contribution to companies' financial performance. Furthermore, given today's low resource prices, companies do not have to internalise the external costs caused by their environmental impact, which again reduces the financial benefit of taking eco-efficiency into account. The current market situation, it is argued, offers financial institutions and their customers precious few distinctive incentives for considering sustainable issues.

However, when assessing the value of companies, many analysts do take future conditions into consideration, and sustainability issues are seen as important variables for determining future developments. Moreover, stakeholders increasingly expect financial institutions to take responsibility. But one undeniable obstacle remains in the persisting lack of adequate instruments to measure, assess and evaluate a company's overall sustainability performance, using qualitative as well as quantitative indicators.

A first step in the right direction would be for financial institutions to identify typical environmental and social risks and opportunities within the financial services sector and bring this knowledge to bear on their handling of clients. Potential company risks include

- Higher costs within the value chain due to lack of efforts toward higher eco-efficiency

- Uncertain effects and risks related to changing legal requirements in the future: for example, limited potential for developing new products or continuing existing production processes

- Higher costs due to existing laws and government restrictions: for example, costs for sewage and refuse disposal

- Risks due to changing environmental conditions in general: for example, the scarcity of natural resources or burdens caused by 'natural' disasters

- Increasing risks through management strategies ignoring internal and external corporate social responsibility: for example, charges of abuses in the supply chain ruin corporate reputation and negatively affect the company's success. Moreover, a company with a bad reputation will have difficulties competing for highly qualified employees.

- Risks resulting from increasing stakeholder expectations and demands. Changed preferences on consumption markets, for instance, lead to products and services having to be in compliance with specific environmental or social requirements. Not meeting these demands spells serious risk for companies.

These factors are crucial for a company's competitiveness and continuity, in generating shareholder value just as much as in destroying it. The major task for companies, therefore, is to forecast future conditions and develop an awareness of changing contexts in their own business field. Understanding the future will enable them to find ways of changing their production systems, products, and perhaps the entire corporate image, to meet upcoming challenges in a way that gives them a competitive advantage over companies that remain rooted in old traditions and fail to recognise the need to change. A sustainably aware company can reduce a large number of specific risks even today, protecting its continuity from unpleasant surprises.

Financial institutions have a certain interface with these sustainability-related risks, in their own role as entrepreneurs on the one hand and, on the other hand, through the catalytic function of various financial products or by direct links to the management of national and international companies. Banks and insurance companies interact with sustainable issues (Delphi and Ecologic 1997)

- As investors—supplying the investment needed to achieve sustainable development

- As innovators—developing new financial products to encourage sustainable development: for example, in material efficiency

- As valuers—pricing risks and estimating returns, from a sustainable perspective, for companies and projects

- As powerful stakeholders—influencing the management of companies as lenders, shareholders or members of supervisory boards of directors

- As polluters—consuming resources and energy through their own internal processes

- As victims of environmental change—for example, the huge environment-based burdens for reinsurance companies (Münchener Rück 2001)

Compared to other sectors the business of financial institutions is neither very resource-intensive nor highly polluting (Jeucken 2001: 148). Nevertheless, a wide range of ecological and social impacts is associated with their internal processes (Street and Monaghan 2001: 77). A survey released by the German Environmental Agency gives a few significant best-practice examples of how financial institutions can enhance their internal processes (Bundesumweltministerium and Umweltbundesamt 2001). To name just some results, efficient resource, energy and waste management could reduce costs, and increasing employee participation would have positive effects on employees' motivation and identification with their own company.

Beyond this internal view, more importantly the risks and opportunities of their customers have a direct impact on the success of financial institutions. Banks and insurance companies should assess each activity according to sustainability risk and opportunity factors; they have to identify these issues and implement appropriate measures, otherwise they have to bear the negative consequences just as much as the primary concerned companies.

Concerning the relevance of sustainable aspects for financial products and services, it is possible to distinguish four main categories: retail banking, asset management, investment banking and insurance business. (Schmid-Schoenbein *et al.* 2001; Schmid-Schoenbein and Braunschweig 2000). Financial institutions need to collect in-depth information if they want to identify existing and new environmentally and socially related aspects within these categories and bring sustainable products and services to commercial reality.

New possibilities to reduce loss due to environmental risks emerged when the Basel Committee on Banking Supervision decided to undertake a second round of consultation on more detailed capital-adequacy framework proposals (Basel Committee on Banking Supervision 2001). This concept, often referred to as 'Basel II', rests on three pillars: minimum capital requirements, a supervisory review process and effective use of market discipline. In a sustainability-oriented context, the most significant changes are in the assessment of credit risks and in the inclusion of explicit capital requirements for operational risk. The Committee's primary goal is to ensure that the regulatory capital generated is sufficient to address underlying credit risks. Through these approaches banks will be motivated to continuously enhance their risk management and show more sensitivity to risk when making decisions about loan conditions (standardised approach or based on internal ratings). Lower loan risks have minimum capital requirements, so banks tend to ask lower interest rates for these loans. If companies achieve a better earnings–risk ratio by reducing risks related to environmental or social issues, banks will offer them better conditions. The result is new opportunities in commercial banking, both for banks and their clients.

Another example of how to bring sustainable products to commercial reality can be seen in the regulations on pension fund disclosure of criteria on SRI. From July 2000 all private-sector pension funds in the UK are legally obliged to declare how they include sustainability issues in their investment screening and overall investment policy. Since January 2002 there has been a similar law in Germany. Private pensions funds and retirement provisions have to disclose the extent—if at all—to which social, environmental or ethical considerations are taken into account in the selection of investments. In addition, NGOs already advocate that the EU should ensure that EU-wide pension funds are also required to disclose how they consider sustainability issues in their investment strategies (EEB *et al.* 2001: 49). This development, as well as recent surveys (e.g. Bartolomeo and Daga 2002), shows that SRI is an increasing and worthwhile business field in international financial markets. Financial institutions have to recognise this increased demand and should take sustainability issues into account in asset management and investment banking.

The role financial institutions play is often, but should not be, underestimated. They have the potential to promote new business practices, products and services that enable them to contribute toward companies' sustainable performance. Their huge influence on companies gives them the unique possibility to enforce overall sustainable development. However, reaching this vision still requires a great deal of research to set up and enhance accurate information tools as well as reliable analysis and assessment instruments.

The examples in the following chapters give a comprehensive account of current best practice and show that banks and insurance companies derive definite economic advantages from striving for environmental and social objectives. These financial institutions examine issues in ways fundamentally different from more conventional approaches. They have a broader perspective of how effectively sustainable strategies can be linked to profitability and a sharper insight into the relationships between economic development and ecological and ethical performance.

20
The challenge of sustainability for financial institutions*

Paul Clements-Hunt
Head of Unit, UNEP Finance Initiatives, Switzerland

In late June 2002 a group of some 70 finance executives, government representatives and members of broader civil society cruised the Danube on a glorious evening blessed by a golden mid-summer dusk. The grand riverside buildings reflecting the historical mercantile wealth of Budapest and the floodlit marvel of the new Hungarian capital theatre were a superb setting for what was a concluding chapter in a 15-month-long global exploration of the role of the finance sector in supporting environmental management and sustainability. The Danube cruise came at the end of a two-day conference for financial institutions from countries with economies in transition.

The Budapest meeting on 24–25 June finalised a 'global dialogue' undertaken by the United Nations Environmental Programme Finance Initiatives (UNEP FI), a unique public–private partnership between UNEP and some 290 financial institutions, between April 2001 and June 2002. In that period a series of regional outreach conferences were held for financial institutions in Asia–Pacific, North America, Latin America and the Caribbean, Africa and the concluding meeting for the transition economies. Midway through the conference series a global roundtable was held in March 2002 in Rio de Janeiro, Brazil, for some 300 participants. Along with the regional conference series, the Rio Roundtable—symbolically returning after a decade to the city of the 1992 Earth Summit—was a critical step preparing the finance sector contribution for the World Summit for Sustainable Development (WSSD) that took place in South Africa in late August 2003.

* This chapter draws from the UNEP FI report for WSSD. Particular thanks go to report authors Tessa Tennant, ASrIA; Sarita Bartlett, Storebrand; Takejiro Sueyoshi, Nikko Asset Management; Walter Jacobi, Gerling Group; Jan Pieter Six, Interpolis; Andrew Dlugolecki, Andlug Consulting; Marcel Jeucken, Rabobank; Iris Gold, Citigroup; and Franz Knecht, Connexis.

The emerging challenges and opportunities of sustainability for the finance sector

The 'end of bull market' scandals raging around the business world and the finance sector have catalysed an intense examination of the way in which the mechanisms of corporate governance, public trading of companies and the accounting practices that underpin our modern markets interact. Since mid-2002 legislative, regulatory and voluntary disciplines guiding corporations, as well as capital and investment markets, have come under intense scrutiny and, almost certainly, will be subject to a major overhaul. Recent legislative changes in the USA overseeing new disciplines for accounting, corporate accountability and the public trading of companies confirm this.

Out of crisis comes opportunity: there is now a rich opportunity in which the benefits of sustainability thinking and action, as both a powerful risk management approach and a predictor of new commercial opportunities, can be fully integrated into corporate governance disciplines. The environmental and social considerations within sustainable development, just as much as the economic ones, must be built into the fabric of corporate governance and the workings of our capital markets and accounting practices.

The finance sector—lending, insurance and asset management communities—should be at the forefront of efforts to ensure that a sustainable development approach, respecting the 'people, planet, prosperity' ethic, provides the foundation stone on which the emerging corporate governance disciplines are based. The UN Secretary General's Global Compact provides an excellent benchmark for the issues that must be driven to the centre of the corporate citizenship debate.

When viewed through a governance lens, the question of how a financial institution moves from eco-efficiency to sustainability is relatively straightforward. If a sustainability approach is built into a financial institution's governance structure and both its management and compliance mechanisms are effective, then a sustainable development ethos, in time, will permeate the institution.

The current reality for the finance sector, and for broader business in general, is that sustainability thinking does not form an integral part of corporate or capital market governance, and this makes the shift from being an eco-efficient institution to a sustainability leader more complicated. UNEP FI believes that governments, business and civil society must work together to change this and to ensure that sustainability is the platform on which modern finance, markets and business are based.

As mentioned above, in 2001–2002 UNEP initiated a global conference series for the finance sector. The purpose of the series was to explore where the banking, insurance and asset management communities, in different parts of the world, stand on the issues of environmental management and sustainability prior to WSSD. It was in the midst of the UNEP conference series that the current brace of corporate, accounting and financial scandals began to unfold and this worked to promote a rich and intense dialogue during the meetings in Asia–Pacific, Latin America and the Caribbean, Africa and the transition economies. The role of sustainability thinking as a foundation for corporate governance was thrust to the centre of the global dialogue between UNEP, the finance sector and a broad array of interested stakeholders.

A series of key findings with respect to the interplay between the finance sector, environmental management and broader sustainability issues emerged during the conference series. The emergence of sustainability as a real issue for the most progressive boardrooms of leading banks, insurance and asset management companies came against a background of dramatic overall transition for the sector as a whole.

Discussions during the UNEP FI global conference series reinforced the fact that the scale, pace and depth of change for the finance sector during the 1990s has been staggering and that the challenges and opportunities presented by sustainability are part of that change. In Manila, New York, Santiago, Midrand, Rio de Janeiro, Belgrade and Budapest, participants in the UNEP FI conferences described how the decade of the 1990s saw the globalisation of financial markets, the emergence of giant 'one-stop-shop' bank-assurance institutions, and system-rattling crises in Asia–Pacific and Russia. Nor was it just regions and countries that created unimaginable shocks for the financial system. The fall, in 1998, of Long-Term Capital Management, a US-based hedge fund which leveraged its way to USD 1 trillion of exposure, sent a powerful warning highlighting the age-old unpredictability of risk to investing institutions. The global information technology (IT) revolution gave us online banking and e-banks and provided access to the type of instant market and corporate information—not always trustworthy—that turned small-time investors into 'day traders'. The most rewarding bull market in history ended as hubris turned to nemesis for many dot.com investors. Questions concerning the role of the financial community with respect to, among others, the Enron, Anderson, Tyco and WorldCom scandals remain to be answered.

In the 1990s many of the largest banking and insurance institutions, serving saturated and highly competitive markets in the industrialised countries where profit margins were tightening, explored new opportunities in emerging economies. Mergers, acquisitions and joint ventures were all the rage as Australasian, European, North American and Japanese financial institutions jostled to establish brand and market presence in industrialising Asia–Pacific, the transition economies, Latin America and to a lesser extent Africa.

Through all of this upheaval in the first post-Cold War decade, the finance sector woke up to, and started acting on, its environmental and broader sustainability responsibilities. The 2001–2002 UNEP FI global meeting series allowed an in-depth, world-roving exploration of how financial institutions are playing their part—or failing to—in the development of responsible capitalism that respects the ideals behind the 'people, planet, prosperity' ethic.

Several broad findings emerged from the global UNEP–finance sector dialogue. These include:

- Institutions within the finance sector worldwide represent a vast spectrum in understanding, learning and implementation with respect to eco-efficiency, environmental and sustainability management. A significant number of companies remain at the very earliest stages of their environmental management journey while a few of the most progressive institutions are tackling the complexities associated with implementing best-practice approaches for corporate citizenship.

- Global capital markets and the mechanisms which support them, such as securities and exchange commissions, are taking—only now—their first tentative steps to address environmental and sustainability questions.

- Distinct challenges remain for eco-efficiency, environmental management and sustainability to be taken mainstream within financial institutions. In many institutions, executives promoting better environmental management and sustainability thinking remain far removed from key decision-makers at the top.

- Where a financial institution has energetically engaged in a sustainability approach this is often driven, sometimes for a short period only, by champions whose influence does not always outlast their tenure.

- Where institutions have effectively integrated environmental management and sustainability thinking into their operations—including many of the leading supporters of UNEP FI—real benefits are being realised in cost savings, higher appreciation of a broader range of socioeconomic and environmental risks and new ways of 'seeing' commercial opportunities. Among the most progressive financial institutions a sustainability approach is recognised as a powerful addition to traditional risk management approaches and a cutting-edge way of achieving new competitive advantages.

- The 'take-up' among financial institutions in using sustainability thinking to identify and realise new business opportunities is limited. The power of sustainability approaches to deliver top-line business and to yield new commercial opportunities is not, generally, appreciated across the finance sector.

- Sustainability entrepreneurs face a difficult task in their capital-raising efforts and many mainstream institutional investors remain wary of sustainability-based business models.

- Critically, the industry must develop products and services to deal with new risks including climate change, depletion of resources, excessive inequality and technological risks created through biotechnology and sub-molecular chemistry.

Further to these broad issues identified during the global dialogue, the finance sector faces a challenge—a conundrum might be a more appropriate term—peculiar to its own seemingly pervasive influence on global and national economies, business sectors, companies and the capital markets that support them.

What is the nature of this challenge? Finance is at the heart of all commercial and industrial activity and, for casual observers, it would seem that the world of finance is supremely placed to influence corporate and institutional clients' behaviour on environment and sustainability. Not so, say many financial institutions, arguing that 'we are in a ferociously competitive industry where our ability to set rigorous conditions on our products and services is limited'. In effect, financial institutions claim, we can police our own internal environmental behaviour and create new financial services and products to support nascent sustainability markets, but the extent to which we can influence our public- and private-sector clients is limited by the highly competitive nature of finance. In short, the finance sector argues: 'We cannot play—and should not be expected to play—a role as an environmental and sustainability policeman.'

For good or for bad, this argument will not suffice as the role of the finance sector, in ensuring globalisation benefits all, in addressing pressing environmental challenges, in tackling worldwide inequity and in dealing with the sector's governance challenges, falls under an intensifying spotlight. The finance sector must become a leader in collective efforts to achieve the targets set out in the Millennium Development Goals (MDGs). Recognising sustainability as the platform for finance-sector governance will be a powerful driver to accelerate the sector's positive role in efforts to realise them.

The role, influence and responsibilities of the finance sector in all aspects of our market system will be brought into question by the media and civil society as never before. The intensity of this questioning will vary, certainly, but the inquisition trend will be upward as the inequalities in the global market and financial system are better understood and given the oxygen of publicity. Every time a major scandal on Wall Street, in the City of London, in Frankfurt or in Tokyo comes to the fore, the interest of opinion-formers, regulators and the engaged elements of the public in OECD countries will be piqued. What is the finance sector doing to deal with environmental degradation, poverty (one of the most vicious environmental toxins), corruption and human rights issues worldwide? This question will not disappear and is not one the finance sector can sidestep. For individual companies in banking, insurance and asset management this challenge will become increasingly difficult as we work deeper into the early years of the new century.

The critical challenge for finance is to ensure that in both perception and actual delivery it is seen as a 'force for good', promoting global sustainability, and not a 'force for bad', placing a brake on the drive to a sustainable development pathway.

Where are we now? Again, the UNEP FI global conference series with the finance sector confirms that, for the mainstream financial community, all things with an environmental or sustainability flavour remain a distinctly acquired taste. It is true that some of the most progressive institutions, many playing a leading role in UNEP FI,[1] are taking significant environmental and sustainability-promoting steps within the core of their operations. However, for the majority of the institutions feeding on investment activity tied up in the world's capital markets and as a result of the deregulation, liberalisation and privatisation that pushes back commercial and financial borders, the prospects of 'carbon lite' industries, a hydrogen economy, or sustainably managed businesses do little to get the corporate pulse racing faster. Quite simply, there are easier ways to make short-term gains than through sustainable development.

1 www.unepfi.net

20. The challenge of sustainability for financial institutions   Clements-Hunt

The raft of international environmental conventions, covering biodiversity, climate change, desertification and persistent organic pollutants, which have become the key foundation of intergovernmental negotiations on the environment during the 1990s, have sparked intense interest among multinational manufacturing companies where policy and regulatory changes may impact core business. For the finance sector, however, intergovernmental deliberations on global warming, biosafety, hazardous wastes, species under threat and ozone-layer depletion will only grab mainstream attention if a tangible commercial risk or a clearly bankable sustainability opportunity—all too rare—emerges. For the insurance and reinsurance sectors the pressing threat of global warming and the commercial liabilities it will pose are creating a deepening interest in the climate change debate, but for finance-sector involvement in environmental issues this remains the exception not the rule.

In short, the sustainability movement's impact on the mainstream banking, insurance, investment and asset management community worldwide is limited. Sustainability issues are just about on the radar screens of the institutions making up the infrastructure of capital markets and, at the other end of the investment spectrum, any budding environmental entrepreneur has a Herculean task to attract private equity interest.

Deutsche Bank chairs the UNEP FI. Writing in the UNEP finance and insurance sector report for WSSD (UNEP FI 2002) Dr Rolf E. Breuer, former spokesman for the Board of Managing Directors of Deutsche Bank, stated:

> In 1992, the Rio Earth Summit outlined the guiding principles for sustainable development that today—ten years later, and in light of the perspective gained from the advances of globalisation—are of ever greater importance. For future-oriented businesses, and especially active members of UNEP, it is clear that a singular focus on economic success is no longer sufficient to ensure long-term, enduring development.
>
> Since Rio, approximately 190 banks have committed themselves to the 'UNEP Statement by Banks on the Environment and Sustainable Development.' Today, an ever-increasing number of sustainability-relevant criteria have become part of the evaluation process in a variety of financial transactions—be it in investment management or project finance. Moreover, many corporations have recognised their responsibility to the community in this area and have begun to understand sustainable development as a fundamental part of corporate citizenship.
>
> Globalisation requires, however, an increasing willingness within the financial industry to actively encourage sustainable development. The challenge faced is spelled out in the preamble of Agenda 21, which calls for 'The elimination of abject poverty and the long-term preservation of our ecosystems.' This challenge can only be met together, through solution-oriented dialogue and the cooperation between businesses, governments and every part of society.

The UNEP FI 2001–2002 conference series did confirm that the direct, internal challenges of environmental management for the finance sector are manageable if the right combination of board-level vision and will, sound planning and systemisation, and the dedicated resources to drive eco-efficiency throughout an institution are committed. UNEP and its private-sector financial partners are working to provide practical tools to promote the adoption of environmental and sustainability best practice. For example, a UNEP FI group is working to finalise an international set of guidelines on environmental management and reporting, allowing any financial institution, anywhere in the world, to take direct steps to address its environmental challenges. These sectoral guidelines, complementing broader systems such as the international EMS ISO 14001 standard, provide the framework in which any institution serious about its environmental performance can take positive action based on practical guidance. The UNEP FI guidelines, engineered to serve a truly global perspective, build on the ground-breaking work of FORGE (FORGE 2002), a working group in the British Insurance Association, and the environmental performance indicators (EPIs) of the Swiss-German banking community (EPI Finance 2000).

Additionally, UNEP FI has co-convened with the Global Reporting Initiative (GRI) a multi-stakeholder group to create a set of finance-sector environmental indicators. This working group hopes to conclude its work and publish the indicator set by mid-2004. These initiatives, providing practical guidance on how an institution can implement key steps toward an eco-efficient approach based on sound environmental management, must now be driven through tens of thousands of financial institutions worldwide in the coming decade if the scaling-up of sustainability is to be achieved in this critical sector. The utilisation of sustainability as the platform on which new approaches to finance-sector governance are based would accelerate the adoption and acceptance of higher environmental standards throughout the banking, insurance and investment communities.

Writing in the UNEP finance and insurance sector report for WSSD (UNEP FI 2002), Dr Jürgen Zech, former Chairman of the Board and CEO, Gerling Group, stated:

> For Gerling, the UNEP Insurance Industry Initiative has been a cornerstone of our public commitment to sustainable development and the environment. It has been, and will continue to be, very helpful in raising awareness among both the public and the financial community. Gerling is proud to be a founding member of this unique partnership between an intergovernmental organisation and the private sector. We are honoured to host the annual conference in 1998 at our headquarters offices in Cologne, Germany and that we have had the opportunity to chair the Initiative's Steering Committee over the past years.
>
> The UNEP Finance Initiatives need, however, to continue to evolve. The recent developments in an increasingly interlinked global financial market, as well as the rise of complex and potentially devastating natural disasters, call for universally responsible and future-oriented risk managers. It is our firm belief that sustainable development is the only long-term process to date able to address global concerns in terms of social equity, environmental justice and economic development. Ignoring any of those factors will be contributing to conflicts and may trigger frustration as well as aggression.
>
> The Johannesburg Summit 2002 has to be a turning point in our understanding of multilateral action on global challenges. We need

a ratified Kyoto Protocol, a renewal of the commitments made in Rio and concrete action. It is unacceptable that the official development assistance has shrunk over recent years, falling short of the goal of 0.7% of industrialised nations' GDP.

A sustainable 21st century only seems possible if we leave behind our traditional ways of thinking. We need to get out of our boxes, with 'evil' multinational companies on one side and 'good' multi-governmental regulatory bodies on the other side. I am convinced that a new world order will need a new multi-stakeholder dialogue plus a mechanism to unleash creative thinking and trust-building steps toward a better future. We stand prepared to work with customers, governments, the UN, our competitors and non-governmental organisations to help shape a more robust, and economically, socially as well as environmentally responsible and just society. As risk managers, we at Gerling have begun to work toward this end. We take our mission statement seriously that our ultimate aim is 'to work in harmony with creation, for the good of man and nature.' In my opinion we cannot afford to fail.

However, despite the steps an institution can take to put its internal house in order, it is the role and responsibilities of financial institutions with respect to their external impacts—via credit for business, corporate and project finance, company shareholdings, insurance and reinsurance products, etc.—that create the most pressing challenge and are at the heart of the finance sector's sustainability conundrum. Without addressing the external impact of its operations and activities, a financial institution lays itself open to the charge that it is not 'walking the talk'.

Because of their intermediary role in economies, the role of lending, insurance and investment institutions in contributing to sustainable development is potentially enormous. In order to take advantage of this potential, the lending sector must continue to come up with innovative financing solutions that are designed to deal with a variety of economic risks and financial requirements, and integrate a range of sustainability factors and divergent stakeholder expectations. Can the fertile minds that have created ever more intricate forecasting models, new approaches to derivative trading and complex hedging strategies fail to think up innovative ways of making the financial business a positive driving force for sustainable development?

Despite the formidable tasks ahead to mainstream sustainability in the financial community and to take it into the heart of our capital market considerations, a range of initiatives and challenges are now emerging that will promote sustainability thinking throughout the finance sector. The next section will highlight several promising developments.

Socially responsible investment (SRI)

The area of SRI has grown exponentially in Europe, Japan and North America in the late 1990s and we are now seeing the first indications of SRI approaches being taken into emerging and transition economies. The Johannesburg Stock Exchange (JSE) marked itself as a leader among emerging-economy capital markets when it launched an SRI index. We are now witnessing the results of innovative work undertaken by a group of visionary investment executives—often working against the mainstream—that has been under way since the 1970s. Already in 1992, in a letter to the Secretary-General of the Rio Earth Summit, the international social investment community described the role of investment in achieving sustainable development as follows:

> Social investors are at the forefront of developing methodologies for the assessment of corporate performance from an environmental and social perspective. This analysis is the bedrock from which companies can evaluate and adjust their activities in relation to environmental and cultural priorities. Such analysis deserves wider recognition as a key mechanism by which sustainability can be achieved (UKSIF 1992).

Today the development of SRI is well advanced in North American and European markets but some major challenges remain. Though SRI has reached the mainstream financial institutions, in most cases its tools and techniques are still segregated from mainstream asset management. What falls under the label SRI may not be a contribution to what most people would consider sustainable finance: for example, shares in alcohol or weapons manufacturers. Moreover, the gap between the financial sector in OECD countries and in the developing world, in awareness of sustainability issues and the capacity to address them, is enormous. All efforts must be made to allow financial institutions in the South to leapfrog to the standards of the most progressive players in the field.

An example of an innovative SRI initiative serving the developing economies of Asia–Pacific is the Hong Kong-based Association for Socially Responsible Investment in Asia (ASrIA), a not-for-profit members association set up to promote SRI in Asian capital markets. After the dramatic crash in 1998 of financial markets in the Asian tiger economies, there was some nascent sustainability action in the region's then, seemingly, irrepressible capital markets. For example, the Stock Exchange of Thailand, following work by the Thai Securities Analysts Association and several Bangkok-based mutual fund management concerns, introduced some limited environmental criteria for Initial Public Offerings coming to the market. Despite the market downturn across the region, however, it appears that an SRI seed, planted following the dark days of 1997–98, took hold and is now firmly rooted. ASrIA now boasts over 60 founding members and is looking to increase its network in 2002.

Tessa Tennant, a founder of ASrIA and a driving force within UNEP FI from its earliest days, explains:

> The Asian market meltdown in 1997 has prompted many institutional investors to become more active in demanding equal rights as minority shareholders, calling for an end to cronyism and greater independence of board directors. Building on the success of the first year, ASrIA aims to increase momentum for sustainable investment by: raising awareness and providing information; facilitating the provision of high quality SRI products and services; driving the development of policies both within the financial and public sectors;

and developing an outreach programme to educate the investment industry in SRI techniques and practices (DresdnerKleinwortWasserstein 2003).

Globally, the emergence of sustainability indices, such as the DJSI and the recently launched FTSE4Good, heralds the start of a process by which SRI will increasingly be seen as part of mainstream investment options.

As noted, SRI has experienced strong growth in the number of funds under management over the last decade as well as in the number and types of SRI products offered. Today, investors can choose from a menu of SRI products that includes negatively screened, positively screened, best-in-class, stakeholder activism and engagement-based portfolios, SRI index-based portfolios, country and regional funds, sector funds, SRI venture capital products, and SRI bond funds. Several asset managers have implemented SRI criteria on real estate portfolios as well.

In future we can expect to see more products focusing on the specific interests of individuals or investor groups and an increase in passive SRI fund products based on the development of a common, more comprehensive global SRI index.

Dedicated sustainability funds for water

In addition to SRI other positive developments are emerging in the investment community.

In September 2001, the Zürich-based independent asset management company Sustainable Asset Management (SAM) launched a Sustainable Water Fund. This targeted investment fund, which allows a portfolio approach to water finance, was created in order to respond to trends facing the sector and to provide a vehicle for diversified investment targeted at companies practising sustainable management by 'adding value in environmental and social as well as economic terms' (SAM 2001). The fund focuses investment in four segments of the industry: distribution and management; advanced water treatment; demand-side efficiency; and water and food. Its scope is wider than many water investment approaches to date.

A joint UNEP–World Bank–International Monetary Fund report (UNEP *et al.* 2002) on financing for sustainable development presented to WSSD describes the SAM water fund approach:

> While the portfolio of investments is largely focused on the developed world, inclusion in the fund will identify those multinational companies operating in distribution and management and advanced water treatment who are deemed by the fund to be operating a sustainable business. Additionally, the fund manager can influence private sector investment in Less Developed Countries (LDCs) by valuing such investment highly in assessing sustainable business practice. In doing so, the fund may lead other global water companies to pursue investment in LDCs and emerging markets.

Financing biodiversity protection

At the other end of the investment spectrum, small, start-up or mezzanine-level biodiversity businesses are not likely to attract strong private equity interest unless they are that all-too-rare creature, the 'sure bet for a quick venture capital killing'. If a business is an African biodiversity-related start-up, its prospects of attracting investor backing are almost non-existent. This is exactly the situation that an innovative programme created by a partnership between the International Union for Conservation of Nature and Natural Resources (IUCN) and the International Finance Corporation (IFC), the private-sector arm of the World Bank Group, has been set up to address. The mission of the Kijani project is to 'promote African biodiversity business'.

The Kijani approach seeks to assist through pre-investment technical assistance for bio-entrepreneurs and private investments in viable biodiversity businesses. Kijani's technical assistance has three basic steps: first, it identifies potential medium-sized bio-business projects; second, it develops triple-bottom-line business plans; and, third, it seeks to connect African bio-entrepreneurs to experts, partners, investors and customers.

The scope of the Kijani fund is to provide private equity and debt finance facilities in the USD0.5–USD10 million investment range with a term of seven to ten years. Sample Kijani projects presented at the UNEP FI Africa conference in Midrand, South Africa (28–30 January 2002) covered eco-tourism, low-intensity shrimp farming, organic tea manufacture and organic fertiliser production.

In addition to an increasing range of initiatives such as ASrIA, the SAM Water Fund and Kijani, which all aim to bring sustainability into the heart of investment decision-making and the operations of capital markets, a range of political, economic, social and technological developments are converging which, increasingly, will ensure the investment community will mainstream sustainability concerns. The wiring-together of the world's capital markets, greater shareholder advocacy by both institutional and individual investors concerned about corporate governance issues, and building hard evidence correlating sound sustainability practices with better investment performance will all act to persuade the mainstream asset management community and the markets in general to adopt and adapt sustainability to their specific needs.

Insurance

Insurance losses from environmental risks have risen sharply in recent decades. Many of the sources of damage are not 'natural' but are related to patterns of development and behaviour. This will be compounded by new challenges in future climate change, resource depletion, excessive inequality, and fresh technological advances.

To manage increases or uncertainty in risk, traditional insurance strategies can only extend so far before the availability of insurance is inadequate to meet the needs of the victims. Already, as much as 80% of the global economic damage from natural events is not remedied through insurance but has to be borne by the victims or alleviated with ad hoc disaster relief. This indicates that a radical rethink is needed to ensure that the approach to managing environmental perils involves all the stakeholders in a way that improves overall efficiency.

The insurance industry response must extend far beyond the traditional underwriting area, into the comprehensive adoption of environmental management systems that ensure the application of sustainability principles to all business processes.

Storebrand chairs the UNEP Insurance Industry Initiative. Writing in the UNEP finance and insurance sector report (UNEP FI 2002) for WSSD, Idar Kreutzer, President and Chief Executive Officer, Storebrand Group, stated:

> All of us who are engaged in asset management, banking, and insurance want a better life for the people we care about: our family, our colleagues, our clients, and our business communities. Less obvious, perhaps, is that we also care about many other constituencies and we take their interests into consideration in how we conduct business. As business leaders, we all want a strong economy, safety in peace, widespread prosperity, and to conserve nature as we know it. That is what corporate social responsibility is all about—seeking to promote these values in our day-to-day business. That is what we mean by sustainable development. We recognise the importance of conducting business in ways that foster environmental protection and social well-being in its largest sense, in addition to creating competitive returns for our shareholders.
>
> We are agreed on the aspiration, but we also know that achieving this is certainly not easy and there are no automatic answers. Like everything else in business, objectives have to be clearly defined, targets must be set, and activities have to be managed in the midst of surprises, unexpected events and constrained resources. Technically speaking, and in financial terms, this translates into reducing risk, securing stable returns over time, developing new forms of insurance and portfolio management, searching for opportunities, being creative, and learning how to integrate environmental and social criteria into financial management, while earning satisfactory returns on investment.
>
> The purpose of the UNEP Insurance Industry Initiative (III), which Storebrand is proud to Chair, is precisely to create a forum for banks, insurance and asset management companies to learn from each other and stimulate each other in pursuing these goals. Our many working groups (including Asset Management, Climate Change, and Environmental Reporting) seek to develop best practices in these areas. We believe there is much to be done in developing pragmatic and effective cooperation between the private sector and the public sector. UNEP III seeks to help make that happen. Our initiative is purely voluntary, but we are not opposed to intelligent regulations that promote sustainable development. This report, by setting forth experiences from representative companies in our initiative, seeks to share with you, the broad interested public at the Johannesburg Summit 2002, what we are doing and hope to achieve.

Lending

Despite being slower to respond to the new challenges presented by sustainability, there is growing awareness in the lending sector that the environment brings both risks and opportunities. Currently, sustainability-related risks are not adequately addressed by the lending sector, as the direct risk assessment method generally used does not take into consideration such things as the environmental clean-up costs of contamination or the labour or human rights standards of suppliers.

Except in the USA, where banks can be held directly responsible for the environmental pollution of their clients and be obliged to pay remediation costs, the focus has been on the development of new products such as environmentally friendly investment funds, instead of on assessing risk.

Despite the lack of attention to dealing with the calculation of risk, addressing sustainability issues is not just a matter of more accurate mathematics. Instead, the solutions must come from within—from the organic development of business standards, accepted best practices and the tools used every day.

Conclusions

To achieve the goals of sustainable development, companies must clarify their economic, environmental and social activities and disclose them to improve transparency. Accordingly, the fiduciary authorities should help to promote disclosure of corporate socially responsible activities among public companies. In principle, companies not committed to disclosure standards should not be targets for investment.

To aid in transparency, governments should provide guidance for disclosure, including the adoption of environmental reporting requirements for initial public offerings and publicly listed companies. In addition, there should be consideration of systemising the publication of sustainability reports. Governments should also follow the example of the handful of European countries leading the way with pension fund disclosure requirements. Continued work on setting standards for environmental and social activities including the introduction of environmental and social criteria for all pension funds, life insurance funds, and government-controlled funds will help to ensure sustainability.

Rating and auditing agencies must also do their bit. Rating agencies must evaluate the environmental and social risks inherent to a company's business activities, not just financial performance when issuing credit ratings. To ensure that company statements are accurate, inspection agencies will need to be created. For this purpose, it is necessary to strengthen the GRI. The reporting style of sustainability and environmental reports must become as universally common as financial reports. International standards must be set for those areas that can be measured quantitatively with methods such as environmental accounting.

The tasks ahead of the finance and insurance community in the years following the Johannesburg WSSD, to move toward full sustainability, will be formidable. It is likely that the finance sector will come under increasing scrutiny from the NGO community, concerned investors and regulatory authorities with respect to the broad social and environmental impacts of their operations.

Portfolio-, project- and technology-focused investment is likely to be examined in greater detail as governance, transparency and disclosure disciplines tighten across the global economy.

The finance sector has a challenging road ahead as it positions itself to be recognised as a foundation block of a sustainable society. Firmly establishing sustainability as the platform on which new governance protocols for the finance sector are developed will smooth and speed this difficult process.

21
Sustainability: the new paradigm in value-based corporate management

Hanns Michael Hoelz
Global Head of Sustainable Development, Deutsche Bank

Many companies may feel that their competitive position will be threatened if they place greater importance on sustainability aspects. Others may possibly see a competitive advantage to be gained by investing in countries with low environmental and social standards. What is needed, however, is a new way of thinking, because a continuous and forward-looking approach to sustainability will increase a company's value and secure this value on a long-term basis.

The Deutsche Bank sustainability concept

In harmony with the guiding principle of sustainability
Sustainability as a synergy of economics, ecology and social commitment has played a major role within Deutsche Bank for over ten years.[1] We understand the term 'sustainability' to mean forward-looking, future-oriented action. The goal is to pass on a healthy environment as well as stable economic and social relationships to coming generations. For us, ecology, economics and social responsibility are inseparable.

---

1   Deutsche Bank at www.environment.deutsche-bank.com.

Acting in harmony with the guiding principle of sustainability is a multi-level task that cuts across organisational lines and has significant benefits. Some examples include:

- We advise business customers in the use of new technologies, on how to benefit from state funding for environmental investments and how to manage operational environmental risks. Among other services, we offer individual customers the opportunity to invest in alternative energy funds set up by DWS Investments.[2]

- Our employees are our most valuable assets. Creating environmentally friendly working conditions for them, promoting their professional advancement and supporting them in their social commitment are important goals of our human resources policy.

- Sustainability as a guiding principle is rewarded by the international stock exchanges, has a positive impact on stock prices and thus increases shareholder value. Our active commitment in the area of sustainability is regularly evaluated by independent rating and research companies. We have been listed in the DJSI[3] and the FTSE4Good Indices[4] since their foundation.

- As an enterprise with global social responsibility, we co-operate on a worldwide basis with internationally recognised partners such as UNEP, the World Bank, and the WBCSD. Such co-operation has a long history, including pioneer work as the first bank to take part in 'debt for nature swaps' in 1988 in Sudan and Madagascar. These swaps made it possible to realise numerous regional environmental projects.

Sustainability as a management challenge

We view sustainability as an all-encompassing topic, which we position accordingly within the corporate group. It is the direct responsibility of the group's senior management, a level where the primary concerns focus on strategic considerations and group development. For us, the integration and implementation of the sustainability concept is a management responsibility. This responsibility rests with various members of the board. Social issues are the responsibility of board members charged with the core business of the bank in the corresponding region. Two members of the board have direct responsibility for the area of environmental issues. Control and/or cross-organisational functions are performed by the Environmental Committee, the Sustainability and Environmental Co-ordination Department, the Group Compliance Officer for the Environmental Management System, the Operating Environmental Protection Department and the Central Environmental Protection Officer.

---

2 www.dws.de
3 www.sustainability-index.com
4 www.ftse4good.com

Financing concepts and the sustainability model

Environmental considerations are key factors in granting loans

The bank's credit policy, which is continuously monitored, states that Deutsche Bank will not participate in financing projects that in its opinion significantly endanger the environment. That includes an examination of the strategic importance of environmental protection and/or environmental risks—for example, possible residual pollution—and these considerations are fully integrated into the analysis process.

Environmentally relevant aspects are also regularly taken into consideration when Deutsche Bank is engaged in financing a customer's export business or cross-border investments. This approach assists in meeting risk management requirements as well as the requirements of government export insurance and environmental standards in the country that will receive the exports or where the investment will be made.

Deutsche Bank organises seminars, workshops and presentations that review environmentally relevant subjects in order to enable Deutsche Bank employees to make competent evaluations of potential environmental dangers. In addition, the in-house newspaper FORUM and Intranet and Internet sites help to communicate the latest information and know-how.

Environmental balance in project finance

Project finance is subject to a large number of decision factors that weigh the opportunities and risks of the project against each other. Economic considerations are always supplemented by an examination of environmental compatibility. Environmental due diligence ensures that the project is in harmony with

- Our environmental principles
- The guidelines of international organisations: for example, the World Bank
- The applicable laws and regulations

The initial step includes an assessment made by bank employees. If considerable environmental risks are noted in this early phase, independent external experts are then brought in to conduct a more specific analysis. This examination of environ-

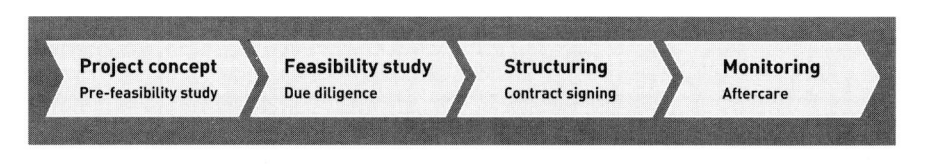

Project concept	Feasibility study	Structuring	Monitoring
Pre-feasibility study	Due diligence	Contract signing	Aftercare

Figure 21.1 Flow chart of a project finance deal

mental risk frequently takes place within the framework of the overall due diligence for the project.

We also review expert opinions submitted by the project partner. This is done either by independent experts or by our internal Technical Support Group. Technical Support Group specialists will also conduct an additional expert study if deemed necessary. Within these reviews, special attention is given to looking ahead to 'tomorrow's legislation': for example, even during the planning phase of a plant, requirements for future upgrading or expansion must be taken into consideration.

This careful, forward-looking examination represents an added value for our customers and our bank. Risks are reduced for both parties and opportunities are realised.

New concepts for municipal environmental protection tasks

Deutsche Bank has formed special marketing and sales units to support investments within the public sector. These units include both banking professionals and experts with public administration experience. The goal is to save municipalities costs while involving all specialised players needed to realise the project and generate an efficient partnership. This can include bringing municipalities into contact with providers of environmental protection technologies, operator companies or auditors.

Deutsche Kommunalinvest GmbH—a subsidiary of Deutsche Bank enterprise Deutsche Immobilien-Leasing GmbH—developed, in co-operation with an engineering firm, a total concept for an environmentally friendly rubbish-tip cover. This innovation achieved cost savings of 30-40% in comparison with conventional procedures.

Another concept, called 'user transference model', offers municipalities solutions they can employ for various problems such as removing asbestos from schools.

Advisory services and the sustainability model

We view our relationships with customers as comprehensive and see ourselves as partners not limited to providing just one service. This approach means that we also provide support to customers to help them to identify environment-related opportunities and risks, because environmental protection is also an important element in defining their business policies. As a result, current environmentally relevant topics are being systematically integrated in the spectrum of services and products we offer to corporate and private customers.

The New Energies and Environmental Technology Competence Team

Innovative companies require innovative support. This is why we have created special innovation and competence teams for supporting technology-oriented companies. One of these teams, the New Energies and Environmental Technology Competence Team, concentrates on the renewable energy, water and waste management markets. The composition of the team—scientists and business specialists—ensures detailed market knowledge and technology know-how. This enables the team to speak the customer's language when discussing the company's strategic direction, possible investors, or adequate financing solutions. The team understands customers' demands and problems, works with a network of internal and external industry experts, analyses projects with respect to their marketability and feasibility, develops individual financing concepts, and accompanies companies in all phases of development.

Know-how transfer in environmental audits

In general, small and medium-sized companies do not have their own staff positions for actively dealing with the environmental risks of their operations, nor are they able to draft strategies for solutions when problems arise. We aim to close this know-how and management gap by acting as intermediaries between enterprises and specialised firms in the environmental area.

Concrete examples of assistance provided are:

- Designing and installing an environmental management system that meets the requirements of the EU Eco-Audit regulations now known as the Eco-Management and Audit Scheme (EMAS) and ISO 14001
- Environmental liability insurance with professional damage management
- Organisation check-up for environmental protection
- Environmental due diligence evaluation

Sustainability for investors

Through our subsidiary, Deutsche Immobilien Leasing GmbH, we offer investors opportunities to invest in 'clean' energy wind-park funds. The Deutsche Erneuerbare Energien GmbH was organised to set up additional funds in the area of renewable energies.

In addition, DWS Investment GmbH, a member of Deutsche Bank Group, with its DWS Invest Sustainability Leaders Fund offers the possibility to invest in companies that are recognised for their efforts to integrate economic, environmental and social criteria into their business policies and decisions. Moreover, DWS, with its New Energies Basket 25+ Fund, gives customers the opportunity to participate in projects involving forward-looking energy generation programmes such as wind, water, solar energy and biomass.

As early as 1997, the Panda Renditefonds was set up by DWS in co-operation with World Wide Fund for Nature (WWF) Deutschland. The DWS Panda Renditefonds enables investors to earn attractive yields by acquiring shares to support the WWF, which receives a portion of the issue premium and can thus finance selected nature protection projects. An example of these projects is the preservation of the habitat of forest elephants in Central Africa.

Systematic internal environmental protection

Areas of action

We recognise that sustainability starts at home. We view internal environmental protection and considerations as matters that always demand a comprehensive view. Our activities are concentrated in:

- Facility management
- Purchasing/logistics
- Production systems
- Closed-loop and waste management

We view our efforts as a process that also involves the independently responsible and environmentally aware behaviour of each individual employee. This applies above all to care in dealing with natural resources (water, energy), office supplies and auxiliary material, as well as waste reduction and removal. Deutsche Bank's various internal communications channels inform employees on topics of environmental relevance and create a higher degree of environmental awareness in the office. In new investments, we employ energy and water-conserving techniques and examine whether the use of renewable and energy-saving technologies—for example, a rainwater recycling system—are feasible.

The environmental management system

To systematise activities we installed an environmental management system based on ISO 14001 in 1997. The system was certified in 1999.

ISO 14001 enables firms to receive certification for their processes, which is especially important for companies with a large number of branches. The framework of certification includes an examination not only of the process functions but also of the proof that these processes are being implemented by employees. The examination takes place within a framework of external audits conducted annually at group headquarters and in different branches each year. Additionally, internal audits are performed at Deutsche Bank to measure the status of implementation of goals and programmes. Results are documented in an internal monitoring programme.

Deutsche Bank's environmental management system aims to establish and enhance the role of the environment in the enterprise and increase the bank's environmental performance. Within the framework of the certification process, goals and actions were agreed on for various areas. Internal and external monitoring reviews the achievement and implementation of these actions.

Worldwide partners for sustainability

We want to do our bit to ensure that future generations live in stable economic and social conditions and an intact environment. We therefore view the concept of sustainable development as a guideline for shaping our present activities so that they can be adapted for the future. No individual, enterprise, city or nation can meet this demand on their own. We need national, international and global partners if we are to do justice to this challenge and develop cross-border strategies and solutions. As a corporate citizen with global responsibility, Deutsche Bank is actively involved in international initiatives and organisations such as the UN Global Compact and UNEP, and also supports national initiatives such as *econsense*.

United Nation Global Compact

The concept of a global compact was first presented in January 1999 when Kofi Annan brought it to the World Economic Forum in Davos. It aims to unite economic goals with comprehensive, universal concepts. The Global Compact challenges corporations to adopt universal norms based on nine principles in the areas of human rights, labour and the environment. Within the framework of this initiative, Deutsche Bank formed the Deutsche Bank Commitment to the Global Compact.

Deutsche Bank was one of the first of approximately 40 companies around the world to join the United Nation Global Compact initiative. Moreover, Deutsche Bank is dedicated to fulfilling the principles as well as promoting awareness and encouraging other corporations to make the same commitment. This has included close work with the UN as well as German multinational corporations.

United Nations Environment Programme

UNEP is a contact partner for nations, NGOs and the business community. Beginning in 1992, Deutsche Bank helped to develop the UNEP Statement by Banks on the Environment and Sustainable Development which today represents the recognised environmental code for the financial industry.

Along with other financial institutions, Deutsche Bank belongs to the steering committee of the UNEP banking initiative that recommends how to use the statement for practical application and develops promising ideas and strategies. As an active partner in UNEP, Deutsche Bank supports and advises other financial institutions at an international level in integrating environmental aspects into various areas of banking activity.

Econsense: forum for sustainable development

Econsense is an initiative of leading national and international enterprises and organisations active in the German economy that have integrated the principle of sustainable development into their overall strategy. The goal of the forum, which was established in 2000, is to develop solutions that will encourage a climate for sustainable innovation via dialogue with political institutions. The ultimate goal is practical implementation of the principle of sustainable development. In the foreground of this effort is the balanced consideration of economic, ecological and social policy questions.

Sustainability in concrete projects

Especially in globally active companies, responsibility does not end with the involvement in international organisations. We are convinced that we must take an active part in a broad spectrum of projects to further the overarching goal of sustainable development. This includes not just increasing environmentally sound business practices but also acting to ensure that an increasing number of the world's population can live in peace, prosperity and dignity. We have therefore committed resources to projects such as the Prototype Carbon Fund, microfinance and peace parks, which serve to support sustainability principles around the world and generate practical contributions to resolving environmental and social problems.

Prototype Carbon Fund

An important sustainability project in which Deutsche Bank has invested along with 22 other companies and countries is the World Bank's Prototype Carbon Fund. With a volume of USD180 million, the fund supports projects in Asia, Eastern Europe, Latin America and Africa that contribute to the reduction of greenhouse gases. The emission rights arising from these projects are available to investors. The idea for the fund bases on the Kyoto Protocol, in which 38 industrialised countries agreed to reduce their emissions of greenhouse gases between 2008 and 2012. The Protocol's goal is to reduce emissions in developed countries by an average of 5.2% below 1990 levels.

Microcredit Development Fund

Microcredits in developing countries have proved to be a positive solution-oriented means to put families in a position to provide for themselves and break the cycle of poverty, so the Microcredit Development Fund of Deutsche Bank Americas Foundation makes an important contribution to the development of stable economic structures. Low-interest loans are made to local microfinance institutions, which use the money as collateral receiving at least double the amount in local currency. Microcredits are granted to entrepreneurs who, among other possibilities, use them to build a small business, acquire better equipment, or operate a retail trade.

Peace parks

Artificial borders in Africa increasingly restrict the freedom of movement of native animals; centuries-old trails and migratory routes have been blocked. This is a threat to biodiversity and the animal population. To protect endangered species, which need biologically meaningful territories, nature preserve areas must be developed and extended beyond national borders. These peace parks were so named because peace is the prerequisite for their development and continued existence. The first peace park, the Kgalagadi Transfrontier Park in Botswana and South Africa, opened in May 2000.

The peace parks are based on ideas suggested by Anton Rupert, president of WWF in South Africa and now chairman of the Peace Parks Foundation, and Joaquim Chissanos, president of Mozambique. The concept of the peace parks initiative focuses on

- Preservation of the environment and biological diversity
- Sustainable economic development/creation of jobs
- Regional stability/ensuring of peace

As a consulting and financially supportive partner of peace parks, Deutsche Bank would like to contribute to preserving the diversity of species, to boost the regional economy, and thus offer indigenous populations better opportunities for the future. Patrons of the peace parks include the presidents of Botswana, Namibia, Malawi, Mozambique, South Africa and Zimbabwe and the kings of Lesotho and Swaziland.

Sustainable development is a process that is constantly being redefined. It is one in which a deep sense of responsibility must be combined with optimism about the inventiveness of human beings. It is about striking a balance between the needs of the present and the needs of the future. There is no doubt, however, that the key to success, as in so many of the challenges we face, lies in our ability to work together.

22
Can pension funds drive sustainable development?

Inge Schumacher
UBS Global Asset Management, Socially Responsible Investments, Switzerland

According to the OECD, the 'emergence of institutional investors as the dominant holders of financial assets and as increasingly important participants in capital markets' is 'one of the distinguishing features of the present financial landscape—and one that is likely to become more prominent in the years ahead' (OECD 1999).

The importance of pension funds as institutional investors derives from the extraordinary amounts of capital managed by these organisations. Table 22.1 shows total managed assets in relation to national GDP and their dominance of local markets.

Country	Total equity holding by pensions (billion USD)	Pension investment as % of GDP	Pension investment as % of market capitalisation
France	91.3	6.4	13.5
Germany	103.2	4.8	12.5
Italy	47.9	4.1	13.9
Netherlands	126.0	32.9	26.9
Switzerland	105.8	40.0	18.4
UK	842.7	62.1	12.3
US	3,761.9	45.8	33.7

Table 22.1 Worldwide pension holdings 1998

Source: Monks and Minow 2001: 82

Differences in Table 22.1 are related not only to country size but also to the different national regulations that affect pension funds, since the characteristics of individual social security systems are based in political decisions. Historically, where the state scheme has been particularly generous there has been little need for alternative options. The three-pillar model gives responsibility to the state, employer and employee for payments into the system. The general consensus is that putting equivalent weight on each pillar best protects pension payments.

Despite the enormous and ever-increasing amount of managed assets, social security systems are facing severe problems resulting from negative demographic developments, unemployment and early retirement. Lower birth rates, a later entry into employment markets due to longer education periods and increasing life expectancies have resulted in fewer contributors supporting more pensioners for a longer time. Contributions decrease while expenses increase, calling into question the sustainability of pension systems.

At present, 16% of Western European populations are older than 65, but by 2030 that percentage will have climbed to 25% and to 30% by 2050. The maintenance of present levels of pensions relative to average earnings under such conditions will prove very expensive, if not impossible. According to calculations by PricewaterhouseCoopers, the break-even contribution rate in France will climb from 16% to 28% of pay over the next 50 years, in Germany from 17% to 28% and in Italy from 20% to 46% (Riley 2000).

Facing these burdens, provision systems are confronted with the pressure of operating more professionally in order to better anticipate and fulfil the growing liabilities. At the same time various activities have been initiated to supplement the systems. Occupational and individual pension schemes are promoted in addition to state insurance. The recent German pension reform reflects this development.

When one considers that increasing amounts of private savings are also managed by investment funds, asset allocation for retirement benefits presents an issue. Regulations affect investment policies, either limiting foreign investments, for example, or setting restrictions on equities or alternative assets. Deregulation has opened some of these barriers, but the result has been a somewhat worrying build-up of the equity ratio over the past few years.

Country	Domestic equities	Domestic bonds	Foreign equities	Foreign bonds	Real estate	Cash/ other
Germany	6	71	3	4	13	3
Netherlands	15	47	19	10	7	2
Sweden	20	64	8	0	8	0
Switzerland	10	25	5	7	16	37[a]
UK	53	9	22	6	2	8

[a] includes loans to employer, mortgages and other short-term loans

Table 22.2 Asset allocation of pension funds

Source: Mercer 1998

There are indications that there is an increasing participation of pension funds in socially responsible investments. The following paragraphs try to evaluate how and why pension funds enter into the market. Economic pressure can be a driver if these investments are shown to provide better long-term returns. Despite its trendiness, it is clear that SRI is still emerging as an investment style and that threats and barriers are hindering its development. Activity patterns and arguments allow comparison with active shareholder involvement toward a better corporate governance by pension funds. This debate has been brought to the forefront by respected multinationals on both sides of the Atlantic. So do SRIs allow pension funds better investments and therefore higher returns, in addition to positive effects on society and their own pensioners?

Institutional market of SRIs: figures and outstanding examples

How can pension funds become involved in SRI?

As there is no common definition of SRI, pension funds have different tools for it (see Burgess 2002: 2).

The oldest method is **negative screening**, which involves the exclusion of certain companies or industry sectors on the basis of environmental, social or ethical criteria. The most common set of negative criteria includes policies against investments in companies involved in weapons manufacturing, tobacco or gambling. Some environmental funds go further and exclude complete sectors such as automobile or oil because of their high environmental impacts. This approach can be implemented quite easily, but imposes higher risks from a portfolio management perspective. Although negative screening enables investors to implement their values in their investment decisions, it does not provide any incentives for excluded companies to improve.

Positive screening is applied to construct investment portfolios from companies that have been actively selected on the basis of their strong performance on environmental, social or ethical issues. Screening is either used to construct portfolios out of the best in class of each sector (which might be defined as the top 20% of companies in a given sector) or to define an over- or under-weight compared to a given benchmark. However, as risk considerations provide an obstacle for institutional investors to invest only in a limited—positively screened—investment universe, and, as the rapid growth of SRI might further reduce liquidity for these selected stocks, this weighting strategy might be an alternative for large pension funds seeking to diversify. On the other hand, this approach lacks transparency and credibility as controversial stocks are included in the portfolios. Therefore it is often combined with the **engagement** of investors conducting robust dialogue with boards or management of companies with the aim of altering corporate behaviour in relation to environmental, social or ethical issues. Engagement can either be exercised as dialogue behind closed doors or also by **share-**

holder activism, the exercise of shareholder powers through general 'protest' voting at annual general meetings or the support of SRI-related shareholder resolutions. An initial survey of 2002 shareholder SRI-related resolutions in the USA showed 251 resolutions submitted to companies.[1]

Engagement should be a process in which investors attempt to persuade companies to implement improvements in identified areas, improving lagging companies instead of cherry-picking leaders. It is also suitable for investors adopting passive investment approaches as there is no deviation from a benchmark. It allows investment companies to use their influence as major investors across their whole portfolio (not just an ethical fund segment) to encourage companies to improve their SRI performance (such as Henderson or Friends Ivory & Sime, which also manage pension money). The main concern about engagement is the lack of transparency: a Deloitte & Touche survey in 2000 pointed out that only very few fund managers measure the success of their active engagement (Burges and Osborn-Barker 2000: 4).

Development of SRI market by institutional investors

Compared to a large number of surveys on the retail SRI fund market,[2] fewer figures are available for the institutional market. This is because many pension funds do not invest in public funds but manage their assets independently or in individual portfolios, which are not usually disclosed.[3] Sparkes (2000: 2) describes the amount of retail SRI investments as the tip of an iceberg: 'you can only see 20% of the total—compared to institutional money'. In addition to the GBP3.3 billion in funds in the UK, GBP23.5 billion are managed by churches and charities and GBP25 billion by pension funds according to socioenvironmental criteria. Cerulli calculated the volume of institutional SRI portfolios to be USD1,336 billion, not including the USD14 million by mutual funds (Cerulli 2001: 3). The US Social Investment Forum (SIF 2001) states that 13% of US assets under professionally managed portfolios are socially screened. This figure is questionable, however, because it includes portfolios that apply only one negative criterion, such as the exclusion of tobacco companies. Institutional investor interest in SRI is also reflected by the launch of specific institutional funds. In Switzerland, for example, all relevant asset classes of pension funds are now available with an SRI screening, either in separated funds or a defined asset allocation strategy.[4]

---

1 See Interfaith Center on Corporate Social Responsibility, www.iccr.org.
2 See Cerulli 2001; Ecoreporter.de 2001; and SiRi 2001, which shows dynamic trend of SRI funds: while in 1999, 159 SRI funds were offered in Europe, the number increased to 251 in 2001, while the managed assets increased by 40%.
3 The Social Performance Indicators (SPI)-Finance working group of German and Swiss banks in 2000 developed an indicator, green assets under management, which also includes individual mandates by financial institutions; see www.spi-finance.com.
4 Institutional funds are offered by Ethos (the Swiss Investment Foundation for Sustainable Development), NEST Sammelstiftung, Prevista, Sarasin and UBS.

Examples of pension funds involved in SRI

The most prominent pension funds involved in SRI are located in the USA, the UK and Switzerland. One can identify a certain pattern as most of them are public funds, often representing academics. The potential of their investment capabilities can be enormous, as the California Public Employees' Retirement System (CalPERS)[5] example shows:

> CalPERS grows about USD1 billion every two months, in a year that is more than four times the median market value of a Fortune 500 industrial company, in a year, enough to buy all the common stock of GM with enough left to buy five tankfuls of gasoline for each vehicle it makes (Monks and Minow 2001: 111).

CalPERS is respected for its pioneering role in corporate governance. The company made its first commitment to corporate governance in 1984, and since then has actively engaged companies. At the end of the 1980s, CalPERS published corresponding investment targets and strategies, also referring to its fiduciary obligations. In 1994, CalPERS announced that it would begin factoring labour management relations and other aspects of human resource management and workplace practices into its analysis of company performance in connection with the fund's investment and voting decisions (Brancato 1997: 67). Recently, CalPERS provoked discussions within the SRI community as it announced that it would blacklist four South-East Asian markets (Thailand, the Philippines, Indonesia and Malaysia) on ethical grounds. Tessa Tennant, the representative of the Asian SRI Forum, criticises the ban as she prefers engagement and the backing of proactive companies within these countries (DresdnerKleinwortWasserstein 2003).

TIAA–CREF (Teachers Insurance Annuity Association–College Retirement Equities Fund), the largest US institutional investor, initiated in 1990 a Social Choice Fund to which beneficiaries can specifically channel their investments. In 1993, TIAA–CREF issued the following statement regarding social responsibility: 'TIAA–CREF believes building long-term shareholder value is consistent with directors giving careful consideration to social responsibility issues and the common ground on the community' (Brancato 1997). The board was asked to develop policies and practices on issues such as equal employment or the environmental impact of corporate operations and products. Based on this policy, TIAA–CREF has supported shareholder resolutions on a number of social issues. The fund has also made an effort to communicate directly with management on those issues it deems particularly important. The sheer size of its equity portfolio and the voting power it exercises in a number of corporations results in a degree of influence unattainable by most institutional investors.

The Universities Superannuation Scheme (USS) is one of the largest pension schemes in the UK, with GBP22 billion in assets. Following an SRI commitment by its academic members in November 2000, three people were hired to address SRI issues.[6] In order to obtain scientific background information and strategic advice

---

5   See www.calpers.com.
6   USS has defined the following SIP: 'The trustee pays regard to social, ethical and environmental considerations in the selection, retention and realisation of fund investments to

for its investment strategy, USS started a series of discussion papers to examine the relationship between financial performance on social, environmental, ethical and governance issues and consequent implications for long-term investors. The first paper, 'Climate Change: A Risk Management Challenge for Institutional Investors' (USS 2001), points out investment implications, as institutional investors are uniquely suited to take particular actions. Surveys on the SRI commitment by UK pension funds also mention the pension funds from the British Broadcasting Corporation (BBC), Nottinghamshire County Council, Lancashire County Council and BT as exceptionally engaged (Sturm and Badde 2001).

In Switzerland two players have stimulated the role of pension funds in SRI, above and beyond involvement in corporate governance and public execution of voting rights: the Geneva civil servants' pension fund CIA and the foundation Ethos.[7] The increasing equity ratio in the strategic asset allocation of the pension fund of teachers and administration staff of Geneva has stimulated a profound discussion about the use of their membership rights. Considering the significance and the value of these rights, it was decided to systematically exercise voting rights for Swiss and foreign equities. CIA was also a founding member of the Ethos foundation, which bases its investment decisions on a socioenvironmental analysis of companies. This procedure reflects not only ideological values but also the target of combining economic with socioenvironmental efficiency to increase a company's long-term value.

Motivation for SRI by pension funds: the same story as corporate governance?

The analysis of active pension funds shows that in most cases their SRI involvement is based on or supplemented by public shareholder activism or direct influence on the corporate governance in their stockholdings. The drivers are quite similar: apart from political considerations the improvement of the governance structures is intended to affect financial performance positively. The pattern of players is also similar, with only a limited number of pension funds involved, mainly public pension funds.

the extent that it is consistent with its legal duties to do so. To this end, having consulted with the participating employers, it has adopted a policy of active engagement with those companies in which the fund is invested concerning the ethical, environmental and social policies pursued by those companies' (Green 2001: 9).
7 In May 2002 Ethos had 92 pension fund members and total assets of CHF750 million (www.ethosfund.ch, accessed 24 May 2002).

Performance potential: links to corporate governance

According to a survey by Credit Lyonnais Securities Asia (CLSA) Emerging Markets, 'Asian companies that rank highest in corporate governance outperformed equity market benchmarks by a 14.4% average'.[8]

The launch of the Dow Jones Sustainability Group Index (DJSGI) was supported by an impressive market entry. A back-test that calculated how the DJSGI would have performed from 1994 to 1999 showed a significant outperformance over the traditional Dow Jones Global Index. The impressive chart should prove that sustainability enhances corporate profitability and investors' return.[9]

The story for pension funds is similar: a better social responsibility and governance structure could lead to higher long-term company performance and more attractive returns for investors. The analysis of soft factors such as non-financial measures and the quality of management gains importance not only because accounting measures are questioned. Surveys of measures determining long-term shareholder value include customer and employee satisfaction as well as social responsibility. Brancanto sums this up: 'These strategic performance measurements will greatly assist institutional investors who invest for the long term and can encourage investors to stay with a company, when sole reliance on financial measurements might suggest otherwise' (Brancanto 1997: 41).

An example of the impact of SRI investors on a set of companies is aptly explained by an official of the Access to Drugs campaign in South Africa: 'We have heard from senior management that they believe this wake-up call helped them to prevent serious reputational damage. The engagement activities, alongside that of the others involved, helped protect a goose that had laid some valuable golden eggs' (Moon and Thamotheram 2000).

The historical experience of a close link between institutional social investing and corporate governance activism explains the geographic differences in SRI activities. The UK and the US favour the engagement approach, while in continental Europe pension funds mainly work by portfolio screening as shareholder activism and the exercise of votes are not yet fully fledged.[10]

Investment capabilities: opportunities to exercise active ownership

Why could pension funds or institutional investors in general be appropriate to exercise active roles as owners of companies? Some authors define pension funds as 'ideal owners':

> Their ownership, by virtue of their size and their time horizons, is as close to permanent as possible. And because of this near-permanent stake, their interest is far-sighted enough to incorporate the long-

---

8   www.tiesweb.org/work/better_corporate_ governance_pays_off.htm, accessed 21 May 2002.
9   See www.sam-group.com/e/susindex/djsi.cfm).
10 Ethos is an often-quoted exception within the Swiss pension funds. (In a Robecco survey of Swiss pension funds 56% of the institutions said that they did not vote.)

term interests of the corporation and (as essential element of those interests) the interests of employees, customers, suppliers and the community. Why should they get involved in SRI? (Monks and Minow 2001: 156).

As the arguments for corporate governance and SRI indicate, shareholder activism in this direction can enhance corporate profits and therefore investor performance. Many investors have a focus on the short term, but pension funds are more concerned about long-term performance. Thus, pension funds are operating on a time-scale that could allow corporate governance and SRI initiatives to pay off.

Because of their size and investment capabilities, institutional investors are better informed and able to monitor management at lower relative cost than small shareholders. The holdings of pension funds are large enough to alleviate the free-rider problem that makes shareholder information and action economically irrational. Pension plans are less restricted by commercial conflicts of interest than are other institutional investors such as banks, insurance companies, mutual funds and other classes of institutional investor.[11] The trend of indexing makes pension funds both universal and permanent shareholders: 'If you can't sell, you must care.' Their holdings are so diversified that they have the incentive to represent the ownership sector (and the economy) generally rather than any specific industries or companies.

One important incentive for shareholder activism is legal obligations such as the duty for US pension funds to exercise their voting rights.[9] Are they also morally compelled?

The investment of such huge sums (GBP830 billion in pension funds) is bound to have an effect on the wider world. As such the nature of investments made on their behalf shapes the world in which fund members live, work and retire. In many ways, whether or not investors are aware of it, investment decision-making has an ethical dimension (Denham, quoted in Sparkes 2000: 5).

From the macro perspective, pension funds should take into account the best interests of society, which cannot be defined only as financial interests. However, if pension promises are to be honoured, we need a peaceful world, an environment that is revered and human dignity that is respected, says Alan Pickering, Chairman of the National Association of Pension Funds (NAPF) (Green 2001: 2). Pensioners can enjoy their retirement only when they live in a healthy environment and a stable society. Pension funds could influence these factors by using investment decisions to push companies in this direction. Looking at the severe financial burden resulting from demographic changes, this discussion is not led with great

11 An example of this conflict of interest is quoted by Monks and Minow (2001: 123): 'We are very reticent to position ourselves as an activist shareholder in domestic or international securities. The problem for us is how we are perceived by our customer base. The risks are such that it probably does not make sense for us to take an aggressive position. I can imagine many of your partners do have a lot more freedom since they apparently have no other business interests with portfolio companies' (Frank V. Cahouet, Chairman, President and Chief Executive Officer of Mellon Bank Corporation).
12 In the Avon Letter, the Department of Labour asserted the fiduciary act of managing plan assets that are shares of corporate stock including voting proxies pertaining to those shares (see Brancanto 1997: 110).

passion. The moral aspect to integrating social and environmental criteria cannot be the only reason for SRI.

Pressure by employees

Surveys show the importance of employee involvement in the decision-making process regarding social and environmental criteria. Oesch (2000: 55) points out that parity management allows employee representatives to put forward their position. Another condition is the profession of the represented employees, which means that a dominant position of sociocultural professions is likely to lead to a higher interest in SRI.

The campaign Ethics for USS is a good example of the pressure brought to bear by scheme members of a large pension fund. It was set up in 1998 to persuade USS to adopt a comprehensive ethical and environmental investment policy. The campaign was supported by 3,500 individual members as well as the Association of University Teachers and seems to have been successful (Sparkes 2000).

Barriers for SRI: why do you always read the same names?

The listed examples of pension funds involved in SRI correspond perfectly with the most prominent players in shareholder activism on corporate governance or other issues. In general, the situation can be described as follows: 'Pension funds and insurance companies have become classic absentee landlords, exerting power with responsibility and making exacting demands on companies without recognising their reciprocal obligation as owners (Short and Keasy 1997: 26).

Problems of active shareholder activism

Although there are a number of encouraging arguments why institutional investors could and should take an active role as shareholders, the number of obstacles is large, which explains the mostly passive behaviour of pension fund managers. The following reasons are given.

The obligation to maximise the value of funds induces fears that the implementation of an SRI policy, by either positive or negative screening, could lead to lower returns because a divesting policy implies higher transaction costs and screening results in less diversification compared to a standard portfolio.

Another form of conflict of interest can occur if, as a result of the engagement process, investment institutions become privy to insider information about the company that could cause the fund to consider insider trading. If they exercise pressure on the companies publicly, they can attract a negative perception by the markets, so that stock prices of their affected holdings might fall.

One general problem is also valid for large pension funds: diversification needs and the tendency to invest in large caps (blue chips) to avoid major stakes in companies in order to keep liquidity reduces governance efforts, as the costs for relatively small holdings are not rewarded.

Stapledon points out another reason for the passive role of pension funds, at least for the UK market. He identified that, in 1993, 78% of directly invested UK occupational pension funds used solely external fund managers while only 14% managed their investments wholly in-house (Stapledon 1996: 34).

In addition, the lack of legal or practical justification for institutional investors to become involved in governance on matters of particular concern to employees or to the public leads to a more passive role, as do practical difficulties with staying informed about foreign holdings.

Legal situation

The debate on shareholder activism and SRI by pension funds often raises the question whether trustees are legally permitted to consider other than purely financial criteria. The legal framework in which pension funds operate generally imposes strict requirements on pension fund trustees to invest pension funds in a prudent fashion while taking the interests of plan members into account. This generally means achieving a reasonable or in some cases a legally defined minimum rate of return for a certain risk (Sturm and Badde 2001: 22). In the USA this debate is particularly controversial because of the experience with the below-average performance of socially targeted investments. Private pension funds are regulated by the US Department of Labor Employee Retirement Income Security Act (ERISA) of 1974, which imposes a 'prudence rule' and 'sole and exclusive benefit rule'. Some authors (e.g. Vieira 1983: 69) see a conflict where the non-economic criteria of social investing relate primarily, if not exclusively, to personal interests of an ideological or political nature. Others (e.g. Leibig 1980; CEP 1980) cannot identify a restriction. Some states even impose an SRI strategy. The California legislature has provided that 'the retirement fund shall be used as much as reasonably possible to benefit and expand the business climate within the State of California, as long as such use would be consistent with sound investment policy' (see Leibig 1980: 18).

The UK guide for trustees and fund managers, *Just Pensions* (Green 2001: 7), sums up the legal question:

> Trustees cannot
>
> - Put their own personal values ahead of acting in the interests of the beneficiaries
> - Follow investment strategies which they are conscious will be to the financial detriment of beneficiaries having no investment choice
>
> Trustees can
>
> - Take account of SRI to deliver improved financial returns, added non-financial benefits

Yve Newbold, who chaired the NAPF Committee of Enquiry into Voting Execution, is quoted in *Just Pensions* as saying that trustees may be in danger of incurring legal risk by not considering social issues.[13]

Performance threats

From a portfolio perspective, the impact of socially based screening and/or exclusion might lead to portfolios that deviate substantially from market portfolios. These ethical portfolios have inefficiencies and lack of diversification, which might result in unsatisfying compensation for the unsystematic risk. To identify the impact of social screening and the correlation of environmental and financial performance, a number of empirical surveys have been conducted mainly in the USA. Schäfer and Stederoth (2001) classify three types of study: event studies; the comparison of a synthetic portfolio with a market portfolio; and the analysis of screened portfolios. Their studies do not identify a significant underperformance of ethical portfolios although the problem remains that the surveys can identify only a correlation between environmental performance and financial performance, but no causality. Therefore it will be difficult to argue that environmental performance is the only driver of higher financial returns. The analysis of screened SRI portfolios shows some typical effects that have a significant impact on fund performance: they have a higher percentage of small companies compared to other funds; they tend to have an overweight in technology stocks; and global portfolios often have an overweight in European stocks. These factors seem to have a high impact on performance. Therefore Sturm and Badde (2001: 20) recommend that the most realistic pension fund strategy is over- and under-weighting combined with shareholder activism unless the pension fund has a large surplus.

Resources

'For many institutional shareholders, the main obstacle to doing so [SRI] is not opposition to the idea, which can often make good business sense, but the apparent difficulty of putting it into practice with the limited resources available' (Green 2001: 2).

SRI is still a recent development. Since only a limited amount of external or standardised information about companies is available, and because of the complexity of social and environmental issues, few pension funds have the capability and resources to deal with these issues. Sturm and Badde (2001: 21) suggest two strategies to implement an SRI strategy, according to the classical 'make-or-buy' decision:

---

13 'The requirement to state in the SIP the extent to which social, environmental or ethical consideration are taken into account in investment decisions means that for all but the smallest trust funds a position of having no such policy would or could be called into question as being unsound in the climate of today's heightened awareness of the influence of such issues on corporate reputation and value' (Yve Newbold, April 2001).

- Develop the skills and know-how needed to screen and analyse stocks and bonds in-house
- Invest in SRI funds without building up in-house know-how on socially responsible investment aspects

Competition, weak equity markets and the additional costs of implementation can make an SRI strategy a difficult burden for pension funds.

As previously mentioned, the combination of these issues provides an obstacle to a policy of relying on institutional investors as a primary mechanism of corporate governance. 'There might be lots of noise and action, and there might be talk about all the new, awakened shareholders and institutional investors, but there's really not much more than a dozen pension funds involved' (Monks and Minow 2001: 122). Legal issues also prevent institutional investors from being informed and activist shareholders: 'What is needed? The current laws are adequate in theory. In practice, they are not being enforced' (Monks and Minow 2001: 186). The following section highlights changes that could speed up pension fund involvement in SRI.

The future: disclosure rules stimulate debate

Governments in different European countries are playing important catalyst roles in SRI pension funds strategies. In order to stimulate public debate on SRI strategies, governments have introduced disclosure rules.

Overview: introduction of disclosure rules for pension funds globally[14]

The first initiative, the UK **Pension SRI Disclosure Regulation**, came into force in July 2000. It requires trustees of occupational pension funds to disclose in their statement of investment principles:

- The extent (if at all) to which social, environmental and ethical considerations are taken into account in their investment strategies
- The policy (if any) directing the exercise of the rights (including voting rights) attached to investments

The goal of the UK government was not to introduce a compulsory integration of SRI criteria and policies of each pension fund but to increase transparency on these issues.[15]

14 Information from K. Franck, 'Perspectives on pension fund disclosure worldwide', presentation at Eurosif Conference, Frankfurt, 24 April 2002.
15 'The private sector has a key role in making globalisation work better for poor people. In recent years, there has been growing public interest in corporate social responsibility. This has brought issues such as child labour, corruption, human rights, labour stan-

If interest from insured and pension funds can be stimulated, the number of funds and shareholder pressure will increase, which could enhance pressure on corporations to achieve a better social and environmental performance. Based on this argumentation the initiative can be understood as part of national environmental policy.

The **German** pension reform introduced in 2002 not only provides financial incentives for occupational pension models and individual savings schemes (Riester-Rente), but also codifies a disclosure regulation. The new certified private and occupational pension schemes will have to report whether ethical, environmental and social aspects are taken into account. The occupational schemes have to fulfil an annual obligation on the application of SRI considerations. The disclosure rule for private schemes has a loophole, however. Those products that are not SRI-registered are relieved from the annual disclosure rule. Therefore few Riester products actually report on social, environmental or ethical considerations.

In **Belgium**, pension institutions will have to issue annual reports on the management of the pension commitment. This will include information on 'how social, ethical and environmental aspects are taken into account'.

France has introduced several new disclosure rules, at both company and investor levels. Based on the history of social reporting, compulsory green reporting will affect French companies. All publicly quoted firms will be required to include data on environmental and social impacts in their annual financial reports. In February 2001 the inclusion of a 'disclosure' amendment in the law on the generalisation of the Employee Savings Plan states that 'investment managers may consider social, environmental and ethical matters'. In addition, the law on the French Pension Reserve Fund makes clear that the fund has to report annually to the board of trustees how it has taken into account social, environmental and ethical considerations.

The **Australian** Senate passed an amendment to the Financial Services Reform Bill in 2002 requiring all financial services product disclosure statements to state 'the extent to which labor standards, environmental, social or ethical considerations are taken into account in the selection, retention or realisation of the investment'. Because the Australian amendment includes all managed investment products, it is the broadest in scope.

In addition to these already implemented rules, similar activities have been started in Canada, Switzerland, Austria and Sweden. As disclosure rules count on market mechanisms by the stimulation of a higher demand, their success can be questioned.

---

dards, environmental and conflict into trade, investment and supply chain relationships. By applying best practice in these areas, business can play an increased role in poverty reduction and sustainable development. Many companies have also realised important commercial benefits, in terms of reputation, risk management and enhanced productivity. Greater business engagement can be encouraged by improving understanding and raising awareness of the potential benefits for business from socially responsible behaviour' (British government position on CSR, in, 'Eliminating World Poverty: Making Globalisation Work for the Poor', Department for International Development White Paper, December 2000, www.dfid.gov.uk).

Impact of disclosure rules: UK example

How important and effective is disclosure regulation as a driver?

A survey undertaken briefly after the UK regulation came into effect found that 49% of pension funds, accounting for 78% of assets, have passed some kind of amendment to their statements of investment principles (SIP) (Mathieu 2000). This United Kingdom Social Investment Forum (UKSIF) survey might lead one to conclude that disclosure rules can stimulate pension fund engagement in SRI. Other surveys come to a less positive conclusion, in particular regarding the implementation of the SRI commitment in their SIP.

A survey by Friends of the Earth (FoE 2001) also found that most occupational pension funds contained SIP including SRI in some form. A total of 90% of their survey respondents made reference to ethics or CSR in their investment principles. They identified the problem 'that many had few or no demonstrable accountability mechanisms to ensure that the fund managers were taking SRI considerations into account (no independent stakeholder verification)'. About 50% had some sort of engagement (i.e. corporate governance policy) and associated monitoring mechanism (voting rights). In the section of their survey entitled 'monitoring', they identified that less than a third of the funds were able to demonstrate how they were monitoring and reporting on environmental, social and ethical (ESE) issues.

At the 2001 NAPF annual meeting, Guptara presented the results of a survey regarding the impact of the July 2000 regulation (Guptara 2001). To the question of whether more money is now being allocated on an SRI basis, he received disappointing answers: 'Though some respondents had the impression that more money "must" be going into SRI-based funding decisions, none of my respondents to date knew of any actual decisions to this effect, specifically as a result of the impact of the legislation.' One of his questions intended to find out whether recruitment/performance criteria have changed for individuals working in fund management. Again only a few respondents felt that recruitment/performance criteria had been influenced, but no one was able to quote anything very specific and the vast majority reported 'no change' in these. Nor did the question regarding structural handling bring more concrete answers:

> Some companies have appointed specialist staff; others have expanded from having one or two staff to several; but most have not changed their internal composition or structure as a result of the legislation, and overall the amount of expansion appears to be limited (Guptara 2001).

These surveys indicate that there seems to be a large gap in implementation, as evidenced by the lack of recruitment of new staff or the application of accounting mechanisms. That monitoring seems to be a non-issue is owing to a lack of interest from employees and the public.

Conclusions and next steps

Returning to the question of whether pension funds can become a new driver for sustainable development, the possible answer can be 'yes, but . . .'. Looking at their financial clout, pension funds represent the largest source of long-term investment in most capital markets. Because of the shift from state pension systems to occupational and individual schemes, their size will tend to increase in the mid-term. The analysis of different markets points out increasing interest and money from pension funds in SRI. This market trend has built on a long tradition in the UK and US and recent initiatives in continental European countries such as Switzerland, France and Italy. Some of the concrete figures provided by certain organisations are questionable, such as the impressive 13% market share of SRI investments reported within the institutional market in the USA.

The introduction of disclosure rules for pension funds to report on their use of ethical and environmental criteria shows the increasing interest from governments in Europe but also in Australia to use the financial market as a driver for sustainable development. The European Commission has also become involved by publishing the White Paper on Corporate Social Responsibility and supporting the European Sustainable and Responsible Investment Forum (EUROSIF). Studies reviewing the recently introduced disclosure rules have identified a large gap between pension fund SRI rhetoric and reality. This gap can be explained in part by the reluctance toward active involvement in shareholder activism regarding corporate governance, as well as financial considerations and a lack of public interest.

As pension funds are bound by a fiduciary duty, risk–return requirements have to be respected. Several surveys (see e.g. Schäfer and Stederoth 2001) have found that SRI portfolios are often characterised by higher risk because of their higher inclusion of SMEs and tech stocks as well as their deviation from benchmark asset allocation. One question that presents itself is whether SRI is appropriate only for pension funds with solid asset liability structures. When one looks at SRI indices such as the DJSGI or the FTSE4Good (which are based on the European approach of positive screening), they also bear higher risk. They cannot be accepted as a benchmark for a pension fund strategy because their deviation from traditional benchmarks is too high (Chan 2001: 16ff.).

From this technical perspective, some experts argue that engagement is the only suitable strategy for institutional investors such as pension funds. Taking into account the lack of accounting and monitoring that has been identified among UK fund managers (FoE 2001), some accompanying measures should be taken to stimulate the public debate and the interests of pension plan members for SRI.

The legal framework affecting pension funds has an important impact on fund size and investment strategy, both on asset allocation and the openness to non-financial criteria such as those in SRI. It has been shown that initiatives such as those taken in Europe can lead pension funds to take on a more active role regarding the social and environmental consequences of their investments. Nevertheless, there is much room for improvement. The involvement of pension funds in SRI should function as a market mechanism to move the targeted companies to become more sustainable. Therefore all market players need to be involved in order to raise awareness. The activities should address three principal target groups (Sturm and Badde 2001: 8-9):

1. Pension plan members and the public. The goal should be to raise awareness with public and pension plan members of SRI issues through better provision of investment information and agenda setting.
2. Pension funds, their managers, trustees and banks. The goal should be to raise awareness and support decisions through training, conducting research, screening, proxy voting and coalitions with institutional investors.
3. Companies. The goal should be to raise awareness about the positive impacts of SRI by rating of companies, providing information on SRI issues, and roadshows.

Some steps have already been taken, at least to facilitate information-gathering on corporate environmental and social performance. Owing to the demand from institutional investors (until now mainly SRI fund managers and churches), fundamental market players have begun to become more engaged in SRI:

1. The number and the service quality of external rating agencies has increased, which is also achieved by European or global networks such as Sustainable Investment Research International (SiRi) Group and Ethical Investment Research Service (EIRIS).
2. The GRI works on social and environmental reporting schemes, which will provide a common standard for the companies' reporting and therefore external evaluation.[16]
3. Sell-side brokers such as DresdnerKleinwortWasserstein and HSBC offer information on the social and environmental performance of companies (see DresdnerKleinwortWasserstein Socially Responsible Investment News and HSBC Sustainability & Securities).
4. Indices based on social and environmental criteria provide an easy access to SRI investments or benchmarking own SRI portfolios (see DJSGI, FTSE4Good and Social Domini Index).

These developments might improve the information exchange between SRI investors and companies, but the crucial question is when the pension plan members will take a stronger interest in the way their money is invested. The success of individual SRI options and initiatives such as Ethics for USS demonstrate the potential of their power.

16 See www.globalreporting.org.

Bibliography

ACEA (European Automobile Manufacturers Association) and Commission Services (2002) 'Monitoring of ACEA's Commitment on CO_2 Emission Reduction from Passenger Cars 2001', final report, www.acea.be/ACEA/publications.html.

AG PVC (1999) *PVC und Nachhaltigkeit: Systemstabilität als Maßstab, Ausgewählte Produktsysteme im Vergleich/Steuerungsgruppe zum 'Dialogprojekt PVC und Nachhaltigkeit' und Arbeitsgemeinschaft PVC und Umwelt eV* (Cologne: div, Dt. Inst.-Verl.).

Ax, C. (1999) *Maßproduktion statt Massenproduktion. Neue Technologien für eine umweltschonende handwerkliche Schuhproduktion: Schlussbericht des Entwicklungsvorhabens* (Hamburg).

Ayres, R., and T. van Leynseele (1997) *Eco-Efficiency, Double Dividends and the Sustainable Firm* (Fontainebleau, France).

Bartolomeo, M., and T. Daga (2002) *Green, Social and Ethical Funds in Europe 2001* (Sustainable Investment Research International [SiRi] Group, www.sirigroup.org).

Basel Committee on Banking Supervision (2001) *Overview of The New Basel Capital Accord* (Basel: Basel Committee on Banking Supervision).

BMBF (Bundesministerium für Bildung und Forschung) (2002) 'Faktenbericht 2002', January 2002, Bonn, www.bmbf.de/digipubl.htm#Allgemeine.

Bosshard, N.G. (1997) 'Die Verbindung von Ökonomie und Ökologie am Beispiel der Rohner Textil AG', thesis, Universität St Gallen, Switzerland.

Brancanto, C.K. (1997) *Institutional Investors and Corporate Governance: Best Practices for Increasing Value* (Chicago: Irwin Professional Publishing).

Braungart, M. (2000) 'Upcycling the World: Chemist Michael Braungart says an eco-conscious future starts with design. Michael Cannell talks to the activist behind the Next Industrial Revolution', *Architecture*, September 2000: 53-55.

—— and J. Engelfried (1992) (1991) 'An "Intelligent Product System" to Replace "Waste Management" ', *Fresenius Environmental Bulletin* 1: 613-19.

—— and W. McDonough (1998) 'The Next Industrial Revolution', *The Atlantic Monthly*, October 1998.

—— and —— (2000a) 'Reinventing the World—Step Two', *Green@work* magazine, May/June 2000.

—— and —— (2000b) 'A World of Abundance', *Interfaces* 30.3: 55-65.

Brown, L. (2001) *Eco-Economy: Building an Economy for the Earth* (Washington, DC: Earth Policy Institute).

Browne, J. (2002) 'Beyond Petroleum: Business and the Environment in the 21st Century', speech by John Browne, Group Chief Executive, BP, 11 March 2002, www.bp.com/centres/press/stanford/highlights/index.asp.

Bundesumweltministerium für Umwelt, Naturschutz und Reaktorsicherheit; Umweltbundesamt (2001) *Green Finance: Environmental Management in Banks, Saving Banks and Insurance Companies* (Berlin: Bundesministerium für Umwelt, Naturschutz und Reaktorsicherheit, www.bmu.de).

Burgess, C. (2002) *Socially Responsible Investment Survey 2002* (London: Deloitte & Touche).

—— and T. Osborn-Barker (2000) *Socially Responsible Investment: Response of Investment Fund Managers* (London: Deloitte & Touche).

Catlette, B., and R. Hadden (1998) *Contented Cows Give Better Milk: The Plain Truth about Employee Relations and your Bottom Line* (Germantown, TN: Satillo Press).

CEC (Commission of the European Commission) (2001a) *A Sustainable Europe for a Better World: A European Union Strategy for Sustainable Development* (COM 2001 264 final 15.5.2001; Brussels: CEC).

—— (2001b) *Innovation Scoreboard* (Commission Staff Working Paper, SEC 2001 1414, 14 September 2001; Brussels: CEC).

—— (2002) 'The Lisbon Strategy: Making Change Happen', Annex 2, SEC 2002 29/2, http://europa.eu.int/comm/barcelona_ council/29annex2_en.pdf.

CEFIC (European Chemical Industry Council) (1998) *Responsible Care. Health, Safety and Environmental Reporting Guidelines* (Brussels: CEFIC).

—— (2002) *Responsible Care 2002* (Brussels: CEFIC, www.cefic.be/Files/Publications/RCreport2003.pdf).

CEP (Council on Economic Priorities) (1980) *Pension Funds and Ethical Investment: A Study of Investment Practices and Opportunities in State of California Retirement Systems* (New York: CEP).

Cerulli Associates (2001) 'Investing for the Future. Socially Responsible Investing Issue', *Cerulli Global Edition*, September 2001.

Chan, L. (2001) *Sustainability Investment* (London: UBS Warburg Global Equity Research).

Charter, M., and U. Tischner (eds.) (2001) *Sustainable Solutions: Developing Products and Services for the Future* (Sheffield, UK: Greenleaf Publishing).

Club of Rome (2001) *Proceedings: Towards a EU Strategy for Sustainable Development* (contribution for the preparation of the Gothenburg Summit of June 2001; Brussels: Club of Rome, 2 May 2001).

Creyer, E., and W. Ross (1997) 'The Influence of Firm Behaviour on Purchase Intention: Do Consumers Really Care about Business Ethics?', *Journal of Consumer Marketing* 14.6: 421-32.

De Simone, L.D., and F. Popoff (1997) *Eco-efficiency: The Business Link to Sustainable Development* (Cambridge, MA: The MIT Press).

Deloitte & Touche (2003) 'Environment and Sustainability', www.deloitte.com.

Delphi and Ecologic (1997) *The Role of Financial Institutions in Achieving Sustainable Development* (Report to the European Commission; London: Delphi; Berlin: Ecologic).

Deutsche Bundesregierung (2002) 'Perspectives for Germany: Our Strategy for Sustainable Development', www.bundesregierung.de.

Doutlik, K. (2000) 'The Role of Public Authorities in the Promotion and Development of Environmental Management Tools', presentation at the International Workshop organised by INETI, Portuguese Directorate-General of Industry and the European Commission, Lisbon, 1-3 March 2000.

DresdnerKleinwortWasserstein (2003) 'UK Treasury to focus on investor activism and trustee training' *SRI News*, 26 February 2003: 2.

Ecoreporter.de (2001) 'Doppelte Dividende: Marktstudie zu Aktien, Fonds und Anlegern des ethisch-ökologischen Investments. Begleitforschung zur Messe Grünes Geld 25.–27.1. in Berlin. Erarbeitet im Auftrag des Öko-Zentrums NRW, Hamm, herausgegeben von der Messe Berlin GmbH, Berlin, January 2001.

EEA (European Environment Agency) (2002) 'Environmental Signals 2002', www.eea.eu.int.

EEB (European Environmental Bureau), Friends of Nature International, Friends of the Earth Europe and Heinrich Böll Foundation (eds.) (2001) *EU Strategy for Sustainable Development: Stakeholders' View* (www.eeb.org/publication/EU_Strategy_for_Sustainable_Development.pdf).
Efa (Efficiency Agency North-Rhine Westphalia) and Wuppertal Institute (eds.) (2001) *Four Elements, Ten Factors, One Goal: Eco-efficiency—Less is More* (Duisburg, Germany: Efficiency Agency NRW).
EIAJ (The Electronic Industries Association of Japan) (1999) *For the Planet Earth: Efforts by Japan's Semiconductor Industry* (EIAJ, July 1999).
Electronics Journal (2000) 'Trends in Lead-free Soldering 2', *Electronics Journal*, January 2000: 89-91.
Elkington, J. (1997) *Cannibals with Forks: The Triple Bottom Line of 21st-Century Business* (Oxford, UK: Capstone Publishing; Gabriola Island, Canada: New Society Publishers).
—— (2001) *The Chrysalis Economy: How Citizen CEOs and Corporations Can Fuse Values and Value Creation* (Oxford, UK: Capstone; New York: John Wiley).
EPI Finance (2000) 'Environmental Performance Indicators for the Financial Industry', www.epifinance.com.
Eurostat (Statistical Office of the European Communities) (1997) *Indicators of Sustainable Development* (Luxembourg: Eurostat).
—— (2001) 'Measuring Progress toward a More Sustainable Europe', http://europa.eu.int/comm/eurostat.
Factor 10 Club (1997–2000) *Carnoules Recommendations 1994, 1995; Carnoules Statement to Government and Business Leaders, 1997; Reports, 1999* (www.factor10.de).
FoE (Friends of the Earth) (2001) 'Top 100 UK Pension Funds: How Ethical Are They?', www.foe.co.uk/pubsinfo/briefings/html/20010828104434.html (accessed 31 January 2002).
FORGE (Financial Organisations Review and Guidance on the Environment) (2002) 'Guidelines on Environmental Management and Reporting for the Financial Services Sector', www.abi.org.uk/forge.
Frazier, C. (1998) *Thoughts on Design* (Hong Kong: Chronicle Books).
Frick, S., R. Gaßner, F. Hinterberger and C. Liedtke (1999) *Öko-effiziente Dienstleistungen als strategischer Wettbewerbsfaktor zur Entwicklung einer nachhaltigen Wirtschaft, Endbericht des Verbundprojekts im Rahmen des Programms Dienstleistung 2000plus des Bundesministeriums für Bildung, Wissenschaft, Forschung und Technologie* (Berlin: IZT).
Fussler, C., with P. James (1996) *Driving Eco-innovation. A Breakthrough Discipline for Innovation and Sustainability* (London: Pitman Publishing).
Gege, M. (ed.) (1997) *Kosten senken durch Umweltmanagement: 1,000 Erfolgsbeispiele aus 100 Unternehmen* (Munich: Vahlen).
German Parliament (2002) *Schlußbericht der Enquete Kommission Globalisierung der Weltwirtschaft: Herausforderungen und Antworten* (Drucksache 14/9200 12 June 2002; Berlin: German Parliament).
Gorman, M.E. (1998) *Transforming Nature, Ethics, Invention and Discovery* (Boston, MA: Kluwer Academic Publishers).
—— and M.M. Mehalik (1998) 'Toward a Sustainable Tomorrow: Three Cases and A Moral', in P. Werhane and L. Westra (eds.), *The Business of Consumption: Environmental Ethics and the Global Economy* (Boston, MA: Rowman & Littlefield).
——, —— and P. Werhane (2000) *Ethical and Environmental Challenges to Engineering* (Englewood Cliffs, NJ: Prentice Hall).
Green, D. (2001) *Just Pensions: Socially Responsible Investment and International Development* (London: Just Pensions).
Green@work (2000) What happens when a manufacturer grants its competitor a license to develop an ecologically sound product? The hope is that it will eventually force an entire industry to clean up its act', *Green@work* magazine, January/February 2000: 52.
GRI (Global Reporting Initiative) (1999) *Guidelines on Corporate Sustainability Reporting* (Amsterdam: CERES).

—— (2002) 'Guidelines on Sustainability Performance Reporting, Version 2002', www.globalreporting.org.

Guptara, P. (2001) 'The Impact, to April 2001, of the UK Government's Summer 2000 Legislation on SRI', paper presented at the National Association of Pension Funds, May 2001.

Hawken, P., A.B. Lovins and L.H. Lovins (1999) *Natural Capitalism: Creating the Next Industrial Revolution* (London: Earthscan Publications; www.natcap.org).

Henkel (2000) *Code of Conduct/Business Ethics Henkel-Group* (Düsseldorf: Henkel).

—— (2002) *Sustainability Report 2001* (Düsseldorf: Henkel).

—— (2003) *Sustainability Report 2002* (Düsseldorf: Henkel).

Hillary, R. (ed.) (2000): *ISO 14001: Case Studies and Practical Experience* (Sheffield, UK: Greenleaf Publishing).

Holliday, C.O., Jr, S. Schmidheiny and P. Watts (2002) *Walking the Talk: The Business Case for Sustainable Development* (Sheffield, UK: Greenleaf Publishing).

ICC (International Chamber of Commerce) (1991) 'The Business Charter for Sustainable Development' (ICC No. 210/356 A), www.iccwbo.org/home/environment/charter.asp.

JEMAI (Japan Environmental Management Association for Industry) (2000) *A Report on Environmental Accounting Research 1999* (Tokyo: JEMAI [Japanese language]).

—— (2001) *A Report on Environmental Accounting Research 2000* (Tokyo: JEMAI [Japanese language]).

Jeucken, M. (2001) *Sustainable Finance and Banking: The Financial Sector and the Future of the Planet* (London: Earthscan Publications).

Kälin, A. (2001) 'Positiv definierter Chemikalieneinsatz als Voraussetzung für die Schliessung von Material- und Wasserkreisläufen: Das Beispiel des Möbelbezugstoffes Climatex® Lifecycle™ der Rohner Textil AG', in E.U. von Weizsäcker, B. Stigson and J.-D. Seiler-Hausmann (eds.), *From Eco Efficiency to Overall Sustainable Development in Enterprises* (Wuppertal, Germany: Wuppertal Institute).

—— and M.M. Mehalik (2000) 'The Development of Climatex® Lifecycle™, a Compostable, Environmentally Sound Upholstery Fabric', in M. Charter and U. Tischner (eds.), *Sustainable Solutions: Developing Products and Services for the Future* (Sheffield, UK: Greenleaf Publishing): 393-401.

Kameda, M. (1999) ' "ECOPAC" New Packaging Made from Waste Paper', *Matsushita Technical Journal* 45.3: 102-109.

Kemp, R. (2000) 'Technology and Environmental Policy: Innovation Effects of Past Policies and Suggestions for Improvement', in OECD (ed.), *Innovation and the Environment*, (Sustainable Development series; Paris: OECD; www1.oecd.org/publications/e-book/9200111E.pdf).

Klinkers, L., W. van der Kooy and H. Wijen (1999) 'Product-Oriented Environmental Management Provides New Opportunities and Directions for Speeding up Environmental Performance', *Greener Management International* 26 (Summer 1999): 91-108.

Klostermann, J.E.M., and A. Tukker (1998) (eds.) *Product Innovation and Eco-efficiency: Twenty-three Industry Efforts to Reach the Factor 4* (London: Kluwer Academic Publishers).

Kodera, T. (2000) 'Responses to the Home Electronics Recycling Law and Development of Recycling-Oriented Products', *Industrial Materials* 48.3: 53.

Kokubu, K. (2001) 'Environmental Cost Accounting in Japan: Two Governmental Initiatives', *Ökologisches Wirtschaften* 6: 12-13.

—— and E. Nashioka (2002) 'Environmental Accounting Information Disclosure Practices of Japanese Companies', *Accounting Progress* 3: 65-76 [Japanese language].

—— and T. Kurasaka (2002) 'Corporate Environmental Accounting: A Japanese Perspective', in M. Bennett, J.J. Bouma and T. Wolters (eds.), *Environmental Management Accounting* (Dordrecht: Kluwer Academic Publishers).

Krcmar, H., G. Dold, H. Fischer, M. Strobel and E.K.Seifert (eds.) (2000) *Informationssysteme für das Umweltmanagement. Das Referenzmodell ECO-Integral* (Munich/Vienna. R. Oldenbourg Verlag).

Kuhndt, M., and C. Liedtke (1998) 'Translating a Factor X into Praxis', in *Centre of Environmental Science Report 148, Substances and Products* (Leiden, Netherlands: Leiden University).

—— and —— (1999) *Die COMPASS. Methodik: Unternehmen und Branchen auf dem Weg zur Zukunftsfähigkeit* (*COMPASS. Companies' and Sectors' Path to Sustainability: The Methodology*) (Wuppertal Paper No. 97; Wuppertal, Germany: Wuppertal Institute, December 1999).

—— and C.T. van der Lugt (2000) 'Der Kalender für effizientes Wirtschaften: Ein innovatives Instrument zur Verbesserung von Umweltleistungen in klein- und mittelständigen Unternehmen im globalen Maßstab' ('The Efficient Entrepreneur Calendar: An Innovative Tool to Improve Environmental Performance in Small and Medium-Sized Enterprises Worldwide'), *UmweltWirtschaftForum* 3 (Berlin/Heidelberg: Springer Verlag).

—— and J. von Geibler (2002) 'Strategies for Sustainable Business Development', in R. Bleischwitz, P. Hennicke, P. Bartelmus, S. Bringezu, M. Fischedick, J. von Geibler, T. Hanke, M. Kuhndt, R. Lukas, F. Merten, S. Moll, W. Sachs, K.O. Schallaböck, E. Seifert, H. Wallbaum and D. Wolters (eds.), *Review of Eco-Efficiency Concepts in Europe: Toward an Application of European-Based Policies on Material Flows and Energy to Japanese Sustainable Development Policies. Part of the Collaboration Projects under the Trust of Nomura Research Institute (NRI) and the Economic and Social Research Institute (ESRI) of Japan Final Report* (Wuppertal, Germany: Wuppertal Institute).

——, —— and C. Liedtke (2002) *Toward a Sustainable Aluminium Industry: Stakeholder Expectations and Core Indicators. Final Report for the GDA (Gesamtverband der Aluminiumindustrie) and the European Aluminium Industry* (Wuppertal, Germany: Wuppertal Institute).

Lee, K.M. (2000) 'Standardisation and Eco-product Development', presentation at the 5th International Conference *Toward Sustainable Product Design*, Design Center, Stuttgart, Germany, 23–24 October 2000.

Lehni, M. (1998) *State of Play Report* (WBCSD Project on Eco-efficiency Metrics and Reporting; Conches–Geneva: WBCSD).

Leibig, M.T. (1980) 'Social Investments and the Law: The Case for Alternative Investments', paper presented at *Conference on Alternative State and Local Policies*, Washington, DC.

Liedtke, C., H. Rohn, M. Kuhndt and R. Nickel (1998) 'Applying Material Flow Accounting: Eco-auditing and Resource Management at the Kambium Furniture Workshop', *Journal of Industrial Ecology* 2.3.

Lomborg, B. (2001) *The Sceptical Environmentalist: Measuring the Real State of the World* (Cambridge, UK: Cambridge University Press).

Luyckx, M. (2001) *Au delà de la modernité, du patriarcat et du capitalisme, la société réenchantée* (Paris: L'Harmattan).

Matsushita (2000) *The Matsushita Group Environmental Report* (Kadoma City, Osaka, Japan: Matsushita Group).

Matthieu, E. (2000) Response of UK Pension Funds to the SRI Disclosure Regulation (UKSIF Report; Social Investment Forum, October 2000).

McDonough, W.A., and M. Braungart (2002) *Cradle to Cradle: Remaking the Way We Make Things* (New York: North Point Press).

——, R. Baumeister, D. Rothenberg, J.E. Towers, M. Braungart, J. Bright, K. Hansen, E. Hüther, A. Jacobson, M. Kalaw, H. Levin, A. Lovins, R. Martinsen, D. Mulhall, J.P. Myers, A. Ott, B. Sang, J. Todd and D. Watson (1992) *The Hannover Principles: Design for Sustainability* (prepared for Expo 2000, The World's Fair Hannover, Germany; Charlottesville, VA: William McDonough + Partners).

McGregor, R.P., and M. Peirce (2000) 'Striving for Success', *AccountAbility*, 3rd Quarter 2000: 2-3.

Mehalik, M.M. (2000) 'Technical and Design Tools: The Integration of ISO 14001, Life-cycle Development, Environmental Design and Cost Accounting', in R. Hillary (ed.), *ISO 14001: Case Studies and Practical Experience* (Sheffield, UK: Greenleaf Publishing): 232-39.

——, M.E. Gorman and P. Werhane (1997) *Case Studies Designtex A–E* (Charlottesville, VA: University of Virginia, Darden Business School).

Mercer, W. (1998) *European Pension Fund Managers Guide*. I. *The Marketplace* (London: Mercer Investment Consulting).

Messner, D. (2000) 'Global Governance: Anpassungsdruck für Nationalstaaten und Anforderungen an Unternehmen', in K. Fichter and U. Schneidewind (eds.), *Umweltschutz im globalen Wettbewerb, neue Spielregeln für das grenzenlose Unternehmen* (Berlin: Springer): 61-72.

METI (Ministry of Economy, Trade and Industry, Japan) (2002) *Handbook of Environmental Management Accounting* (Tokyo: METI).

Mizuno, S. (1998) 'Applications of Magnesium and Trends in Demand', in *Magnesium Manual 1999* (Japan Magnesium Association).

MOE (Ministry of the Environment, Japan) (1999) *Grasping Environmental Cost: Draft Guidelines for Evaluating Environmental Cost and Publicly Disclosing Environmental Accounting Information* (Interim Report; Tokyo: MOE).

—— (2000) *Developing an Environmental Accounting System* (Report; Tokyo: MOE).

Monks, R., and N. Minow. (2001) *Corporate Governance* (Oxford, UK: Blackwell Publishing, 2nd edn).

Moon, P., and R. Thamotheram (2000) 'Corporations become "socially responsible" ', *The Independent*, 12 December 2000.

Munich Re Group (2001) *Jahresrückblick Naturkatastrophen 2000* (Munich: Munich Re Group, www.munichre.com/pdf/topics_2001_e.pdf).

Myers, N., and J. Kent (1998) *Perverse Subsidies* (Winnipeg, Canada: International Institute for Sustainable Development).

Nakajima, M., and K. Kokubu (2002) *Material Flow Cost Accounting* (Tokyo: Nippon Keizai Shinbun-sha [Japanese language]).

Nakano, K. (1999) 'Recycling of Plastics and Environmental Impact Evaluation', *Environmental Management Using LCA* (Japan Environmental Management Association for Industry) 35.3: 10.

Nattrass B., and M. Altomare (1999) *The Natural Step for Business* (Gabriola Island, Canada: New Society Publishers).

Nishikawa, Y., K. Matsunaga and K. Matsumura (1999) 'Application of Thixomolding Technology for Recycling-Oriented Products', *Matsushita Technical Journal* 45.3: 101.

OECD (Organisation for Economic Co-operation and Development) (1999) *Institutional Investors 1998* (Statistical Yearbook; Paris: OECD).

Oesch, D. (2000) *L'intégration des critères sociaux et écologiques dans la politique d'investissement des caisses de pension en Suisse: Une étude mandatée par le Réseau pour la responsabilité sociale dans l'économie* (Bern, Switzerland: NSW/RSE).

Orbach, T., and C. Liedtke (1998) *Eco-Management Accounting in Germany: Concepts and Practical Implementation* (Wuppertal Paper No. 88; Wuppertal, Germany: Wuppertal Institute).

——, —— and H. Duppel (1998) 'Umweltkostenrechnung: Stand und Entwicklungsperspektiven' ('Environmental Cost Accounting: Status Quo and Prospects'), in U. Lutz, K. Döttinger and K. Roth (eds.), *Springer Loseblattsystem Betriebliches Umweltmanagement: Grundlagen–Methoden–Praxisbeispiele*; Loseblattsammlung 8 (Berlin/Heidelberg: Springer).

Osawa, N. (1985) *The New Age of Soldering Technology* (publisher unknown).

Österreichische Bundesregierung (2002) *Österreichs Zukunft Nachhaltig Gestalten: Die österreichische Strategie zur nachhaltigen Entwicklung. Eine Initiative der Bundesregierung* (Vienna: Entwurf).

Pallas, B. (1999) 'Chemische Reinigung: Das dritte Ranking des Hamburger Umweltinstituts der 50 größten Chemie- und Pharmaunternehmen', *Manager* magazine 9: 128-43.

Riess, G. (1998) 'Rohner Textil massgeschneidertes Beurteilen', *Bulletin ETH Zürich* 268 (January 1998).

Riley, B. (2000) 'Ageing upsets calculations', *Financial Times Survey, Pension Fund Investment*, May 2000.

Rivière, A., J. Soth, R. Ketelhut, J. Rinkevich and M. Braungart (1997) 'From Life-cycle Assessment to Life-cycle Development', paper presented at the *Air and Waste Management Association's 90th Annual Meeting and Exhibition*, Toronto, 8-13 June 1997.

RNE (Rat für Nachhaltige Entwicklung) (2001) 'Ziele zur Nachhaltigen Entwicklung in Deutschland: Schwerpunktthemen', *Dialogpapier des Nachhaltigkeitsrates*, Berlin, www.nachhaltigkeitsrat.de.

Roach, S. (2001) 'Back to Borders', *Financial Times*, 28 September 2001.

Robins, N. (2002) 'Reforming Foreign Capital Flows', www.sbi-w.com/SBI%20Web/sbiw12002/Robins.htm.

SAM (Sustainable Asset Management) (2001) *Sustainable Water Prospectus* (internal report; Zürich: SAM).

Schäfer, H., and R. Stederoth (2001) *Portfolioselektion und Anlagepolitik mittels Ethik-Filtern: ein Überblick zum Stand der empirischen Kapitalmarktforschung* (Forschungsprojekt ethische Kapitalanlagen; Siegen, Germany: Universität Siegen).

Schmidheiny, S. (1992) *Changing Course: A Global Business Perspective on Development and the Environment* (Cambridge, MA: The MIT Press).

—— and F. Zorraquín (eds.) (1996) *Financing Change: The Financial Community, Eco-efficiency and Sustainable Development* (Cambridge, MA: The MIT Press).

Schmid-Schoenbein, O., and A. Braunschweig (2000) *EPI-Finance 2000: Environmental Performance Indicators for the Financial Industry* (Zürich: EPI-Finance, www.epifinance.com).

——, —— and G. Oetterli (2001) *SPI-Finance 2001: Social Performance Indicators for the Financial Industry* (Zürich: SPI-Finance, www.spifinance.com).

Schmidt-Bleek, F. (1993) *Wieviel Umwelt braucht der Mensch? MIPS, das Maß für ökologisches Wirtschaften* (*The Fossil Makers: Factor 10 and Beyond*) (Boston/Basel/Berlin: Birkhäuser; www.factor10-institute.org/publications.htm).

Shell International (1998) *Profits and Principles: Does There Have to Be a Choice? The Shell Report* (London: Shell)

Short, H., and K. Keasey (1997) 'Institutional Shareholders and Corporate Governance', in K. Keasey and M. Wright (eds.), *Corporate Governance: Responsibilities, Risks and Remuneration* (Chichester, UK: John Wiley): 23-58.

SIF (Social Investment Forum) (2001) *2001 Report on Socially Responsible Investing Trends in the United States* (SIF Industry Research Program, November 2001, www.socialinvest.org/areas/research/trends/2001-Trends.htm).

SiRi Group (Sustainable Investment Research International Group) (2001) *Green, Social and Ethical Funds in Europe 2001. Report as of June 30* (SiRi Group, www.sirigroup.org).

Sparkes, R. (2000) 'A Business Outlook on SRI: Or Seeing The Wood For The Trees', speech at *Triple-Bottom-Line Investing Conference*, Rotterdam, 2 November 2000.

Stapledon, G.P. (1996) *Institutional Shareholders and Corporate Governance* (Oxford, UK: Clarendon Press).

Steger, U., and S. Alikhan (1999a) *Case Studies Rohner Textil AG: Surviving the Impossible* (Lausanne, Switzerland: IMD Business School).

—— and —— (1999b) *Case Studies Rohner Textil AG: Leveraging Sustainability* (Lausanne, Switzerland: IMD Business School).

Steilmann Commission (2000) *The Wealth of the People: A Framework for an Intelligent Economy* (Oxford, UK: Oxford University Press).

Street, P., and P.E. Monaghan (2001) 'Assessing the Sustainability of Bank Service Channels', in J.J. Bouma, M. Jeucken and L. Klinkers, *Sustainable Banking: The Greening of Finance* (Sheffield, UK: Greenleaf Publishing): 72-87.

Strobel, M., and C. Redmann (2001) *Flow Cost Accounting* (Augsburg, Germany: Institut für Management und Umwelt).

Sturm, A., and M. Badde (2001) *Socially Responsible Investment by Pension Funds: A State-of-the-Knowledge Report* (Basel: Ellipson AG).

SustainAbility (2001) *Buried Treasure: Uncovering the Business Case for Corporate Sustainability* (London: SustainAbility).

—— and IBLF (International Business Leaders Forum) (2001) *The Power to Change: Mobilising Board Leadership to Deliver Sustainable Value to Markets and Society* (London: SustainAbility).

UKSIF (United Kingdom Social Investment Forum) (1992) 'Rio Resolution on Social Investment', www.uksif.org/Z/Z/Z/lib/1992/05/archv-rio/index.shtml.

UNEP (United Nations Environment Programme), World Bank and International Monetary Fund (2002) 'Financing for Sustainable Development', www.unepfi.net/pubs/FSDfinal_08.2002_unepfi.pdf.

UNEP FI (United Nations Environment Programme Finance Initiatives) (2002) 'Finance and Insurance: Industry as a Partner for Sustainable Development, UNEP's Finance Industry Initiative, Report for WSSD', www.unepfi.net/pubs/WSSDReport_03.02_UNEPFI.pdf.

UNSD (United Nations Division for Sustainable Development) (2001) 'Indicators of Sustainable Development: Guidelines and Methodologies', www.un.org/esa/sustdev/natlinfo/indicators/isd_guidelines_note.htm.

USS (Universities Superannuation Scheme) (2001) 'Climate Change: A Risk Management Challenge for Institutional Investors', www.usshq.co.uk/INVMENT/climch/framclim.htm.

Vieira, E. (1983) *'Social investing': Its Character, Causes, Consequences, and Legality under the Employee Retirement Income Security Act of 1974* (Washington, DC: US Department of Labor, Labor-Management Services Administration).

Von Weizsäcker, E.U., A.B. Lovins and L.H. Lovins (1997) *Factor Four: Doubling Wealth, Halving Resource Use* (London: Earthscan Publications).

WBCSD (World Business Council for Sustainable Development) (2000a) 'Eco-efficiency: Creating More Value with Less Impact', www.wbcsd.org.

—— (2000b) 'Measuring Eco-efficiency: A Guide to Reporting Company Performance', www.wbcsd.org.

—— (2000c) 'Corporate Social Responsibility, Meeting Changing Expectations', www.wbcsd.org.

—— (2001) 'Sustainability through the Market', www.wbcsd.org.

—— (2002) 'Sustainable Development Reporting Project', www.wbcsd.org.

WCED (World Commission on Environment and Development) (1987) *Our Common Future* (Oxford, UK: Oxford University Press).

Weaver, P., L. Jansen, G. van Grootveld, E. van Spiegel and P. Vergragt (2000) *Sustainable Technology Development* (Sheffield, UK: Greenleaf Publishing).

WI (Wuppertal Institute) (2002) *Review of Eco-Efficiency Concepts in Europe: Toward an Application of European-Based Policies on Material Flows and Energy to Japanese Sustainable Development Policies* (Final Report; Wuppertal, Germany: WI).

Wirth, C. (1999) *Unternehmungsvernetzung, Externalisierung von Arbeit und industrielle Beziehungen: Die 'Negotiation of order' von ausgewählten Netzwerkbeziehungen einer Warenhausunternehmung* (Munich: Hampp).

World Bank (2001) 'World Development Indicators 2000', www.worldbank.org.

WRI (World Resources Institute), WBCSD (World Business Council for Sustainable Development) and UNEP (United Nations Environment Programme) (2002) 'Tomorrow's Markets: Global Trends and Their Implications for Business', www.wbcsd.org.

Wrisberg, N., and H.A. Udo de Haes (eds.) (2002) *Analytical Tools for Environmental Design and Management in a Systems Perspective* (Leiden, Netherlands: Leiden University Centre of Environmental Sciences [CML]).

WWF (2000): 'Living Planet Report', www.panda.org.

Biographies

Jacqueline Aloisi de Larderel joined the United Nations Environment Programme (UNEP) in March 1987 as the Director of the Industry and Environment Centre, and in 1998 assumed her position as Director of the Division of Technology, Industry and Economics (DTIE). In June 2001 she was appointed Assistant Executive Director of UNEP. Before joining UNEP, she worked for the French Ministry of the Environment. She is the author of numerous articles on renewable energy, technology transfer, environmental management tools, corporate responsibility, environmentally responsible investing and other sustainable development themes. In 1986, Mrs Aloisi de Larderel was decorated 'Chevalier de l'Ordre National du Merite', and in 2003 was officially nominated for the 'Chevalier de l'Ordre National de la Légion d'Honneur', in honour of her lifetime achievement in the field of sustainable development. Mrs Aloisi de Larderel is now retired.

Michael Braungart founded EPEA in Hamburg, Germany, in 1987 and in 1995 co-founded MBDC with designer and dean William A. McDonough in Charlottesville, Virginia. After completing his studies in Process Engineering in Darmstadt, Germany, he went on to explore industrial production techniques with the Chemistry Department at Constance, Germany. He subsequently spearheaded the formation of the Chemistry Section of Greenpeace International by the time he completed his PhD in chemistry at the University of Hannover in 1985. He is currently professor of Process Engineering at the Technical University of Northeast Lower Saxony and guest professor at the Darden Business School in Charlottesville, Virginia. At the heart of his work is the 'Intelligent Products System' (IPS) which earned the Océ-van der Grinten Award in 1993. His work, addressing topics from particles to policy, has been published in numerous journals on science, public affairs, design and environment in Europe and the US.
Braungart@epea.com
Braungart@mbdc.com

Hans Martin Bury has been a member of the Social Democratic Party since 1988 and a member of the German Bundestag since 1990. In 2002 he became Minister of State for Europe at the German Foreign Office. At the European Convention he participated in the creation of a European constitution. From 1999–2002 he was Minister of State to the Federal Chancellor. He was spokesman for the SPD Parliamentary Group for economy and technology and for post and telecommunications. He is the author of *Das Bankenkartell* (Knaur, 1996) and numerous contributions to periodicals.
team@bury.de

Timo Busch has been working as research fellow and project manager at the Wuppertal Institute's Working Group on Eco-efficiency and Sustainable Enterprises since 1999. His fields are resource efficiency, sustainable finance, stakeholder approaches, life-cycle assessment and climate change. He studied business administration with majors in accountancy, corporate governance, strategic management and controlling. Since 2002 he has been working on his PhD on the topic of 'Financial markets and sustainable development'.
Timo.Busch@wupperinst.org

Paul Clements-Hunt is Co-ordinator for the United Nations Environment Programme Finance Initiatives (UNEP FI), based in Geneva. UNEP FI is a voluntary initiative of close to 275 banks, insurers and asset management companies worldwide partnering with UNEP to extend environmental and sustainable development best practice throughout the finance sector. Prior to joining UNEP in 2000, Paul represented the International Chamber of Commerce in Paris on energy, environment and sustainable development policy matters. From 1991-98, he was based in Bangkok, engaged in environmental business issues in the South-East Asia region. He lives near Geneva with his wife and their two children.
pch@unep.ch

Volker Hauff holds a PhD in economics. A member of the German Parliament for over 20 years, he was formerly a Federal Minister for Traffic and for Research from 1978 to 1982 and was Mayor of the City of Frankfurt am Main. Leaving the role of active politician, Volker Hauff began a career in consulting and is currently Senior Vice President of BearingPoint. Volker Hauff was a member of the UN World Commission on Sustainable Development chaired by Gro Harlem Brundtland, which in 1987 introduced the idea of sustainability as a political concept.
volker.hauff@nachhaltigkeitsrat.de

After successfully completing an apprenticeship at Deutsche Bank and thereafter studying business management at the University of Mannheim, **Michael Hoelz** joined Badische Kommunale Landesbank Mannheim as Head of the Board of Management's Office. Since 1986 he has been working for Deutsche Bank Group and is currently the Global Head of Public Affairs and Sustainable Development. He is a board member of several Deutsche Bank organisations including Alfred-Herrhausen-Society for International Dialogue, Deutsche Bank Americas Foundation and Deutsche Bank Africas Foundation. His responsibilities include representing Deutsche Bank in national and international committees, i.e. UNEP Finance Initiatives (chairman), the UN Global Compact (representative of Deutsche Bank, Advisory Council), the Global Reporting Initiative (member of board of directors), the Bellagio Forum for Sustainable Development (chairman), and the World Business Council for Sustainable Development, among others.
mailbox.environment@db.com

Born in 1944, **Nobuhisa Itoh** has a bachelor of engineering from Osaka University, Japan. In 1967 he joined Matsushita Electric Industrial Co. Ltd and held various managerial positions in Room Air-Conditioner Design and Product Planning, including the position of Director of the Air Conditioning Research Laboratory as well as Director of the Environmental Energy Research Laboratory. In 2000 he was appointed Director of the Corporate Environmental Affairs Division. In 2003 he was awarded the position of President of the Japan Audit and Certification Organisation for Environment and Quality.
itoun@jaco.co.jp

Claude Fussler runs a farm and vineyard with his wife Martina in Provence where they live with their son Fabrice. He is also a director of the World Business Council for Sustainable Development. He principally acts as Special Advisor to the UN Global Compact. Claude wrote the business book *Driving Eco-innovation: A Breakthrough Discipline for Innovation and Sustainability* (Pitman, 1996) where he articulates his proposals for strengthening competitive advantage and innovation through a business vision of sustainable development. He produced the business book *Walking the Talk: The Business Case for Sustainable Development* (Holliday, Schmidheiny and Watts; Greenleaf Publishing, 2002), in which prominent business executives express the opportunities in and responsibilities of globalisation. He often speaks at top-management briefings.
Fussler@wbcsd.org

Albin Kälin is CEO of the textile company Rohner Textil AG. The company was rewarded in the 1990s with several international design awards, and it has taken a pioneering role in addressing economic and ecological issues and their combination. The development of Climatex®Lifecycle™ and Climatex®LifeguardFR™ was subject of press features in *Time*, *The Wall Street Journal*, *Manager* magazine, *Facts*, *Schöner Wohnen*, *Arte*, *Forbes* and *Business Week*. The sustainable strategy of the 30 employees in the company became the subject of academic case studies (Darden Business School, Virginia and IMD, Lausanne). In 2001, Albin Kälin was awarded with the UBS Key Trophy, Rhine Valley Entrepreneur of the Year.
Albin.Kaelin@ria.com

Ralf Ketelhut has been working as a senior scientist in projects related to the assessment and improvement of materials, material flows and processes in various fields, including textiles, cosmetics, plastics, pigments, paper, leather, building materials, electric and electronic appliances, and automotive products. In particular, he has analysed the environmental impacts of production and recycling processes in the frame of approval procedures or reviews of quality insurance programmes. He obtained a degree in environmental engineering at the University of Applied Sciences in Hamburg in 1994. In early 2003, Ralf Ketelhut established his own company, but still contributes to EPEA projects.
ketelhut@stoffstromdesign.de

Andreas Kicherer studied chemical engineering at the Universities of Karlsruhe and Stuttgart (Germany). In Stuttgart he was awarded a PhD with a thesis on 'Combustion of biomass in dust firing'. He started his career at BASF in Ludwigshafen in 1995 where he first worked in the technical development of the combustion of solids. Two years later he moved to the group 'Eco-efficiency, Life-cycle Assessment and Eco-profiles', of which he became the leader in 2000.
andreas.kicherer@basf-ag.de

Katsuhiko Kokubu is Professor of Social and Environmental Accounting at the Graduate School of Business Administration, Kobe University, Japan, having completed his PhD at Osaka City University. Professor Kokubu has been involved with many governmental projects on environmental accounting, serving as a member of the Committee of Ministry of the Environment, Ministry of Economy Trade and Industry, etc. He is currently appointed as Steering Committee Member of Environmental Management Accounting Network-Asia Pacific (EMAN-AP), an International Associate of the Centre for Social and Environmental Accounting Research at University of Glasgow, UK, and Director of Environmental Economics and Policy Association. His main publications include *Material Flow Cost Accounting* (Nippon Keizai Shinbun-sha, 2002), *Environmental Accounting* (Shinseisha, 2000) and *Social and Environmental Accounting* (Chuo-Keizaisha, 1999).
kokubu@rokkodai.kobe-u.ac.jp

Michael Kuhndt studied chemical engineering and environmental management and policy. He worked as a research assistant for an automobile company developing and applying environmental information for decision support and also worked for the European Commission on linking environmental information demand and supply in industry and science. Currently, he is a senior consultant at the Wuppertal Institute and director of Triple Innova. Since 1999 he has been a permanent consultant at the United Nations Environment Programme. He is at present project manager in the field of new technologies and sustainable development, the assessment of product value chains, triple-bottom-line innovation management and the design of a sectoral sustainability indicator set based on multi-stakeholder approaches.
Michael.Kuhndt@wupperinst.org

Markus Lehni is a Director for Deloitte's Environment and Sustainability Services Group (since 2002). He provides advisory and assurance services on corporate sustainability reporting. Dr Lehni developed the Deloitte Sustainability Reporting Scorecard and conducted several sector studies on sustainability reporting. Before joining Deloitte & Touche, Markus was a programme manager for the World Business Council for Sustainable Development (WBCSD), responsible for the 'Eco-efficiency', 'Sustainability through the Market' and 'Reporting' programmes (1997–2000), and a senior Vice President and Corporate Environmental Affairs Manager for the electronic equipment manufacturer, Landis & Gyr Group (1990–97). Between 1998 and 2001, Markus was a member of the steering committee of the Global Reporting Initiative (GRI) and acted as a co-chair of the Measurement Working Group for the 1999 Exposure Draft and as a senior advisor for the 2002 Version of the Guidelines.
mlehni@deloitte.com

Dr **Christa Liedtke**, born in 1964, studied biology and theology. Since 1993, she has been working as project leader at the Wuppertal Institute, Division for Material Flows and Structural Change, advancing in 1995 to team leader for product-related material flow analysis and sustainable management systems. Since 2000 she has been working as head of the Working Group 'Eco-efficiency and Sustainable Enterprises', now 'Research Group Sustainable Production and Consumption', which is concerned with developing workable concepts, tools and management systems that support economic, ecological and social sustainability in industries, enterprises and product lines.
Christa.Liedtke@wupperinst.org

Michiyasu Nakajima is Associate Professor of Cost Accounting, Faculty of Commerce, at Kansai University, Japan. He serves as a member of the Committee of Ministry of Economy Trade and Industry, among others. He is co-founder of the Institute for Environmental Management Accounting (Consulting and Research Company). His main publications include *Material Flow Cost Accounting* (Nippon Keizai Shinbun-sha, 2002), which earned the prize of the Japan Cost Accounting Association in 2003.
nakajima@ipcku.kansai-u.ac.jp

Thomas Orbach studied business administration with majors in financing, taxes and environmental economics. From 1996 to 2003 he worked in the Working Group on Eco-efficiency and Sustainable Enterprises as a project manager and representative head of the working group. He is currently Head of Scientific Services and Organisation at the Wuppertal Institute. His main fields are environmental management accounting, integrated management systems and sustainable finance.
Thomas.Orbach@wupperinst.org

Rainer Rauberger joined Henkel in 1999, where he currently works at Corporate Sustainability Management as Head of Reporting and Stakeholder Dialogue. Previously, he was a Management Partner in Environmental Consulting. He holds an MSc in Environmental Technology from the University of London and a PhD in Business Administration from the University of Augsburg.
Rainer.Rauberger@henkel.com

Michaela Raupach joined Henkel in 2001, where she deals with Sustainability Reporting at the department of Corporate Sustainability Management. She holds a degree in economics and social sciences from University of Lüneburg and has been focusing on the topic of sustainability reporting in her thesis as well as in her previous position as a researcher.
Michaela.Raupach@henkel.com

Alain Rivière has been working as a senior scientist in projects related to material flows and their management, waste reduction, toxicological assessment of products and chemicals, environmental product optimisation, and life-cycle development in various fields. He is responsible for projects and the development of scientific tools for assessment and information management. Alain Rivière studied biology in France at the Universities of Caen, Paris XI and Lyon III. After a degree thesis at the university hospital of Hamburg, Germany, and a training as Environmental Expert Europe, he joined EPEA in 1994.
riviere@epea.com

Ingeborg Schumacher-Hummel studied ecology and business administration at the Universities of Lüneburg (Germany) and Avignon (France). In 1995, she began her career in the former Swiss Bank Corporation's ecology department. Currently, she is responsible in the area of Socially Responsible Investments (SRI) for the construction of mandate portfolios complying with environmental and social standards. She represents UBS in the board of the Forum Nachhaltige Geldanlagen and in the European organisation EUROSIF. Besides her job, she is working on a PhD at the University of St Gallen, analysing the role of pension funds in socially responsible investments.
ingeborg.schumacher@ubs.com

Jan-Dirk Seiler-Hausmann was project leader in the Working Group 'Eco-efficiency and Sustainable Enterprises' at the Wuppertal Institute for Climate, Environment and Energy. Together with Ernst Ulrich von Weizsäcker, he published a collection of essays on eco-efficiency (*Ökoeffizienz: Management der Zukunft*; Birkhäuser, 1999). He organised the international conference 'From Eco-efficiency to Sustainability in Enterprises' held alongside the ENVITEC trade fair in Düsseldorf in 2001. The proceedings of the conference are documented in a book of the same name published with Ernst Ulrich von Weizsäcker and Björn Stigson. In 2001–2002 he spent six months as a visiting researcher at the Institute for Global Environmental Strategies in Japan before joining sustainability communications at Henkel.
Jan-Dirk.Seiler-Hausmann@arcor.de

Raymond van Ermen is Executive Director of European Partners for the Environment (EPE). EPE is a European multi-stakeholder network whose purpose is to accelerate the transition towards sustainability. To 'accelerate', we need to change our 'mental map' and innovate. Change the way we think about the world, the way we address security issues, the way we design governance, the way we invest, and the way we trade, purchase and consume. Raymond van Ermen is also rapporteur of the Permanent Forum of Civil Society on European Citizenship and Identity. He is in charge of a proposed 'European Contract for a Well-being Society' and a European Participatory Budget.
raymond.vanermen@epe.be

Dr **Ernst Ulrich von Weizsäcker** is a member of the German parliament, and, since 2002, chairman of the Parliamentary Committee on Environment, Nature Conservation and Nuclear Safety. He has also been chairman of the Parliamentary Study Commission 'Globalisation of the Economy: Challenges and Answers' (2000-2002), and, previously, president of the Wuppertal Institute for Climate, Environment and Energy from 1991 to 2000. He is a member of the Club of Rome and of the ILO Commission on the Social Dimension of Globalisation. With Amory Lovins and L. Hunter Lovins, he wrote the landmark book, *Factor Four: Doubling Wealth, Halving Resource Use* (Earthscan Publications, 1997).

Jürgen Zech, with a master and doctorate in business economics from the University of Cologne, worked in the 1960s for Uniroyal and McKinsey & Co., receiving an MBA while at INSEAD. From 1975 to 1985 he was a member of the Executive Board of Colonia Versicherungs AG, Cologne, and from 1986 to 1992 Chairman of the Executive Board of Cologne Reinsurance AG. In 1993 he moved to Gerling-Konzern where he was Deputy Chairman of the Executive Board, becoming Chairman in 1996. He is currently on the board of, or chairs, a number of corporations and institutions.
j.zech@denkwerk.de

Peter Zollinger is SustainAbility's Executive Director, based in the Zürich office, with a focus on financial markets and governance. In his previous career, he held various posts. Peter was executive assistant of Swiss industrialist Stephan Schmidheiny, founder of the Business Council for Sustainable Development (now WBCSD). His emphasis has been on strategic management and communication. He was seconded to the World Resources Institute (WRI), Washington, DC, to help it engage the business community. He was also Director Strategic Development of FUNDES International (part of Schmidheiny Group), and co-managed this network for small-business development in nine countries of Latin America. He co-authored *The Power to Change: Mobilising Board Leadership to Deliver Sustainable Value to Markets and Society* (SustainAbility/IBLF, 2001).
zollinger@sustainability.com

Abbreviations

ACEA	European Automobile Manufacturers Association
Ag	silver
AI	Amnesty International
APG	alkyl polyglycoside
ASrIA	Association for Socially Responsible Investment in Asia–Pacific
BASD	Business Action for Sustainable Development
BASF	Badische Anilin- & Soda-Fabrik AG
BBC	British Broadcasting Corporation
BCSD	Business Council for Sustainable Development
BDI	Bundesverband der Deutschen Industrie (Federation of German Industry)
BMBF	Bundesministerium für Bildung und Forschung (German Ministry of Education and Research)
BS	Broadcasting Satellite
BUND	Bund für Umwelt und Naturschutz (Association for Environmental and Nature Conservation, Germany)
CalPERS	California Public Employees' Retirement System
CEC	Commission of the European Communities
CEFIC	European Chemical Industry Council
CEO	chief executive officer
CEPE	Centre for Energy Policy and Economics (Switzerland)
CFC	chlorofluorocarbon
CH_4	methane
CHF	Swiss franc
CLSA	Credit Lyonnais Securities Asia
CO_2	carbon dioxide
COMPASS	Companies' and Sectors' Pass to Sustainability
COP3	Conference of the Parties 3 (UNFCCC)
CP7	Seventh International High-Level Seminar on Cleaner Production (UNEP)
CRT	cathode-ray tube
CSR	corporate social responsibility
Cu	copper
DAX	Deutsche Aktienindex

DGB	Deutscher Gewerkschaftsbund (German Federation of Trade Unions)
DIN	Deutsches Institut für Normung (German Institute for Standardisation)
DJSI	Dow Jones Sustainability Index
DLG	Deutsche Landwirtschafts-Gesellschaft (German Agricultural Society)
DNR	Deutscher Naturschutzring (German League for Nature Conservation)
EBIT	earnings before interest and tax
EEB	European Environmental Bureau
EEEI	European Eco-Efficiency Initiative
EH&S	environmental, health and safety
EIA	environmental impact assessment
EIAJ	Electronic Industries Association of Japan
EIRIS	Ethical Investment Research Service
EMAS	Eco-Management and Audit Scheme
EMS	environmental management system
EnTA	environmental technology assessment
ENVITEC	Environmental, Technology and Services Trade Fair
EPE	European Partners for the Environment
EPEA	Environmental Protection Encouragement Agency
EPI	environmental performance indicator
ERISA	Employee Retirement Income Security Act (US Department of Labor)
ERP	enterprise resource planning
ESE	environmental, social and ethical
ETH	Eidgenössische Technische Hochschule (Switzerland)
ETUC	European Trade Union Confederation
EU	European Union
EUR	euro
EUROSIF	European Sustainable and Responsible Investment Forum
FDI	foreign direct investment
FoE	Friends of the Earth
FORGE	Financial Organisations Review and Guidance on the Environment
FTSE	Financial Times Stock Exchange
GBP	pound sterling
GDP	gross domestic product
GNESD	Global Network on Energy for Sustainable Development
GNP	gross national product
GRI	Global Reporting Initiative
HFC	hydrofluorocarbon
IBLF	International Business Leaders Forum
ICC	International Chamber of Commerce
IFC	International Finance Corporation
IGES	Institute for Global Environmental Strategies
IISD	International Institute for Sustainable Development
ILO	International Labour Organisation
IMU	Institut für Management und Umwelt (Institute for Management and Environment, Germany)
IPU	International Parliamentary Union
ISI	Fraunhofer Institute for Systems Technology and Innovation Research

ISO	International Organisation for Standardisation
ISS	International Space Station
IT	information technology
IUCN	International Union for Conservation of Nature and Natural Resources
JEMAI	Japan Environmental Management Association for Industry
JIS	Japanese Industrial Standards
JPY	Japanese yen
JSE	Johannesburg Stock Exchange
KPI	key performance indicator (Shell)
KRC	Kansai Research Center (Institute for Global Environmental Strategies)
LCA	life-cycle assessment
LCD	life-cycle development
LDC	less-developed country
MBDC	McDonough Braungart Design Chemistry
MD	minidisc
MDG	Millennium Development Goals
METI	Ministry of Economy, Trade and Industry Japan
MFCA	material flow cost accounting
MIPS	Material Input per Service Unit
MOE	Ministry of Environment, Japan
N_2O	nitrous oxide
NABU	Naturschutzbund Deutschland (Association for the Protection of Nature, Germany)
NAPF	National Association of Pension Funds (UK)
NCPC	National Cleaner Production Centre
NGO	non-governmental organisation
NH_3	ammonia
NO_x	oxides of nitrogen
ODA	official development assistance
OECD	Organisation for Economic Co-operation and Development
PC	personal computer
PFC	perfluorocarbon
PRTR	Pollutant Release and Transfer Register
PSS	product service systems
PVA	polyvinylalcohol modified polyacrylate
R&D	research and development
RNE	Rat für Nachhaltige Entwicklung (National Council for Sustainable Development, Germany)
SAFE	Sustainability Assessment for Enterprises
SAI	Social Accountability International
SAM	Sustainable Asset Management
SANet	Sustainable Alternatives Network
SEK	Swedish kronor
SETAC	Society of Environmental Toxicology and Chemistry
SF_6	sulphur hexafluoride
SHE	safety, health and environment
SIGN	Sustainable Investments—Global Network for Asia

SIP	statement of investment principles
SiRi	Sustainable Investment Research Institute
SME	small or medium-sized enterprise
Sn	tin
SO_2	sulphur dioxide
SRI	socially responsible investment
STD	sustainable technology development
STIC	Sustainable Trade and Innovation Centre
TIAA–CREF	Teachers Insurance Annuity Association–College Retirement Equities Fund
TV	television
UKSIF	United Kingdom Social Investment Forum
UN	United Nations
UNCED	United Nations Conference on Environment and Development
UNCSD	United Nations Commission on Sustainable Development
UNEP	United Nations Environment Programme
UNEP FI	United Nations Environmental Programme Finance Initiatives
UNFCCC	United Nations Framework Convention on Climate Change
UNGASS	United Nations General Assembly Special Session
UNGC	United Nations Global Compact
USD	US dollar
USS	Universities Superannuation Scheme
VCR	videocassette recorder
VOC	volatile organic compound
WBCSD	World Business Council for Sustainable Development
WCED	World Commission on Environment and Development (UN)
WEEE	Directive on Waste Electrical and Electronic Equipment
WEHAB	water and sanitation, energy, health, agriculture and biodiversity
WI	Wuppertal Institute for Climate, Environment and Energy
WI AGZU	Wuppertal Institute for Climate, Environment and Energy, Working Group Eco-Efficiency and Sustainable Enterprises
WRI	World Resources Institute
WSSD	United Nations World Summit for Sustainable Development (UN)
WTO	World Trade Organisation
WWF	World Wide Fund for Nature
ZEW	Zentrum für Europäische Wirtschaftsforschung (Centre for European Economic Research, Germany)
Zn	zinc

Useful websites

AccountAbility . . . . www.accountability.org.uk
ACEA (European Automobile Manufacturers Association) . www.acea.be/ACEA/index.html
Amnesty International . . . . www.amnesty.org
Association for Socially Responsible Investment in Asia–Pacific . . . . www.asria.org
BASF . . . . www.basf.com
BDI (Bundesverband der Deutschen Industrie) . . . . www.bdi-online.de
BMBF (German Ministry of Education and Research) . . . . www.bmbf.de
COMPASS . . . . www.oekoeffizienz.de/english/index.html
DIN (German Institute for Standardisation) . . . . www.din.de
DJSI (Dow Jones Sustainability Indices) . . . . www.sustainability-index.com
EMAS . . . . http://europa.eu.int/comm/environment/emas/index_en.htm
Environmental Protection Encouragement Agency (EPEA) . . . . www.epea.com
European Environmental Bureau (EEB) . . . . www.eeb.org
European Eco-Efficiency Initiative (EEEI) . . . . www.epe.be/programmes/eeei
Ethical Investment Research Service (EIRIS) . . . . www.eiris.org
European Partners for the Environment (EPE) . . . . www.epe.be
European Sustainable and Responsible Investment Forum (EUROSIF) . . www.eurosif.org
European Trade Union Confederation (ETUC) . . . . www.etuc.org
European Union . . . . http://europa.eu.int
FTSE4Good www.ftse4good.com
Global Reporting Initiative . . . . www.globalreporting.org
Institute for Global Environmental Strategies, Kansai Research Center
 . . . . http://host-3.iges.or.jp/iges_kansai/english
IMU (Institute for Management and Environment, Germany) . . . . . www.imu-augsburg.de
International Business Leaders Forum . . . . www.pwblf.org
International Chamber of Commerce . . . . www.iccwbo.org
International Institute for Sustainable Development . . . . www.iisd.org
International Labour Organisation (ILO) . . . . www.ilo.org
International Organisation for Standardisation (ISO) . . . . www.iso.ch

International Space Station . . . . http://spaceflight.nasa.gov/station
IUCN (International Union for Conservation of Nature and Natural Resources)
. . . . www.iucn.org
Japan Environmental Management Association for Industry . . . . www.jemai.or.jp
METI (Ministry of Economy, Trade and Industry, Japan) . . . . www.meti.go.jp/english
Millennium Development Goals . . . . www.undp.org/mdg
MIPS (Material Input per Service Unit) www.factor10-institute.org
MOE (Ministry of Environment, Japan) . . . . www.env.go.jp/en/index.html
Nitto Denko Co. www.nitto.com/index2.html
OECD (Organisation for Economic Co-operation and Development) . . . . www.oecd.org
Pollutant Release and Transfer Register
. . . . www.m-kagaku.co.jp/english/aboutmcc/RC/prtr1
RNE (German National Council for Sustainable Development) www.nachhaltigkeitsrat.de
SAFE (Sustainability Assessment for Enterprises) . . . . www.wupperinst.org/safe
SAM Sustainable Asset Management . . . . www.sam-group.com
Social Accountability International (SAI) . . . . www.cepaa.org
Sustainable Investment Research Institute (SiRi) . . . . www.sirigroup.org
Tanabe Seiyaku Tanabe Seiyaku Co. . . . . www.tanabe.co.jp/english/index.html
United Nations . . . . www.un.org
The United Nations and Business . . . . www.un.org/partners/business
United Nations Division for Sustainable Development . . . . www.un.org/esa/sustdev
United Nations Environment Programme . . . . www.unep.org
United Nations Environment Programme Finance Initiatives . . . . http://unepfi.net
United Nations Framework Convention on Climate Change . . . . www.unfccc.org
United Nations General Assembly Special Session . . . . www.un.org/esa/earthsummit
United Nations Global Compact . . . . www.unglobalcompact.org
United Nations World Summit for Sustainable Development
. . . . www.johannesburgsummit.org
World Business Council for Sustainable Development . . . . www.wbcsd.org
Wuppertal Institute for Climate, Environment and Energy . . . . www.wupperinst.org
Wuppertal Institute for Climate, Environment and Energy,
Working Group Eco-Efficiency and Sustainable Enterprises . . . . . . www.eco-efficiency.de
World Resources Institute . . . . www.wri.org
World Trade Organisation . . . . www.wto.org
WWF . . . . www.panda.org

Index

Access to Drugs Campaign 211
AccountAbility 72
Accounting, environmental 100-12, 155
  see also Reporting
Adhesives 104-107, 166-67, 170-72
Advertising 44
Africa, biodiversity of 192, 201, 204
Agenda 21 28, 65, 187
Agriculture 42, 44-45
Air conditioners 156, 160-61
Allianz 49
Amnesty International (AI) 67
Animal testing 170
Annan, Kofi, UN Secretary-General 15, 202
Asia, investment in 55, 190-91, 209
Asia–Pacific Development Centre 55
ASrIA (Association for Socially Responsible Investment In Asia) 190-91, 209
Asset management
  see Financial services sector; Investment; Pension funds
Association of University Teachers 213
Audi 86
Australia 217
Austria 29
Automotive industry
  reporting practice of 85-92
  see also Cars; Transport
Aventis Pasteur 24
Avon Letter 212

Banking
  see Deutsche Bank; Financial services sector
Basel II concept 180
BASF AG 10, 33, 49
  eco-efficiency method 113-22

Batteries 154, 157
Bayer 49
BBC 210
BDI
  see Federation of German Industries
Belgium 217
Berger, Roland 113
Bio-capacity 23
Bioaccumulation 142
Biodiversity 191-92, 201, 204
  industrial 134
BMW Group 49, 86
Bosch 49
BP 16
Brandt, Willy 46
Braungart, Michael 133-34, 139
Breuer, Rolf E. 187
British Insurance Association 188
Brown, Lester 52, 54
Brundtland, Gro Harlem 39, 46
Brundtland Commission (WCED) 28, 39, 46, 93, 163
BT 210
Budapest, conference 2002 182
Buildings, energy use 43
Business Charter for Sustainable Development 164-65
Business Council for Sustainable Development (BCSD) 9-10, 29

Cahouet, Frank V. 212
CalPERS 209
Canon 102
Carbon dioxide 16, 25, 30, 42, 153-54
Cargill Dow 24
Carnegie Textiles 131
Cars
  emissions from 30, 42

manufacturers, reporting by 85-92
markets for 25-26
paint spraying 172-73
suspension systems 117-18
see also Automotive industry; Transport
Cellasto® 117-18
Cellulose fibre 137-38
Changing Course 29
Chemical industry
see BASF; Ciba; Clariant; Henkel
Chissanos, Joaquim 204
Ciba SC 137, 138
Clariant AG 137
Cleaner Production, Seminar on (CP7) 20
Climate change 187
see also Greenhouse gases
Climate Change, Framework Convention on (UNFCCC) 28, 153
Climatex® upholstery fabrics 10, 130-45, 146
design prizes/awards 135-36
and fire standards 136-38
Closed-loop systems 134-35, 147-48, 150-51
Commission of Enquiry on Globalisation 127
Commission of the European Communities (CEC) 29, 65
Commission on Sustainable Development (UNCSD) 65
Commonwealth Science Council 55
Computer chips 154, 157
Conference on Environment and Development 1992 (UNCED) 16, 28, 182, 187, 190
Container and Package Recycling Law 154
Corporate governance
and shareholder activism 207-14
Corporate social responsibility (CSR) 65, 67, 193, 216-17, 219
see also Reporting
Cosmetics 169-70
Cotton fabrics, sizing 119-21
Council for Sustainable Development (Germany) 29, 37, 38-47
'Cradle to cradle' concept 148
Credit ratings 194

Daikin Industries Ltd 161
DaimlerChrysler 49, 86
'Debt for nature swaps' 197
Deloitte Sustainability Reporting Scorecard 75-92
and automotive industry 85-92
criteria for 77-79, 80
scoring levels 79
use of 81-84
Deloitte Touche Tohmatsu 76, 80-85

Design 130-45, 146-51, 166-73
eco-effective 134-35, 147-49
Index of Sustainability™ 131, 141-42, 145
prizes/awards 135-36
for recycling 158-60
see also Innovation; Life-cycle analysis; Products
DesignTex 131, 133, 141
Detergents 168-69
Deutsche Bahn 49
Deutsche Bank 49, 187, 196-204
sustainability concept 196-97
Deutsche Bundesbank 144
Deutsche Immobilien Leasing GmbH 200
Deutsche Kommunalinvest GmbH 199
Deutsche Telekom 49
Dialogue on Sustainable Development 36-37
Dow Jones Sustainability Index (DJSI) 10, 57, 66, 191, 211, 219
DresdnerKlinwortWasserstein 220
DuPont, case study 25-26
Düsseldorf Trade Fair 9
DWS Investment GmbH 197, 200
Dye chemicals 131, 137, 143

E-Parliament 14-15
Earth Policy Institute 52
Eco-effectiveness 134-35, 141-42, 146-51
Eco-efficiency, definition of 10, 29, 123-24
Eco-efficiency analysis 113-22
Eco-Management and Audit Scheme
see EMAS
Eco-services 127-28
Eco-tourism 192
Ecofunds
see Investment
Eco-labelling 131, 161, 171
Econsense Forum for Sustainable Development 48-51, 203
Electrolux 127-28
Electronics industry
cleaner processes in 154, 156-58
energy efficiency of 153-54, 155-56
recycling in 154-55, 158-62
'Eliminating World Poverty' 217
EMAS (Eco-Management and Audit Scheme) 71, 133, 200
EMICODE EC1 label 171
Emissions
greenhouse gases 153-54, 203
carbon dioxide 16, 25, 30, 42, 153-54
trading systems 16, 203
Employee Retirement Income Security Act (ERISA) 214
Endocrine disrupters 142, 154

Index   243

Energy
  efficiency
    of electronics industry   153-54, 155-56
    and market share   25-26
    of old buildings   43
    and productivity   35-36
    of products, improving   155-56
    standards for   155-56
  management systems, domestic   156
  policies, Germany   31, 35-36, 42, 43, 200
  production, global   22
  renewable   36, 197, 200
  use, CO_2 emissions   154
Energy Conservation Law, Revised   155-56
Energy Star Home Electronics   156
Environmental management
  tools for   70-72
Environmentally intelligent products   133-35
E.ON   49
EPEA Internationale Umweltforschung GmbH   131, 133, 136, 137, 141, 145, 146
Ethical investment
  see Investment
Ethical Investment Research Service (EIRIS)   220
Ethics for USS campaign   213
Ethos foundation   208, 210
European Automobile Manufacturers Association (ACEA)   30
European Eco-Efficiency Initiative (EEEI)   53, 57
European Environmental Bureau (EEB)   56-57
European Partners for the Environment (EPE)   54, 57, 60
European Sustainable and Responsible Investment Forum (EUROSIF)   219
European Trade Union Confederation (ETUC)   56
European Union (EU)   55, 219
  Directive on Waste Electrical and Electronic Equipment (WEEE)   157
  governance of   56-57
  Sustainable Development Convergence Initiative   62
  sustainable development strategies of   29, 58-59, 60-63
Export businesses   55, 198

Fabrics
  see Climatex®
Factor 10 concept   23, 29, 30
Federation of German Industries (BDI)   49, 164
Fiat Group   86
Fibres, as raw materials   136-37

Financial services sector   177-81
  challenges/opportunities for   178-79, 183-89
  changes in   184
  and environmental legislation   178, 187, 194
  influence of   179, 180, 185-86, 188-89, 210-14
  UNEP FI 2001–2002 conference series   66, 182-88
  UNEP Statement by Banks on the Environment and Sustainable Development   187, 202-203
  see also Deutsche Bank; Investment; Pensions
Fire regulations   136
First International Eco-Efficiency Conference   9
Flame retardants
  in electronics industry   157-58
  for textiles   136-38
Flasbarth, Jochen   39
Food   42, 44
  packaging   172
Ford Motor Company   86, 98, 146, 172-73
Forests   22
FORGE group   188
France   217
Franck, K.   216
Frank, Horst   39
Franz, Wolfgang   39
Frazier, Craig   24
Friends of the Earth   218
'From Eco-Efficiency to Overall Sustainability in Enterprises'   9
FTSE (Financial Times Stock Exchange)   174
FTSE4Good Index   174, 191, 197, 219
Fuel cells   156
Furnishing fabrics
  see Climatex®
Fussler, Claude   60

Gemeinschaft emissionskontrollierter Verlegewerkstoffe   171
General Motors   86
Geneva civil servants' pension fund   210
Gerling Group   49, 188-89
German Ministry of Education and Research (BMBF)   167
Germany
  Council for Sustainable Development   29, 37, 38-47
  pension reform in   15, 180, 217
  sustainable development strategy of   29-33, 34-37, 38
  see also Deutsche Bank
Giroflex   131
Girsberger   131
Global Compact (UNGC)   15, 17, 65, 202

244 Eco-efficiency and Beyond

Global Network on Energy for Sustainable Development (GNESD)   18, 19
Global Reporting Initiative (GRI)   17, 66, 75, 88, 188, 194
Global warming   187
see also Greenhouse gases
Globalisation   13-17, 37
and corporate social responsibility   216-17
origins of   13-14
and sustainability   46-47, 59-60, 187
Governance
corporate   207-14
European Union (EU)   56-57
global   14-15
Greenhouse gases   153-54, 203
carbon dioxide   16, 25, 30, 42, 153-54
Greenpeace   15, 16, 133
Grohe, Rainer   39
Growth, economic   21, 22
Guptara, Prabhu   218

Hair colorant   170
Halogen compounds   157-58
Hamburg Environment Institute   174
Hatzfeldt, Hermann Graf   39
Hauff, Volker   37, 39
Hazardous materials   156-58
Heerbrugg, Switzerland   130-31, 145
Heidelberg Cement   49
Heinisch, Roland   39
Henderson Global Investors   59
Henkel Group   10, 49, 163-76
Herman Miller Inc.   131, 146
Hipp, Claus   39
Home Appliance Recycling Law   160, 162
Honda   86
Hong Kong   190
Household appliances   127-28, 155-56, 160-62
HSBC   220
Human rights   67, 96, 186, 202

Index of Sustainability™   131, 141-42, 145
Indicators, sustainability   30-32, 35, 45, 61, 65, 125
see also Dow Jones; Reporting; Standards
Indonesia   209
Industrial estates   62
Innovation   24-27, 30-32
by DuPont   25-26
by Henkel Group   166-67
Institut für Management und Umwelt (IMU)   103
Institute of Social and Ethical Accountability   66
Insurance companies   177-81, 188, 192-93
see also Financial services sector
Insurance Industry Initiative (UNEP III)   188, 193

Intelligent Materials Pooling concept   149
Intelligent product systems   133-35
International Chamber of Commerce (ICC)   67, 163-64
International Corporate Governance Network   17
International Finance Corporation (IFC)   192
International Institute for Sustainable Development (IISD)   26
International Labour Organisation (ILO)   65
International Monetary Fund (IMF)   191
International Organisation for Standardisation (ISO)   66, 71
International Parliamentary Union (IPU)   14
International Space Station (ISS)   52
International Union for Conservation of Nature and Natural Resources (IUCN)   192
Internet
for environmental reporting   87, 155
forums   36-37, 45
and government   14-15
and 'pay as you use' products   128
product instruction manuals on   160
Investment, socially responsible (SRI)   155, 189-92
in Asia   55, 190-91, 209
in biodiversity businesses   191-92
in carbon funds   203
as microcredits   203-204
new frameworks for   59-60
by pension funds   59, 205-20
barriers to   213-16
disclosure rules for   15, 180, 216-18
examples   209-10
motivation for   210-13
portfolios, screening of   207, 208, 213
and shareholder activism   207-14
ISO 14000 series   71
ISO 14001   100, 153, 166, 201-202
ISO 14031   66

JAB Anstoetz   131
Japan
electronics industry in   152-62
sustainable accounting in   100-12
Japan Energy Conservation Centre   155
Japan Environmental Management Association for Industry (JEMAI)   101
Japan Steel Works Ltd   159
Jochem, Eberhard   39
Johannes Wellmann Textilverlag   144
Johannesburg Stock Exchange (JSE)   189
Johannesburg Summit 2002 (WSSD)   18, 34, 38, 42, 55, 188, 193

Index

Just Pensions 214-15

Käßmann, Margot 39
Kijani Project 192
Kreutzer, Idar 193
Kwik Fit 98
Kyoto Protocol 28, 189, 203

Labour
  productivity of 35
  standards for 65, 66, 96, 202
Lady Brazil 139
Lancashire County Council 210
Land use 31, 41, 44-45, 62
Lantal Textiles 139, 140, 145
Lead-free solder 156-57
Lenzing AG 137
Life-cycle analysis (LCA) 18-20, 114, 115, 160
Life-cycle development (LCD) 150-51
Life-cycle Initiative (UNEP/SETAC) 18, 20
Life expectancy 22
Light bulbs 26
Living Planet Report 2000 (WWF) 23
Lomborg, Bjørn 22-23
Long-Term Capital Management 184
Love the Earth campaign 153
Lovins, Amory B. 29, 57
Lovins, L. Hunter 29
Lufthansa 49
Lycra® 25
Lyons, Susan 133

Madagascar 197
Magnesium alloys 159-60
Malaysia 209
Management, sustainable 93-99
  Deutsche Bank 196-204
  Henkel Group 163-76
  strategies for 97-98
  tools for 70-72
  see also Material flow cost accounting;
    Reporting
Markets
  for cars 25-26
  future trends in 22
Material flow cost accounting (MFCA) 100-12
  case studies, Japan 104-11
  definition of 103-104
Material flows, closing loops in 134-35, 147-48, 150-51
Material input per service unit (MIPS) 125
Matsushita Ecotechnology Centre 161
Matsushita Group 10, 153, 154
Matsushita Product Assessment 160
McDonough, William 133-34, 139

McDonough Braungart Design Chemistry (MBDC) 133, 139, 146
  Index of Sustainability™ 131, 141, 145
Media, globalisation of 95
Mellon Bank Corporation 212
Microfinance 203-4
Millennium Development Goals (MDGs) 18-19, 186
Ministry of Economy, Trade and Industry, Japan (METI) 101-104, 112
Monet, Jean 56
Moosa, Valli, Minister 55
Müller, Edda 39
Munich Re 49

Nanotechnology 167
National Association of Pension Funds (NAPF) 212, 218
National Cleaner Production Centres (NCPCs) 19
National Council for Sustainable Development (Germany) 29
National Strategy for Sustainable Development (Germany) 34-37
NEST Sammelstiftung 208
Newbold, Yve 215
Ngubane, Ben, Minister 55
Nike Inc. 146
Nissan 86
Nitto Denko Co. 102, 104-7
Normalisation factors 121
North–South Commission 46
Nottinghamshire County Council 210
Novatex SA 25

Oeko-Tex Standard 100 131
Opel 86
Organic farming 192
Organisation for Economic Co-operation and Development (OECD) 65
Ozone 115, 116, 154, 187

Packaging 154, 160
  for food 172
Paint 172-73
Panda Renditefonds 201
'Pay per wash' 127-28
Peace parks 203, 204
Pension funds 59, 205-20
  asset allocation of 206
  and corporate governance, influence on 210-14
  disclosure rules for 15, 180, 216-18
  examples of 209-10
  portfolios, screening of 207, 208, 213
  worldwide holdings 205, 208
  see also Financial services sector;
    Investment
Pension SRI Disclosure Regulation, UK 216-17

PFCs (perfluorocarbons)   153, 154
Pharmaceuticals production   107-11
Philippines   209
Pickering, Alan   212
Plastics   157-58
Platzeck, Matthias   39
Politics, sustainable   28-33
Pollutant Release and Transfer Register (PRTR)   154
Polypropylene   158
Population, global   22
Porter, Michael   24, 57
Poverty   22, 23, 61, 186, 187, 216-17
Prevista   208
Prince of Wales Business Leaders Forum   67
Pritt Sticks   172
Prodi, Romano, EC President   57
Product for Consumption™   142, 143
Products
  electrical, standards for   155-56
  end of life, recycling   160-61
  environmentally intelligent   133-35
  green, information on   161
  leasing/lending   124, 127-28
  see also Design; Eco-effectiveness; Innovation
Prospects for Germany strategy   34
Prototype Carbon Fund   203
PSA Peugeot Citroën   86
Public goods   15
Public sector   199
Purchasing, sustainable   60-61
Putzhammer, Heinz   39
PVC (polyvinyl chloride)   157-58

RAG   49
Rail transport   42
Recycling
  in electronics industry   154-55, 158-62
  end-of-life products   160-61
  packaging   154, 160
Redesigned LenzingFR™   137-38, 143
Redmann, C.   103-4
Refrigerators   158, 160-61
Relevance factors   121
Renault Group   86
Renewable Energy Act (Germany)   36
Reporting, environmental/social   17, 30, 66, 67, 73-74, 155
  Deloitte Sustainability Reporting Scorecard   75-92
    and automotive industry   85-92
    criteria for   77-79
    use of   81-84
  Global Reporting Initiative (GRI)   17, 66, 75, 88, 188, 194
  Japan   100-101
  social, developments in   72
  see also Accounting; Indicators; Management

Ricardo, David   13
Rimpau, Jürgen   39
Rio Earth Summit 1992 (UNCED)   16, 28-29, 182, 187, 190
Rio Roundtable, March 2002   182
Robins, Nick   59, 60
Rohner Textil AG   130-45, 146
  design awards   135-36
Ruhrgas   49
Rupert, Anton   204
RWE   49

SA8000   66, 72
SAM (Sustainable Asset Management)   66, 191
Sarasin   208
Sayer, Josef   39
Scandals, financial   183, 184, 186
Sceptical Environmentalist, The   22-23
Schmidheiny, Stephan   28-29
Schröder, Gerhard, German Chancellor   37
Schwarzkopf   170
Services, eco-efficient   127-28
Shareholder activism   207-14
Shell   15, 16, 95, 98
Shock absorbers   117-18
Shrimp farming   192
Siemens   49, 128
SIGN Asia   55
Sitag   131
Sizing agents   119-21
Smith, Adam   13, 14
Soap formulations   170
Social accountability   94-96, 166, 176, 207-10
  see also Corporate social responsibility; Reporting
Social Accountability International (SAI)   66, 72
Social Domini Index   220
Social Investment Forum, US   208
Social reporting, corporate
  see Corporate governance; Reporting
Socially Responsible Investment In Asia, Association for (ASrIA)   190-91
Socially responsible investment (SRI)
  see Investment
Society of Environmental Toxicology and Chemistry (SETAC)   18, 19-20
Solar power   156, 200
Solder, lead-free   156-57
Solvents   110, 160, 170, 172-73
Sontora®   25
South Africa
  Access to Drugs Campaign   211
  see also Johannesburg
SRI
  see Investment

Index

Standards
  environmental   155-56, 161
  labour   65, 66, 96
  see also EMAS; Indicators; ISO
Steelcase Inc.   133
Storebrand Group   193
Strobel, M.   103-104
Strong, Maurice   28
Styrofoam   154
Subsidies   26, 33, 62
Sudan   197
SustainAbility   94, 96
Sustainability, Index of ™   131, 141-42, 145
Sustainability indicators   30-32, 35, 45, 61, 65, 125
  see also Dow Jones; Reporting; Standards
Sustainability management
  see Management
Sustainability reporting
  see Reporting
Sustainable accounting   100-12
Sustainable Alternatives Network (SANet)   18
Sustainable development
  business case for   96, 174-76, 211
  definition of   28, 50-51, 94
  strategies for   97-98
    Germany   29-33, 34-37
  see also Design; Indicators; Innovation; Investment; Management; Reporting
'Sustainable Development, Dialogue on'   36-37
Sustainable Development, *econsense* Forum for   48-51
Sustainable Investment Research International (SiRi) Group   220
Sustainable Investments–Global Network for Asia (SIGN)   55
Sustainable Solutions   30
Sustainable Trade and Innovation Centre (STIC)   55
Sustainable Water Fund   191
SusTech Darmstadt   167
Switzerland
  see Rohner Textil AG

Takiron, Japan   102
Tanabe Seiyaku Co.   102, 107, 110-11
Tebo, Paul   25
Televisions   157, 158, 159, 160-61
Tennant, Tessa   182, 190, 209
Terathane®   25
Tetra Pak   49
Textiles
  sizing agents for   119-21
  upholstery fabrics   130-45
Thailand   190, 209
Thixomoulding   159-60
ThyssenKrupp   49

TIAA–CREF   209
Toiletries   169-70
Töpfer, Klaus   39
Toshiba Corp.   161
Toy Story (movie)   11-12
Toyota   24, 25, 86
Trade, sustainable   55, 60-62
Transparency
  see Reporting
Transport   42, 43-44
  see also Automotive industry; Cars
Tschense, Holger   39
TU Darmstadt   167
TUI   49

UBS   208
United Kingdom
  Department for International Development   217
  Pension SRI Disclosure Regulation   15, 180, 216-17, 218
  Social Investment Forum (UKSIF)   218
United Nations (UN)
  Agenda 21   28, 65, 187
  Commission on Sustainable Development (UNCSD)   65
  Conference on Environment and Development 1992 (UNCED)   16, 28, 182, 187, 190
  Environment Programme (UNEP)   18, 19-20, 55, 66, 191, 197
  Finance Initiatives (UNEP FI)   66, 182-90
    Africa conference 2002   192
    Insurance Industry Initiative (UNEP III)   188, 193
    'Statement by Banks on the Environment and Sustainable Development'   187, 202
  Framework Convention on Climate Change (UNFCCC)   28, 153
  General Assembly Special Session (UNGASS)   29
  Global Compact (UNGC)   15, 17, 65, 202
  and global governance   14-15
  Secretary-General   15, 65, 202
  World Commission on Environment and Development 1987 (WCED)   28, 39, 46, 93, 163
  World Summit on Sustainable Development 2002 (WSSD)   18, 55
    and financial institutions   182, 188, 193
    and German policies   34, 38, 42
United States
  Department of Labor   212, 214
  Employee Retirement Income Security Act (ERISA)   214
  Environmental Protection Agency   156

Upholstery fabrics
    see Climatex®

Vahrenholt, Fritz   39
Vauxhall Motors   86
VCI (Association of the Germany
    Chemical Industry)   49
Victor-Innovatex   139, 140
Viscose fibres   137, 138
Volkswagen   25, 49, 86
Volvo Car Corporation   86
Von dem Bussche, Philip Freiherr   39
Von Weizsäcker, Ernst Ulrich   10, 29
Voscherau, Eggert   39

Washing machines   127-28, 160-61
Washing powders   168-69
Waste
    hazardous   157, 199
    management   138, 200
    as nutrient   134-35
    plastics   157-58
    solvents   110
    see also Eco-effectiveness; Recycling
Waste Electrical and Electronic
    Equipment, EU Directive on (WEEE)
    157
Water
    consumption   22, 36
    sustainability funding for   191
Weinzierl, Hubert   39

Wellmann Inc.   131
White goods   127-28, 156, 160-61
Wind power   156, 200
Wool   142
World Bank   191, 192, 197
    Prototype Carbon Fund   203
World Business Council for Sustainable
    Development (WBCSD)   9-10, 29, 56,
    60, 197
    core mission of   67
World Commission on Environment and
    Development 1987 (WCED)   28, 39,
    46, 93, 163
World Commission on Sustainability and
    Globalisation   42, 46-47
World Economic Forum   202
World Summit on Sustainable
    Development 2002 (WSSD)   18, 55
    and financial institutions   182, 188, 193
    and German policies   34, 38, 42
World Trade Organisation (WTO)   42, 55
WWF   23, 201, 204
Worldwatch Institute   23
Wuppertal Institute   9, 33

Xerox   98

Zahrnt, Angelika   39
Zech, Jürgen   188-89
Zero impacts, goal of   25-26, 155